TIME-BOUND / TIMELESS

Understanding Eternal Truth In a Temporal World
Through the Letter to the Romans
& the Letter of James

SCOTT SIMPSON

innovo
PUBLISHING
innovopublishing.com

Published by Innovo Publishing, LLC
www.innovopublishing.com
1-888-546-2111

innovo
PUBLISHING

Innovo Publishing LLC is a Christ-centered publisher located near Memphis, TN. Since 2008, Innovo has published quality books, eBooks, audiobooks, music, screenplays, and online and physical curricula that support the Great Commission, equip believers, and help create a positive Christian worldview. Innovo's capabilities and global reach provide Christian authors, artists, and ministries access to the world for Christ. To learn more about Innovo Publishing, visit our website at innovopublishing.com. To connect with other Christian creatives and to learn best practices for creating, publishing, marketing, and selling Christian titles, visit the Christian Publishing Portal at cpportal.com.

TIME-BOUND / TIMELESS
Understanding Eternal Truth In a Temporal World
Through the Letter to the Romans & the Letter of James

Unless otherwise noted, all Scripture was taken from the New American Standard Bible®, Copyright © 1960, 1971, 1977, 1995 by The Lockman Foundation. All rights reserved.

Scripture marked "HCSB" was taken from the Holman Christian Standard Bible. Copyright © 1999, 2000, 2002, 2003, 2009 by Holman Bible Publishers, Nashville Tennessee. All rights reserved.

Scripture marked "KJV" was taken from the King James Version of the Bible. Public domain.

Scripture marked "GNV" was taken from the 1599 Geneva Bible. Public Domain.

Library of Congress Control Number: 2026901383
ISBN: 979-8-88928-126-9

Cover Design & Interior Layout: Innovo Publishing, LLC

Printed in the United States of America
U.S. Printing History
First Edition: 2025

to John Fey
my friend and my teacher
The man who discipled me when I was lost.
The man who continued to disciple me after Jesus saved me.
Thank you for the time and the effort.

CONTENTS

PART 1: THE LETTER TO THE ROMANS

PART 2: THE LETTER OF JAMES

AUTHOR'S NOTE

The man who discipled me is skilled in ancient languages and is an impossibly well-read world history expert. While he is also well versed in Western philosophy, he is no fan of Aristotle and Plato. For a while after my salvation, I experienced a steadily developing, overarching biblical theology while remaining blissfully ignorant of Western-style systematic theology. I did not have to deal with what the early university systems set in motion and Thomas Aquinas drove home until I went to Christian undergraduate college, followed by the completion of three seminary programs.

Throughout my undergraduate and graduate studies, I kept finding myself returning to the hermeneutic my mentor used as a baseline for my interpretations. The *Time-bound / Timeless* model presented here formed the underpinning of my interpretive stance for my initial exposure to the Bible. I present it here as both a foundational contextual stance for reverentially approaching the Bible and as a response—in essence—to my four Aristotle-style theological degrees.

INTRODUCTION

TIME-BOUND

T he Bible states that the time-bound universe we temporarily exist in had a beginning. Before Creation, the time-bound-ness we experience in this universe did not exist. At Creation, universe-style time-bound-ness began. We exist in the midst of everything we do and don't know about time.

Our experience with time is based in an ongoing series of *nows* that we call *the present*. Everything that has happened before any given *now* we call *the past*. When we project our thoughts into times that have not happened yet from our position in the *now*, we call those thoughts *the future*.

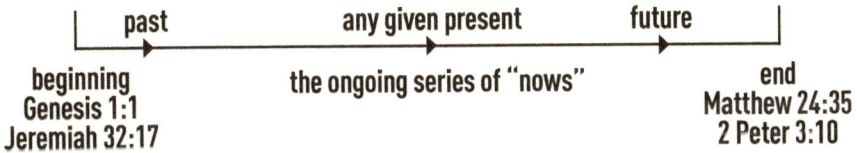

past	any given present	future
beginning Genesis 1:1 Jeremiah 32:17	the ongoing series of "nows"	end Matthew 24:35 2 Peter 3:10

Figure 1: The big time-bound picture

- The Bible states that the time-bound universe had a single moment of beginning at some distant point in the past.
- The time-bound aspect of the Bible's story shows humanity moving from the past, through an ever-changing present that is always in motion, toward a series of futures.
- The Bible states that at some point in the future, this version of the time-bound universe we inhabit will have an end.

Figure 2: Human perception in time

- We are unique in God's creation. We have the ability in any given present moment to recall and reflect on the past, and the ability to project our minds speculatively into possible futures.

In some places, the Bible asserts that in any given *now* we have moral agency and that we are responsible for the decisions we make and the directions we take. The Bible states that we are accountable for the decisions we have made and the directions we have taken. In many places, the Bible insists that we are making real and meaningful choices in time that are ours to make.

TIMELESS

In many places, the Bible says that God is holy and sovereign. In some places, the Bible states that God preexists the universe. God existed, and exists, outside of the bounds of His universe, beyond any constraints imposed on us by our time-bound existence. Therefore,

- God is not bound by space-time. He is present everywhere in His universe all the time; there is no place you can go where God is not.
- God is all-powerful. He created the universe and everything in it.

In some places, the Bible says that God is all-knowing; He has perfect foreknowledge of the entire panorama of time-bound-ness that He created. Among other things, this means that while any given human is perceiving time this way . . .

Figure 3: Human perception in time (repeated)

God is seeing something like this:

Figure 4: Sovereign overview

Sovereign God exists in a state of being we can call *timeless* as a contrast to *time-bound*.

> *I am God, and there is no one like Me, declaring the end from the beginning. (Isaiah 46:9b-10a)*

> *I am the Alpha and the Omega, the first and the last, the beginning and the end. (Revelation 22:13)*

TIME-BOUND-NESS IN CONTEXT OF TIMELESSNESS

That which is time-bound only exists in context of that which is timeless.

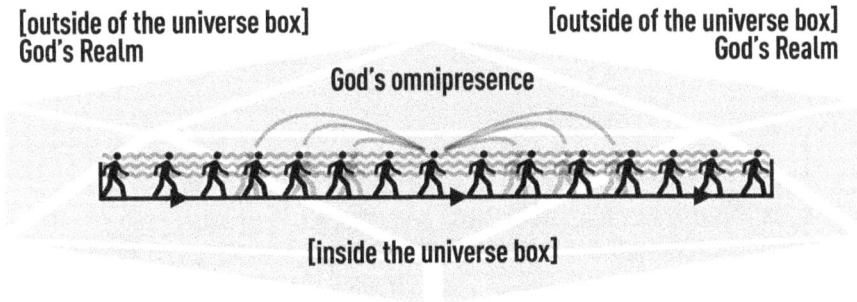

Figure 5: The big picture

Humanity, and the entire universe, exists surrounded and encompassed by God. God as Trinity exists outside of His universe box in a place we call heaven.

Where can I go from Your Spirit? Or where can I flee from Your presence?

If I ascend to heaven, You are there;
if I make my bed in Sheol, behold, You are there.
If I take the wings of the dawn, If I dwell in the remotest part of the sea,
even there Your hand will lead me and Your right hand will lay hold of me.

If I say, "Surely the darkness will overwhelm me,
and the light around me will be night,"
even the darkness is not dark to You and the night is as bright as the day.
Darkness and light are alike to You.

For You formed my inward parts; You wove me in my mother's womb.
I will give thanks to You, for I am fearfully and wonderfully made;
wonderful are Your works and my soul knows it very well.

My frame was not hidden from You when I was made in secret
and skillfully wrought in the depths of the earth;
Your eyes have seen my unformed substance;
and in Your book were all written the days that were ordained for me
when as yet there was not one of them. (Psalm 139:7-16)

THE PARADOX

TIME-BOUND: The Bible states in many places that humans have moral agency to make real and meaningful decisions in time. Our future with God is the result of this ongoing decision-making process. Some people call this ability free will.

TIMELESS: The Bible states in many places that sovereign God knew/ knows everything that would/will ever happen in His universe from beginning to end down to the smallest detail of every life. Our future with God was/is predetermined before we knew we existed. Some people categorize this phenomena as predestination and God's act of choosing as election.

The Bible presents both of these viewpoints in various places, each presentation asserting its truth. Nowhere do the biblical authors attempt to reconcile the two positions or apologize for the logical impasse the presentation creates. To address the mystery inherent in time-bound humanity being surrounded and encompassed by timeless sovereign God, the Bible simply presents both viewpoints, thus creating an intentional time-bound paradox.

paradox: *noun*

1. A statement that seems to contradict itself but may nonetheless be true.
2. A person, thing, or situation that exhibits inexplicable or contradictory aspects.
3. A statement that is self-contradictory or logically untenable, though based on a valid deduction from acceptable premises.

This matter is addressed tersely and succinctly in various places in the Bible. Here are two examples:

"For My thoughts are not your thoughts, nor are your ways My ways," declares the Lord. (Isaiah 55:8)

How unsearchable are His judgments and unfathomable His ways! (Romans 11:33)

THE SYSTEMATIC PROBLEM: PART 1

The Bible presents variations on the following time-bound viewpoint in several places:

> **Free will:** I learn about the gospel of Jesus Christ. The Holy Spirit helps me, but I either choose God or reject God by my own convictions. If I choose God, God then responds to my choice with justification and regeneration.

Likewise, the Bible presents variations on the following God-level viewpoint in several places:

> **Predestination:** God chose me from before the creation of the universe. I appear to respond to the gospel, but God had already established the moment of my salvation before I had any awareness of the gospel of Jesus Christ or any notion of repenting. My choice to accept (or reject) Jesus has already been made for me at the sovereign level despite time-bound appearances.

One of the free will solutions (among many) is that God can know everything that has happened and have a God's-eye view of everything that could happen, but He doesn't know exactly what will happen in any given life. The time-bound logic problem with all free will solutions is that they make God something less than sovereign. God is sort of all-knowing, but not really.

The predestination position (taken at its most basic premise) is that God has already ordained every human's eternal destiny regardless of how things appear to us as we experience time-bound-ness. The logic problem with time-bound notions of predestination is that humans, then, have no more ability to choose or reject God than characters at some point in a book have the ability to change what's on the next pages. Humans become nothing more than pre-programmed biological robots.

Brilliant theologians from all sides of this issue and from every Western and Eastern theological tradition have been fiddling about with attempts to solve this paradox since God revealed Himself in writing. Every effort always ends up either limiting God's sovereignty in some way, robotizing humanity, and/or elevating human control over God's word. That should tell you something.

TIME-BOUND: The human view from within the universe box.

TIMELESS: God's sovereign view from outside of the universe box.

Question: In essence, which viewpoint is correct?

Answer: Yes, the Bible presents us with both essence viewpoints.

We must remember that even when we are reading about timeless things in the Bible, immersing in states of worship, or communing with God in prayer, we are experiencing these things with a time-bound central nervous system and from within the confines of a time-bound universe. God tells us about His sovereign viewpoint; we don't have His sovereign viewpoint.

Remember that even when we are reading about time-bound things in the Bible, those things only exist in context of timelessness. God tells us about certain time-bound things; He is in no way bound by the time-bound-ness He created.

The foundations of both systematic positions are conditionally true, even though to Aristotelian style intellection they seem contradictory. While the biblical presentation of these two viewpoints is self-contradictory and logically untenable, the reality of both positions existing in an intellectually unreconcilable, time-bound spiritual tension is a valid deduction from biblical premises acceptable to the regenerate mind.

Deeply contemplate everything the Bible teaches about time-bound humanity. Deeply contemplate everything the Bible teaches about timeless, Sovereign God. Immerse in both viewpoints in essence, and let each exist on their own biblical tracks in your mind. Live by the Spirit while existing continuously, spiritually stretched by the intellectual tension the biblical presentation intentionally creates.

THE SYSTEMATIC PROBLEM: PART 2

Life in the Spirit is decidedly non-ordinary in relation to life in the world. As Christians, we stand astride the paradox of humanity moving through the time-bound universe in context of divine sovereignty—the paradox of time in context of timelessness.

Part of the trouble is that our intellects don't like a paradox. We tend to place what we can intellectually understand in time through direct contact with the fallen world above what and how we learn spiritually—we tend to trust the physical more than the spiritual. And while pure intellect is very powerful for digging out incredibly useful stuff from the world, it is near to useless when it comes to surrendered living in the hope of faith.

Why do we think about these things the way we do? As Westerners, we have to start with the origin of our learning systems: the ancient Greeks. They loved reasoning and intellection.

Most of the ancient Greek philosophers believed that there was an intellectual path to perfect certainty and ultimate knowledge. Greek thinkers had known for a long time that sensory data was fallible, and they invented dozens of experiments to demonstrate it. They proved out the reality that our senses can be fooled, directed, misdirected, shut off, and manipulated. They proved that our senses can't be trusted.

The Greek thinkers knew that engaging sensory data with the intellect was not a path to the certainty they wanted, but they were convinced they had found a way. They called it *pure reason*. The two parts of the argument go like this:

1. Humanity has an inner, higher awareness that is not fallible and that can know the ultimate truth of any situation in spite of the fallibility of the human sensory system.
2. And, this perfect inner awareness knows the truth of any given situation or event, even before being confronted with the situation or event.

So, in the pure reason model,

> **sensory data + infallible inner human awareness = certitude and all knowledge**

In Christian terms, the ancient Greek thinkers idolized the human mind and elevated the human spirit to godhood. Through their models, they became as gods in their minds. The pure reason model fell apart over the centuries for a variety of reasons. But the biggest was that most of the truths these philosophers arrived at using the pure reason model eventually turned out to be untrue.

Then, in the thirteenth century, there was a Christian named Thomas Aquinas who was thoroughly intoxicated with all things Greek philosophy. He liked the idea of arriving at truth through intellectual certainty but saw the problems with the ancient pure reason model. He decided that he could fix the model by adding the Bible to it.

For Aquinas,

> **sensory data + infallible inner human awareness + the Holy Bible = certitude and all knowledge**

Aquinas instituted the model of systematizing theology outside of the Bible. The problem was, and still is, that whenever theology is systematized, some fallible human is doing the systematizing.

Ever since then, large numbers of Christians have been trying to lock down the Bible systematically via human command and control. If you need help understanding how that went, read a comprehensive church history book. The short answer: it hasn't gone well.

Along the way, the Western scientific method developed and proved useful for all sorts of things in the world. Scientific method is sensory data, refined and amplified by instruments and devices mixed with variations on the old pure reason model. Over time, this new pure reason model has become religion for large chunks of humanity.

The scientific method has its place and uses in time, but at its best, it's next to useless for dealing with the biblical paradox of time-bound human existence in relation to timeless sovereign God. And yet, generation after generation of theologians keep trying to solve the biblical paradox with some combination of refined and amplified sensory data + infallible human awareness + the Holy Bible. And the hoped-for result is still intellectual certitude and all knowledge.

The problem with all of the systematized theologies is that they rely on the principles of Greek philosophic thought and categories. This approach almost always ends up with some human misrepresenting or flat-out abusing one side of the paradox or the other. Christians who over-invest in systematic theology often get to the point where their understandings obscure their trust in the Lord and their relationship with the Lord.

Sensory data, refined or not, and inner human awareness can both deceive us. Leaning on our own understandings won't get us where God wants us. Even with computers and tons of data at our disposal, we are still chained to our time-bound human-ness.

Engaging the Holy Bible without the Holy Spirit will not result in sanctifying growth, but we keep trying to conquer the Bible through the intellect. Why? It's all about control. The need for intellectual certitude is an expression of our fundamental fallen human desire to be in control. Certitude is seized by the fallen mind because of the emotional need of our fallen minds to have complete certainty and complete control of our lives. But intellectual certitude is not faith, and faith is not intellectual certitude.

Reason and intellection are involved in the process of faith, but saving faith is not a product of reasoning and intellection or anything else experienced with the senses. Faith based on sensory knowledge is what I call *head faith*. Head faith is the kind of faith that both justified and non-justified believers can have. A person running on head faith while claiming to be a Christian can be lost in their certainty of who they think Jesus is and isn't. A lost person running on head faith can sincerely believe that Jesus was real, wise, and wonderful, walked the earth, helped people out, and even performed miracles, but they stop short of surrendering their lives to Jesus as God and Lord of their lives.

A regenerate Christian stuck in head faith tends to read the Bible like it's a math book and can recite biblical data about the Holy Spirit but exists deeply troubled by the idea of walking under the influence of the Spirit. A head-faith Christian believes in the Bible as revelation but tends to routinely agonize over the condition of his faith while living secretly terrified of ever directly experiencing the power and presence of the Holy Spirit.

A head-faith regenerate Christian may even regularly read the Bible, study it, and chew on it, but they would rather default to leaning on their own understandings than to trusting in the Lord through a life given over to prayer, worship, and surrendered immersion in the Bible. I've known a lot of biblically literate Christians who long for a Holy-Spirit kick in the head, but it seems to me that they wouldn't hear the Spirit if He was screaming in their ear with a megaphone. Too many Christians that I meet, at all levels of intellectual ability and accomplishment, seem to be living in the pure reason style Christian haze of head faith.

The way to maintain a solid Christian walk is to embrace the word of God by faith alone through a faith firmly rooted in biblical truth, without that faith becoming dependent on pure reason style intellection. Whether it was read or heard, biblical faith is how we got started; faith had potential when we authentically heard the gospel. In time-bound terms, faith began when the will of God was sufficiently known to the mind to be accepted by the heart.

At my current level of ignorance and understanding, it seems reasonable to me that if you were saved by grace through faith, then you ought to live out your Christian life by grace through faith. Embrace the word of God by faith. Cultivate as much biblical understanding as you can, just don't rely on the Greek reasoning model we have all inherited. We should have understandings—we can and should progress through different levels of understanding—but after, and before, all is said and done, trust in the Lord.

We can then learn to exercise biblical faith by reading, accepting, and acting upon the word of God completely independent of our feelings, intelligence level, cultural biases, or any evidence that our senses demand. As a Christian, to only act after we have some sort of evidence is decidedly not walking on faith. When we decide to run on sensory data and intellectual evidence, we don't need faith. When we give substance to belief that's not physically substantial, that's faith.

The heart of this mystery isn't the paradox. That's the best we can do to intellectually look at it. The heart of this mystery is God's heart—and God judges the heart. Once we are saved, God engages His faithful through faith and holiness—His heart to our hearts. The Fall separated us from that faith and altered our hearts and our ability to love, but through Christ we are rejoined to God and in the process of renewing our broken hearts. The Word made flesh puts us back in right relationship with God; the Word as Spirit indwells us and teaches us; the Spirit made Bible informs us in the classroom of the Spirit that is in our lives.

In light of all this, here is my recommended hermeneutic baseline for engaging the Bible:

> **reverential fear of God + humility before God + respect for the paradoxical mystery of time existing only in context of timelessness**

Part 1:

THE LETTER
TO THE ROMANS

INTRODUCTION:

THE LETTER TO THE ROMANS

The letter to the Romans stands as one of the most theologically dense writings in all of Scripture. Penned by the apostle Paul under divine inspiration, Romans develops and deepens key elements of Jesus' teachings found in the Gospels—illuminating the power of grace, the necessity of faith, and the righteousness that comes from God alone.

This letter is essential for anyone seeking to understand how the Old and New Testaments are intricately connected. Paul, trained in the Law and transformed by Christ, reveals how God's covenant promises to Israel find their fulfillment in Jesus, and how Gentiles are graciously grafted into the redemptive plan. It is here that the relationship between Law and grace, judgment and mercy, time and timelessness, is brought into reverent harmony.

From the sixteenth verse of chapter one onward, Romans unfolds with tightly packed, sequential arguments that demand thoughtful attention. Theological truths are not presented in isolation—they build upon one another with precision and purpose. Each layer prepares the heart and mind for the next. For this reason, readers are encouraged to become intimately familiar with the entire epistle before drawing systematized conclusions from individual verses or sections.

Romans is not a letter to skim. It is a book to be studied, meditated upon, and prayed through—until its truths become part of the believer's spiritual reflex. To engage with this letter is to draw near to the very heart of God's redemptive plan. It is an invitation to be transformed by the renewing of the mind, rooted in the gospel which is "the power of God for salvation to everyone who believes" (Romans 1:16).

You will be well-served to learn the letter to the Romans inside and out.

COMMENTARY:

THE LETTER TO THE ROMANS

1:1-17 THE OPENING

1:1-7 Introduction

1:1 Paul, a bond-servant of Christ Jesus, called as an apostle, set apart for the gospel of God.

Paul presents himself as a bond-servant of Christ Jesus. Roman readers of that time understood that a bond-servant surrendered his will to his master and served with no regard for self; only death could break the bond. Hebrew readers would have connected this with the *'ebed*—the indentured Hebrew servant who voluntarily became the permanent bond-slave of a master he loved and respected.

Paul's baseline model for his Christian life is the total surrender of a bond-servant. In this same sense, Christians should live in a daily state of total surrender to Jesus. As His bond-servants, we are to submit our wills to the will of God as a way of life.

An apostle was an envoy or ambassador sent with a specific message on the authority of their master. In the New Testament, *apostle* is primarily used as a unique title for the specific group of men personally chosen and trained by Jesus to preach and teach the gospel.

Paul's writings are a part of Scripture because he was divinely called, personally instructed, and specifically commissioned by the risen Christ.

Before Saul became Paul, he was a Pharisee. The Aramaic term *Pharisee* has a common root with the word translated here as "set apart." The Pharisees were set apart according to the standards of their own traditions. Paul, originally set apart as a Pharisee, was now set apart to serve Jesus. All true Christians have been set apart from the world for the gospel of God.

1:2 ... which He promised beforehand through His prophets in the holy Scriptures.

The gospel did not originate with Paul or with Jesus's earthly ministry—it was promised "through [God's] prophets." Prophets were the Old Testament spokesmen for God. The gospel is the fulfillment of the Hebrew Scriptures. Everything Jesus taught aligns with and is in agreement with the Old Testament.

1:3 ... concerning His Son, who was born of a descendant of David according to the flesh.

"Flesh," here, refers to human existence and emphasizes the transitory and frail nature of that existence. This verse presents Jesus as the fulfillment of Old Testament prophecy according to the *merely human* aspect of His genealogy. Jesus fulfilled all of Old Testament messianic prophecy.

1:4 ... who was declared the Son of God with power by the resurrection from the dead, according to the Spirit of holiness, Jesus Christ our Lord.

In the incarnation, the second person of the Trinity willingly surrendered His glory and the prerogatives of deity. During His humanity, Jesus willingly submitted to the will of the Father and to the power of the Holy Spirit ("with power . . . according to the Spirit"). It was the Holy Spirit working in Christ that accomplished the incarnation at the virgin conception, the miracles of Jesus's ministry, and the resurrection.

Jesus demonstrated His power to conquer death, a power belonging only to God. Jesus established that He was beyond all doubt the Son of God ("declared the Son of God . . . by the resurrection"). If Jesus had not risen from the dead, we would have nothing. Because Jesus rose from the dead, we have everything.

The name "Jesus" was a common name in biblical times, and it means "Jehovah saves." "Christ" is a title, like "Lord," and it means "the Messiah" and "anointed one."

Jesus's earthly life (verse 3)	Jesus as God (verse 4)
"was a descendant"	"was declared"
"of David"	"the Son of God in power"
"according to the flesh"	"by the resurrection . . . according to the Spirit of holiness"

1:5-6 . . . through whom we have received grace and apostleship to bring about the obedience of faith among all the Gentiles for His name's sake, among whom you also are the called of Jesus Christ.

Grace is God's favor given at salvation. God gives it; all we can do is receive it. Human achievement has no place in the divine work of saving grace. This is about surrender and obedience. We can transform our thinking and behavior; only God can transform our nature.

In this sense, all saved believers are called as apostles and sent into the world as messengers of and witnesses to Jesus Christ. We don't have the original apostolic office, but we are still called to be ambassadors of Christ.

"Obedience of faith" is synonymous with salvation. To claim faith in Jesus Christ and then to live in utter disobedience to God's word is to live a lie. Faith is obedient. Faith that doesn't manifest itself through obedient living is fake and worthless.

Because God loves the world, the salvation of humanity is important to God for our sake. But the main thrust of God's plan is His glory. Why have we been given grace? For the glory of God—"for His name's sake." Followers of Jesus Christ should live and exist for the glory of God.

1:7 . . . to all who are beloved of God in Rome, called as saints: Grace to you and peace from God our Father and the Lord Jesus Christ.

"saint"—a noun meaning "set apart," which references the distinct blessings on believers

"called as saints"—to be set apart for God

As saints, we are learning to live set apart from sin by abiding in Christ.

> "peace from God"—inner tranquility due to God's grace; spiritual joy despite earthly circumstances

In Phillipians 4:7, Paul calls it "the peace that surpasses all understanding." Paul always mentions grace first, then peace—it's a divine order. There can be no spiritual peace without God's grace.

1:8-15 Thanksgiving and Occasion

1:8 First, I thank my God through Jesus Christ for you all, because your faith is being proclaimed throughout the whole world.

The first thing Paul does is thank God.

1:9a For God, whom I serve in my spirit.

In the original language, this phrase conveys a sense of sincere and passionate investment derived from the joining of Paul's (small *s*) spirit with the (big *S*) Holy Spirit. Paul is all-in with God.

1:9b . . . in the preaching of the gospel of His Son.

Paul is totally committed to the gospel.

1:9c-10a . . . is my witness as to how unceasingly I make mention of you, always in my prayers making request.

Paul prays a lot.

1:10b . . . if perhaps now at last by the will of God I may succeed in coming to you.

Paul had intended to visit the Roman church for a while but God kept giving him other places to go and other things to do. The second part of the phrase shows that Paul knows that ultimately it is not up to him. The only way he will succeed is by the will of God. Therefore Paul tries to stay in the world of God's will—God's way all of the time.

1:11 For I long to see you so that I may impart some spiritual gift to you, that you may be established.

Paul wants to go to the church at Rome to share "some spiritual gift"—whatever that may be—as his ministry unfolds, and in so doing, to strengthen their faith.

1:12 . . . that is, that I may be encouraged together with you while among you, each of us by the other's faith, both yours and mine.

"That is" signals verse 12, clarifying verse 11. Paul makes it clear that everyone, including Paul, benefits from Christian fellowship—"each of us by the other's faith"—regardless of differences in gifting and ability.

1:13 I do not want you to be unaware, brethren, that often I have planned to come to you (and have been prevented so far) so that I may obtain some fruit among you also, even as among the rest of the Gentiles.

This is a reemphasis of verse 11 and of Paul's unique apostolic mission, even in context of an already thriving Roman church.

1:14 I am under obligation both to Greeks and to barbarians, both to the wise and to the foolish.

Even though his calling is unique, he wants the Romans to understand that Paul is not about Paul. He is motivated by the divine obligation he is under. He has a deep sense of missionary obligation to both "Greeks and barbarians"—the wise and the unwise. Paul will teach anyone and everyone who will listen to him. The gospel can be received by anyone.

1:15 So, for my part, I am eager to preach the gospel to you also who are in Rome.

Paul makes disciples of anyone and everyone he can, wherever he goes and in whatever spiritual condition he finds them. The gospel mandates discipling.

1:16-17 The Theme

Paul transitions from his ministry to focusing on the gospel. The letter now becomes a formal theological exposition.

1:16 For I am not ashamed of the gospel, for it is the power of God for salvation to everyone who believes, to the Jew first and also to the Greek.

The gospel's message of hope is not merely a religious idea; it is the very power of God for salvation. Without the gospel, there is no salvation—no rescue from sin, no reconciliation with God, and no eternal life. What began as a promise to Israel has been graciously extended to all of humanity. The gospel breaks through every barrier—national, cultural, racial—and reaches every person who believes, offering the same saving grace to Jew and Gentile alike. Paul is not ashamed of the gospel of Jesus Christ. We shouldn't be either.

1:17a For in it the righteousness of God is revealed.

This verse is intended to be understood in a few different ways:

> **Paraphrase 1:** *For in the gospel, the faithfulness of God to His promises of salvation is revealed.* Taken in this sense, "righteousness" emphasizes God's own character—His justice and faithfulness in keeping His covenant promises.

> **Paraphrase 2:** *For in the gospel, the righteous status that is from God is revealed.* Taken in this sense, "righteousness" refers to the believer's standing before God. It is a judicial declaration of justification, not an inner transformation (which belongs to regeneration and sanctification).

> **Paraphrase 3:** *For in the gospel, the saving action of God is revealed.* Taken in this sense, "righteousness" highlights God's activity—His powerful intervention to deliver and redeem His people.

Throughout the letter, all three dimensions of righteousness appear. Whether describing God's justice and faithfulness, the believer's justified standing, or God's saving work, any presentation of the righteousness of God in Romans is always closely linked to faith and always concerns the gift of righteousness God grants to those who believe.

1:17b ... from faith to faith.

"Faith" is the quality of absolute reliance on God and His revealed word instead of relying on human abilities or activities. Faith and nothing but faith can put us in right relationship with God.

1:17c ... as it is written, "But the righteous man shall live by faith."

The justified sinner is now in a relationship with God in which all sins—future and past—are forensically accounted for by the blood of Jesus.

This whole of verse 17 can be paraphrased in the following way:

> **Paraphrase:** *For in the gospel, the saving action of God, which brings people into right relationship with Him, is revealed by faith and from nothing but faith, as it is written, "Those justified by the saving action of God will live by faith."*

In Paul's writings, it is always God who justifies and the human being who is justified. When viewed through the time-bound biblical presentations regarding human willful ability and moral agency, the moment a sinner places saving faith in Jesus Christ, the sinner is justified by and before God. When viewed through the time-bound biblical presentations regarding the timeless sovereignty of God, the moment a sinner is justified by and before God, that sinner places saving faith in Jesus Christ.

EXCURSUS: THREE KEY TERMS

1. *Justification*—God's righteous act and decision by which we are declared innocent. It is an activity on God's part that declares our status before God.

2. *Regeneration*—the justifying activity of God that results in, and includes within it, the gift of the Holy Spirit. The spiritually awakened believer can now have a relationship with God.

3. *Sanctification*—a believer's growth in Christ-likeness. While justification, regeneration, and sanctification are inseparable, they are distinct. Do not confuse or combine them. There is a mysterious mix of divine activity and human receptivity occurring in the moment of salvation, but the justifying work is all of God.

1:18-3:20 SIN AND THE LAW

1:18-32 God's Wrath and Human Unrighteousness

This passage has three main parts:

1. Verses 18-20: People suppress God's truth.
2. Verses 21-28: Three ways people suppress God's truth:
   i. People exchange the truth of God for idols.
   ii. People exchange the truth of God for a lie.
   iii. People embrace unnatural sexual practices.
3. Verses 29-31: People not only engage in sin, they indulge it and celebrate it.

1:18a For the wrath of God is revealed from heaven.

Contrast this verse against verse 17: "For in [the gospel] the righteousness of God is revealed."

1:18b . . . against all ungodliness and unrighteousness of men who suppress the truth in unrighteousness.

Ungodliness is any attack on the majesty of God. Unrighteousness is any violation of God's desired order. People willfully, mindfully commit ungodly and unrighteous acts as they suppress whatever knowledge of God they have. This upsetting of God's truth justifies His wrath. Everything that is under heaven and not under the gospel is under the wrath of an all-seeing and angry God.

1:19 . . . because that which is known about God is evident within them; for God made it evident to them.

People have a God-given conscience that is informed by the natural revelation inherent in God's design of the universe.

1:20 For since the creation of the world His invisible attributes, His eternal power and divine nature, have been clearly seen, being understood through what has been made, so that they are without excuse.

Therefore (tying back to verse 18), ungodly and unrighteous people make conscious decisions to suppress God's truth. Relying on natural revelation in and of itself always leads to negative results. Without the gospel, people inevitably turn knowledge of (big *G*) God into (small *g*) gods of their own making.

No one is saved by natural revelation. Natural revelation serves to demonstrate that God's wrath is justified. Making the inevitable choice to rebel against God makes humans without excuse before God.

1:21 For even though they knew God, they did not honor Him as God or give thanks, but they became futile in their speculations, and their foolish heart was darkened.

Humans are hard-wired for worship; we are designed to worship God. We all have some knowledge of God, but that knowledge is obscured by our fallen condition.

1:22 Professing to be wise, they became fools.

God's wisdom versus human foolishness—God's reality versus human illusions.

1:23 . . . and exchanged the glory of the incorruptible God for an image in the form of corruptible man and of birds and four-footed animals and crawling creatures.

Pagan religions do not represent non-Christians aspiring to know God; they represent a falling away from God's truth. They represent the tragic predisposition of people to corrupt whatever knowledge of God they possess into false gods of their own.

1:24 Therefore God gave them over in the lusts of their hearts to impurity, so that their bodies would be dishonored among them.

The result? "God gave them over." God essentially said to humanity, *You want it? You insist? You got it. Your will be done, human.* God gives the unrepentant sinner over "to impurity, so that their bodies would be dishonored" (given over to uncleanness—see Leviticus).

1:25 For they exchanged the truth of God for a lie, and worshiped and served the creature rather than the Creator, who is blessed forever. Amen.

Putting some aspect of God's creation in place of God is the essence of idolatry. Any worldly thought or mental wave of worldly thoughts that you cannot turn off at will, becomes an idol. The time and energy that you invest in it becomes idol worship.

1:26a For this reason God gave them over to degrading passions.

The result? "God gave them over." God to humanity: *You want it? You insist? You got it. Your will be done, human.* God gives the unrepentant sinner over "to dishonorable passions." Idolatry is the essence of fornication.

1:26b-27 . . . for their women exchanged the natural function for that which is unnatural, and in the same way also the men abandoned the natural function of the woman and burned in their desire toward one another, men with men committing indecent acts and receiving in their own persons the due penalty of their error.

Idolatry gives birth to sexual perversion. Sexual perversion feeds on itself and becomes ever more perverse. This verse illustrates idolatrous, sinful humanity taking the powerful, natural, life-giving gift of sexuality and thoroughly and completely ruining it. All sexual perversion is sinful—all the time.

1:28 And just as they did not see fit to acknowledge God any longer, God gave them over to a depraved mind, to do those things which are not proper.

The result? "God gave them over." God to humanity: *You want it? You insist? You got it. Your will be done, human.* God gives the unrepentant sinner over "to a depraved mind, to do those things which are not proper." This represents the bottom of the barrel: sin completely rules.

1:29-31 . . . being filled with all unrighteousness, wickedness, greed, evil; full of envy, murder, strife, deceit, malice; they are gossips, slanderers, haters of God, insolent, arrogant, boastful, inventors of evil, disobedient to parents, without understanding, untrustworthy, unloving, unmerciful.

The harm that sin does to others is added to idolatry and sexual perversion. Paul describes the general societal results of living with a debased mind:

- "unrighteousness" manifesting as "wickedness, greed, evil"
- "envy" manifesting as "murder, strife, deceit, malice"
- "gossips, slanderers"—everything from whispering rumors to public defamation
- "haters of God"—self-exaltation manifesting as "insolent" [action], "arrogant" [thought], "boastful" [word]
- "inventors of evil"—total self-absorption; I am my own god
- "disobedient to parents"—even the biological family unit breaks down

And then we are shown the baseline spiritual result of not acknowledging God. Those given over to a depraved mind are "without [spiritual] understanding, [spiritually] untrustworthy, unloving [the way God wants us to love], unmerciful [by God's standard]."

1:32 . . . and although they know the ordinance of God, that those who practice such things are worthy of death, they not only do the same, but also give hearty approval to those who practice them.

"the ordinance of God"—what all people can know about God through natural revelation

"worthy of death"—divinely imposed punishment

"they not only do the same, but also give hearty approval"—a place beyond temptation that lapses into sin, where the sinful actions are enthusiastically embraced; willful, mindful rebellion against God

Sin must be seen as the dominating, ruling force that it is. Then it can become clear why God's righteousness can only be received as a gift by way of faith.

2:1-11 God's Righteous Judgment

2:1 Therefore you have no excuse, everyone of you who passes judgment, for in that which you judge another, you condemn yourself; for you who judge practice the same things.

"Therefore" continues the main argument from 1:18-20—humanity is without excuse. Here, the same accusation is brought against anyone who acts as the ultimate judge of others based on their access to the knowledge of God. This is a warning against self-righteousness.

2:2 And we know that the judgment of God rightly falls upon those who practice such things.

Final judgment is left to God, and God will judge rightly. We are supposed to "know" this about God's justice. This is part of trusting in God and being all-in with His biblical word.

2:3 But do you suppose this, O man, when you pass judgment on those who practice such things and do the same yourself, that you will escape the judgment of God?

No one has earned the right to be self-righteous, even the people of God. Being specifically judgmental of sinful actions and being sovereignly judgmental of the sinner are two different things. The first is part of Christian fellowship; the second is the sole right of God.

O man, when you pass judgment on those who practice such things.

Paul is accusing the Jews of earning for themselves the same wrath that falls on Gentile sinners. Contrary to popular Jewish belief at the time, the sins of the Jews will not be treated differently from those of the Gentiles. The impartial "judgment of God rightly falls" on both Jew and Gentile.

2:4 Or do you think lightly of the riches of His kindness and tolerance and patience, not knowing that the kindness of God leads you to repentance?

God's purpose in His mercy and kindness is not to excuse sin so that everyone gets a prize, but to lead individual sinners to repentance.

2:5 But because of your stubbornness and unrepentant heart you are storing up wrath for yourself in the day of wrath and revelation of the righteous judgment of God.

God's patience with sin as we move through time must not be taken as a sign that God will go easy in the final judgment. People who presume on God's kindness by refusing to repent are storing up the wrath of God against themselves.

2:6-7 . . . who will render to each person according to his deeds: to those who by perseverance in doing good seek for glory and honor and immortality, eternal life.

It is not the works that earn eternal life; it is the condition of the person doing the works. For all-knowing, all-seeing God, the outward works reflect the inner condition.

2:8-9 . . . but to those who are selfishly ambitious and do not obey the truth, but obey unrighteousness, wrath and indignation. There will be tribulation and distress for every soul of man who does evil, of the Jew first and also of the Greek.

Lost people are self-seeking—they do not obey the truth of God but obey unrighteousness. People unaligned with God are aligned with evil in the big picture, regardless of how their works appear to us. There is no contrast of works across these verses. Whatever good social works lost people do are of no account when it comes to God's righteous judgment.

2:10 . . . but glory and honor and peace to everyone who does good, to the Jew first and also to the Greek.

No one gets special treatment on the basis of people group or denominational affiliation. The power of sin prevents anyone from doing good to the degree necessary to earn or sustain salvation. God's act of regeneration is the spiritual cause of the works God sees as done by "those who by perseverance in doing good seek for glory and honor and immortality."

God's justifying salvation verdict of "not guilty" will be confirmed by the "render[ing] to each person according to his deeds" at the final judgment. Our Spirit-driven, sanctifying works will stand as testimony to God's "not guilty" verdict. Our works in and of themselves do not afford us any special spiritual merit or earn us any elevated status in relation to God.

2:11 For there is no partiality with God.

. . . because God is perfectly impartial in this regard. God's way is the only way.

2:12-29 God's Judgment and the Law of Moses

2:12 For all who have sinned without the Law will also perish without the Law, and all who have sinned under the Law will be judged by the Law.

> The (big *L*) Law: The body of commandments given by God through Moses to Israel at Mt. Sinai.
>
> "under the Law"—The Jews have the Law of Moses.
>
> "without the Law"—the Gentiles (read: everyone else)

The Jews believed that outside of the Law there is no salvation, but that they were virtually assured of salvation as God's chosen people living within the domain of the Law. But verse twelve makes it clear that "all who have sinned . . . will be judged."

2:13 . . . for it is not the hearers of the Law who are just before God, but the doers of the Law will be justified.

This verse does not tell us that people can be justified by keeping the Law; it shows the standard that would have to be met for a person to be justified by the Law.

> "doers of the Law"—those able to perfectly, sinlessly keep the Law

Paul affirms the principle that, theoretically, "doing the Law" can lead to salvation. But when taken with the previous verse, he denies that anyone can actually do it.

The Law was given to regulate the covenant relationship already established by God's grace. Neither reading, studying, nor hearing the Law—nor all of these together—could ever justify a person. Paul puts Jews and Gentiles on equal footing with regard to works and judgment.

It has never been enough to seek to do the Law. It has always been faith in the promise of God—and only faith—that justifies. This was a departure from the traditional Jewish view of the time.

2:14 For when Gentiles who do not have the Law do instinctively the things of the Law, these, not having the Law, are a law to themselves . . .

> **Amplification:** *For when [non-Jews] who do not have [access to] the Law [of Moses] do instinctively the things [required] of the Law [by way of general revelation], these, not having the Law, [by giving clear evidence of knowledge of the demands of God,] are a [small l] law to themselves, [and are therefore accountable to God].*

2:15 . . . in that they show the work of the Law written in their hearts, their conscience bearing witness and their thoughts alternately accusing or else defending them . . .

> **Amplification:** *. . . in that they show [some moral aspects of] the work of the Law [of Moses] written in their hearts [by way of natural revelation], their conscience bearing [judgmental] witness and their [conflicting] thoughts alternately accusing or else [finding ways of] defending them.*

Paul is leveling the playing field. He applies the word "Law," a term usually reserved in this context only for the Jews, to the Gentiles. Some knowledge of the work of the Law is written even on Gentile hearts, but not the grace to fulfill this Law.

2:16 . . . on the day when, according to my gospel, God will judge the secrets of men through Christ Jesus.

The accusing and excusing games we play on ourselves in our thoughts will be exposed when God judges the secrets we keep in our hearts. You can't fool—or fool with—God.

2:17-18 But if you bear the name "Jew" and rely upon the Law and boast in God, and know His will and approve the things that are essential, being instructed out of the Law . . .

Five blessings God gave the Jews:

1. "bear the name 'Jew'"—belonging to the chosen people
2. "the Law"—The Jews had possession of the Law.
3. The Jews could "boast in God," carrying the personally neutral meaning, "glory in" (see Jeremiah 9:23-24a).
4. The Jews could "know His will," having more than the natural revelation of verse 1:17.

38

5. The Jews could "approve [discern] what is excellent" through their exposure to the Law.

While possession of the Law was definitely a blessing, Paul's choice of words here ("rely upon the Law") hints at the root problem. This is similar to the accusation in Micah 3:11:

> Her leaders pronounce judgment for a bribe,
> Her priests instruct for a price
> And her prophets divine for money.
> Yet they lean on the Lord saying,
> "Is not the Lord in our midst?
> Calamity will not come upon us."

The Jews thought that just having the Law, whether they lived it or not, would exempt them from judgment.

2:19-20 . . . and are confident that you yourself are a guide to the blind, a light to those who are in darkness, a corrector of the foolish, a teacher of the immature, having in the Law the embodiment of knowledge and of the truth.

Four privileges God gave the Jews:

1. "guide to the [spiritually] blind [Gentiles]"
2. "a light to those [Gentiles] who are in [spiritual] darkness"
3. "a corrector of the [spiritually] foolish [Gentiles]"
4. "a teacher of the [spiritually] immature"

It was the Jews' privilege and responsibility to radiate God's Law out into the Gentile world. Even though they failed miserably at this, the Jews continued to boast pridefully about their privileged status.

2:21-22 . . . you, therefore, who teach another, do you not teach yourself? You who preach that one shall not steal, do you steal? You who say that one should not commit adultery, do you commit adultery? You who abhor idols, do you rob temples?

Four rhetorical questions pointing at the failure of the Jews:

1. "[Y]ou, therefore, who teach another, do you not teach yourself?"— Is your faith authentic? This is the main question. The next three questions provide representative sins.

2. "You who preach that one shall not steal, do you steal?"—a Ten Commandment violation

3. "You who say that one should not commit adultery, do you commit adultery?"—a Ten Commandment violation

4. "You who abhor idols, do you rob temples?"—It was widely known that some Jews would loot a pagan temple and sell the idols or the precious metals, which was a violation of Deuteronomy 7:25. This also violated Roman law. Jews robbing pagan temples, when the secular Roman legal system protected the Jewish Temple, would paint inauthentic Jews as even bigger hypocrites in the eyes of the Gentiles.

Paul exposes spiritual inconsistency and hypocrisy. These listed sins are representative of the contradiction between claim and conduct that pervaded Judaism at the time of Paul. All of the blessings and privileges of being God's people were rendered meaningless without sincere and consistent obedience.

All of the personal pronouns are singular. Accountability before God is an individual matter. Salvation, then, is also an individual matter.

What are you outwardly teaching? What are you inwardly living? The passage may draw on the mental sin represented in Jesus's teaching in Matthew 5:27-28. There is no way not to sin.

2:23 You who boast in the Law, through your breaking the Law, do you dishonor God?

Driving home the accusation of verses 17-22, boasting about God does not bring honor to God; faithful obedience brings honor to God.

2:24 For "the name of God is blasphemed among the Gentiles because of you," just as it is written.

Paul employs irony by drawing on Isaiah 52:5. In the Isaiah passage, God's chosen people are "taken away without cause" by foreign powers, causing God's name to be profaned by Israel's oppressors. Using the Isaiah passage in context of Romans 2, Paul accuses the Jews of eliciting the same response from the Gentiles.

2:25 For indeed circumcision is of value if you practice the Law; but if you are a transgressor of the Law, your circumcision has become uncircumcision.

Think about circumcision like believer's baptism. The symbol of baptism, and its effect on the believer and the surrounding world, is of use if the believer is faithfully following Christ.

The symbol of baptism, like the symbol of circumcision before it, is rendered meaningless in the world if the believer disregards Jesus's commandments—and for all intents and purposes lives like a lost person.

2:26-27 So if the uncircumcised man keeps the requirements of the Law, will not his uncircumcision be regarded as circumcision? And he who is physically uncircumcised, if he keeps the Law, will he not judge you who though having the letter of the Law and circumcision are a transgressor of the Law?

> **Paraphrase:** *If there happened to be an uncircumcised person who perfectly kept the Law, that person would be a full member of the people of God. And that person would be in a position to righteously condemn the sinful actions of God's covenant people who have the Law and circumcision, but break the Law.*

Jews, despite their covenant privileges and covenant rituals, are ultimately in the same position as Gentiles. Disobeying the Law cancels out any salvific advantages the Law and rituals could potentially, theoretically, bring.

Jewish teachers believed that only a radical and insistent denial of the faith could invalidate circumcision. Paul argues that any transgression of the Law can have the same effect.

2:28 For he is not a Jew who is one outwardly, nor is circumcision that which is outward in the flesh.

No one can depend on covenant status, Law, circumcision, (and by extension) ritual, mechanical obedience, church membership, or works for salvation. Any mixing or synergism of faith and works with regard to salvation is damaging to the grace of God.

2:29 But he is a Jew who is one inwardly; and circumcision is that which is of the heart, by the Spirit, not by the letter; and his praise is not from men, but from God.

Ritual circumcision, like ritual believer's baptism, is a matter of the heart. It is only circumcision "by the Spirit" that ultimately counts.

Paul is drawing a line between faith and doing the Law. In two roughly parallel paragraphs (2:17-24 and 2:25-29), Paul makes the argument that the sins of the Jews make them just as liable as Gentiles to God's judgment, despite possession of the Law and circumcision.

"[C]ircumcision . . . of the heart . . . by the Spirit" is what made a Jew a real Jew in the Old Testament and what makes a Christian a real Christian in the New Testament. The solution to sin is, and always has been, saving faith.

"God will judge the secrets of men through Christ Jesus" (Romans 2:16). God's final judgment over humanity is based solely on the work of Jesus Christ. Our standards of works and judgment need not apply. God knows the heart, and God judges the heart by His holy standard.

3:1-8 God's Righteousness Upheld

3:1-2 Then what advantage has the Jew? Or what is the benefit of circumcision? Great in every respect. First of all, that they were entrusted with the oracles of God.

What advantage (value toward salvation) did the Jews have? The Jews had a tremendous advantage—they had the revealed word of God.

3:3-4 What then? If some did not believe, their unbelief will not nullify the faithfulness of God, will it? May it never be! Rather, let God be found true, though every man be found a liar, as it is written, "That You may be justified in Your words and prevail when You judge."

The Bible stands whether or not God's people are faithful to it. God's faithfulness to His biblical word stands even when His followers are unfaithful. God is honoring the terms of the contract.

"[L]et God be [made] true." The Lord's Prayer: "Let Your name be [made] holy." In contrast, God is always reliable and trustworthy even if all of humanity is faithless.

Verse 4 is a restatement and amplification of the faithfulness/unfaithfulness contrast in verse 3. The truthfulness of God in 4a includes His judgment of sin expressed by the quote from Psalm 51:4b. David is confessing his sin with Bathsheba and acknowledging that God is right in judging him.

Alternate translation: "blameless when You judge" or "pure when You judge."

3:5 But if our unrighteousness demonstrates the righteousness of God, what shall we say? The God who inflicts wrath is not unrighteous, is He?

Paul presents a false human logic premise—a human way of subjecting God to human standards of right and wrong: If Jewish faithfulness and sin both cause the manifestation of God's righteousness, and God's righteousness is good even when He judges sin, then it would be unrighteous to condemn any Jewish sinner for contributing to God's righteousness.

> **Question:** Do Jews, as God's chosen people, get a special pass on sinful behavior?

3:6 May it never be! For otherwise, how will God judge the world?

> **Answer:** No. All sin is abhorrent to God, and God is a just Judge. God's righteousness in this sense designates God's faithfulness to His own person and word. The verse 6 question points out the absurdity and impossibility of the false human-logic premise of verse 5. The biblical premise is that God is always holy and just, otherwise the entire system collapses.

3:7 But if through my lie the truth of God abounded to His glory, why am I also still being judged as a sinner?

Human-logic premise: If our unrighteousness serves to show the righteousness of God, then God is unrighteous if He punishes us for our unrighteousness, as our unrighteousness actually results in righteousness.

> **Question 1:** How is it fair for God to judge me if my sin brings Him glory?

3:8a Let us do evil so that good may come.

> **Question 2:** Paul, aren't you encouraging us to sin?

Paul's critics accused him of teaching a cheap and lawless grace.

3:8b Their condemnation is just.

> **Answer:** That is how some are misinterpreting the gospel message—either to slander it or to exploit it. In either case, they are wrong. God's judgment is just, and God's holiness will manifest regardless of what humans do.

God is faithful in His promises to His covenant people, but we can't pick and choose the promises we like and ignore or discard the others. God remains true to the entirety of His biblical word, but only as viewed by Him.

God's grace should not exempt us from any concern over our sin. God's ultimate concern is His glory and not our blessing. "If saved, always saved" is true, and God promises in both the Old and New Testaments to rebuke and chastise His people for sin as well as bless them out of His grace. Saved people should not be in the business of testing the lines God draws for us.

Many people claiming to follow Jesus are ultimately going to find out that "[t]heir condemnation is just."

3:9-20 No One Is Righteous

3:9 What then? Are we better than they? Not at all; for we have already charged that both Jews and Greeks are all under sin; . . .

This complements verses 3:1-2. Did Jews have some advantages given to them by God? Yes. Did that make them better humans in the eyes of God? No.

3:10-12 . . . as it is written, There is none righteous, not even one; there is none who understands, there is none who seeks for God; all have turned aside, together they have become useless; there is none who does good, there is not even one.

"as it is written"—Paul's way of introducing Old Testament quotes

Paul paraphrases Psalm 14:1-3 and Psalm 53:1-3 and changes "good" to "righteous," referencing Romans 1:17. These psalms develop the folly of humanity. Paul points the two psalms to this conclusion: No one is right before God on their own merits. Without God's grace, humanity is doomed.

3:13-14 Their throat is an open grave, with their tongues they keep deceiving, the poison of asps is under their lips; whose mouth is full of cursing and bitterness; . . .

Verse 13 is from Psalm 5:9; verse 14 is from Psalm 10:7.

> "throat is an open grave"—the effects of sin on human speech and thought
>
> "tongues" to deceive . . . venom "under their lips" . . . "mouth . . . full of cursing and bitterness"—deceivers who flatter humanity with their tongues but who intend evil

3:15-17 . . . their feet are swift to shed blood, destruction and misery are in their paths and the path of peace they have not known.

The Isaiah 59:7-8 reference is directed against the unrighteous in Israel. Verses 10-12 describe humanity as a whole, verses 13-14 describe the speech of lost people, and verses 15-17 imply that all Israel is lumped in with those in verses 10-14.

3:18 There is no fear of God before their eyes.

This verse is taken from Psalm 36:1.

---

reverential fear: *noun phrase*

terror-filled, dreading, respectful, humbled, surrendered, obedient, awestruck, worshipful

---

You can't understand or access holy love without a deep and abiding reverential fear. The core human error: people do not reverentially fear God.

3:19 Now we know that whatever the Law says, it speaks to those who are under the Law, so that every mouth may be closed and all the world may become accountable to God; . . .

Because of the Law, "every mouth may be closed." There is nothing left for any defendant—Jew or Gentile—to say in response to the charges. God as Plaintiff has been offended. God as Judge weighs the evidence and pronounces the verdict. All humanity is held accountable for willful rebellion against God.

3:20 . . . because by the works of the Law no flesh will be justified in His sight; for through the Law comes the knowledge of sin.

"works of the Law"—things done in obedience to the Law

There is no justification by works—by good deeds, by good deeds done in the name of God, by good deeds done with some sort of enabling grace, etc. The Law was given to define sin and to make us specifically aware of sin. By interacting with the Law and experiencing our inability to keep it, the friction of sin is amplified. This dynamic should drive us into ever more dependance on the grace of God.

All people are charged with being under the power of sin. All of humanity stands condemned before God's holy standard of judgment. No one can escape condemnation by doing works, including Jews doing "works of the Law." The Law offers no hope for defense.

The stage is now set for the proclamation of the gospel of Jesus Christ.

3:21-4:25 JUSTIFICATION BY FAITH

3:21-31 The Righteousness of God Through Faith

3:21 But now apart from the Law the righteousness of God has been manifested, being witnessed by the Law and the Prophets, . . .

"But now"—two words that mark the cross of Christ as the transition point in salvation history

Through the death and resurrection of Jesus Christ, God's righteousness is now revealed directly by Him—from His initiative in the redemptive work, rather than through the Law or human striving.

"Behold, days are coming," declares the Lord, "when I will make a new covenant with the house of Israel and with the house of Judah. (Jeremiah 31:31)

The covenant with Moses was a temporary structure to order the lives of the people of God and to reveal sin until Christ initiated the new covenant.

When He said, "A new covenant," He made the first one obsolete. But whatever is becoming obsolete and growing old is ready to disappear. (Hebrews 8:13)

COMMENTARY: THE LETTER TO THE ROMANS

Jewish national and religious identity markers such as circumcision, dietary laws, festivals, and sabbaths are no longer needed for God's righteousness to be made manifest. They have been made obsolete by the work of Jesus Christ.

> "the Law and the Prophets"—the Pentateuch and everything else; the entire Old Testament

> *Do not think that I have come to abolish the Law or the Prophets; I have not come to abolish them but to fulfill them. (Matthew 5:17)*

> *And beginning with Moses and all the Prophets, [Jesus] interpreted to them in all the Scriptures the things concerning himself. (Luke 24:27)*

The Old Testament anticipated and predicted the saving work of Jesus Christ on the cross. Even though there is a transition point at the cross, there is continuity between the old era and the new era.

3:22a . . . even the righteousness of God through faith in Jesus Christ for all those who believe; . . .

> **Paraphrase:** *The righteousness of God from the human side of the transaction is only available through faith in Jesus Christ but it is available for all those who believe.*

3:22b-23 . . . for there is no distinction; for all have sinned and fall short of the glory of God.

> "glory"—the magnificent presence of the Lord

There is no spiritual difference in anyone's standing before a righteous and holy God. No one is justified by the quality of their obedience. No one gets a pass on sin. Everyone has sinned; everyone falls short of the glory of God. Everyone sins; everyone is continuously falling short of the glory of God.

3:24 . . . being justified as a gift by His grace through the redemption which is in Christ Jesus; . . .

> "justified"—to be declared righteous (not guilty) by God

> "grace"—unmerited favor; the will of God towards us

> "gift"—you didn't earn it; you don't deserve it; someone else paid for it
>
> "redemption"—liberation through payment of a price

God is the Judge who renders the verdicts. God is the originator of the liberating process. God is the receiver of the price (ransom).

3:25 . . . whom God displayed publicly as a propitiation in His blood through faith. This was to demonstrate His righteousness, because in the forbearance of God He passed over the sins previously committed; . . .

> "displayed publicly"—Christ is the New Testament mercy seat. The Old Testament mercy seat was hidden behind a veil in the Temple; Christ has been displayed publicly. The Old Testament mercy seat ritual is fulfilled, completed, and ended in the sacrifice of Christ.
>
> "propitiation"—the sacrifice of atonement; the covering and forgiving of sins as well as the removal of God's wrath
>
> "by His blood"—the means by which God's wrath is covered
>
> "through faith"—the means by which a person takes advantage of the sacrifice

Redemption takes place by the will of God the Father. God the Father and God the Son are viewed distinctly in this process, but they are not separate. God's holy love and holy wrath meet in the atoning sacrifice, but it is not a case of Jesus's holy love taking the initiative against the Father's holy wrath.

God's wrath is the reaction of God's perfect holiness to sin—the wrath of God is inevitable. The atoning sacrifice is God's holy-love answer to the problem of sin in humanity in light of His holy wrath and as an answer to His holy justice.

> *For it is impossible for the blood of bulls and goats to take away sins.*
> *(Hebrews 10:4)*

The temple sacrificial system was never meant to last. God, in His consistent righteousness, was always looking forward to the cross of Christ as He "passed over sins previously committed" by postponing the full penalty of sin due under the old covenant. Christ on the cross was God as Trinity resolving the sin problem at the timeless, sovereign level, while providing an accessible resolution for humanity in time.

3:26 . . . for the demonstration, I say, of His righteousness at the present time, so that He would be just and the justifier of the one who has faith in Jesus.

God is just—the penalty for sin is not removed; it is paid for by Christ. God is the Justifier: the one who provides the means of justification and the one who declares sinners "not guilty." God's holy justice, holy love, and holy mercy meet at the cross and satisfy God's holy wrath.

3:27 Where then is boasting? It is excluded. By what kind of law? Of works? No, but by a law of faith.

In this verse, (small l) "law" means "principle."

> *Where then is boasting? It is excluded. By what kind of [principle]? Of works? No, but by a [principle] of faith.*

Since justification is all of God, and salvation comes by faith, no one can take pride in repentance or boast about it as any kind of human accomplishment. Any principle of works is contrasted against the principle of faith.

3:28 For we maintain that a man is justified by faith apart from works of the Law.

No works of any kind have any part in making a sinner right with God. Luther was not the first person since apostolic times to figure this out. Justification by faith alone was understood and taught by many Western theologians from the early church up until the time of the Reformation.

3:29a-30 Or is God the God of Jews only?

If justification is by covenantal works of the Law, then God would be the God of the Jews only.

3:29b-30 Is He not the God of Gentiles also? Yes, of Gentiles also, since indeed God who will justify the circumcised by faith and the uncircumcised through faith is one.

There is one God over all humanity. The Law of the Torah is no longer a dividing wall between God's people as the Jews and the rest of humanity. All humanity now has equal access to God through faith in Jesus Christ. There is only one way of justification: by faith.

3:31 Do we then nullify the Law through faith? May it never be! On the contrary, we establish the Law.

Christ perfectly fulfilled the Law and achieved righteousness. His atoning death on the cross allows salvation for all who believe. The Christian relationship to Jesus Christ through faith fully meets the judicial demands of God's Law.

> *Do not think that I have come to abolish the Law or the Prophets; I have not come to abolish them but to fulfill them. (Matthew 5:17)*

The Law was fulfilled, not abolished. "Do we then nullify the Law through faith?" No. Faithful, obedient Christians are expected to uphold the moral norms of the Law.

4:1-22 "By Faith Alone" in the Old Testament

Abraham was revered by the Jews as their father and progenitor (see Isaiah 51:1-2). He was looked to as a model of obedience to God. In chapter 4, Paul uses Abraham as a test case for justification by faith alone. His argument centers on Genesis 15:6, which is quoted in verse 3 and then quoted or alluded to in every paragraph of the chapter.

In a four-part argument, Paul defends the point he made in 3:27-28.

1. Part 1 (4:1 and 4:2) argument—Abraham is not an exception to justification by faith.
2. Part 2 (4:3)—scriptural support for the argument
3. Part 3 (4:4 and 4:5)—development of the argument
4. Part 4 (4:6 and 4:8)—secondary scriptural support

Paul defends his arguments with Scripture, draws his supportive arguments from exegesis, and then supports his reasoning with more Scripture. This is our model.

4:1 What then shall we say that Abraham, our forefather according to the flesh, has found?

Paul is about to use the history of Abraham to develop and reinforce the points he made in 3:27-31. The expression "according to the flesh" places the limitation of humanity on "our forefather" Abraham.

4:2 For if Abraham was justified by works, he has something to boast about, but not before God.

> **Amplification:** *For if Abraham was justified by works, he has something to boast about, [and the claim in 3:27-28 does not stand], but not before God [when God's point of view is considered].*

If Abraham's righteousness was based on his works, his relationship to God would be based on sinless obedience. Since he has no grounds for boasting before God, he has no grounds for boasting before humanity. There is then also no grounds for idolizing him.

4:3 For what does the Scripture say? "Abraham believed God, and it was credited to him as righteousness."

Paul quotes Genesis 15:6 to explain "but not before God" from the previous verse. Genesis 15:6 is the first time the word *believe* is used in the Bible and one of the few times the Old Testament directly links belief to attaining righteousness. The Jews missed the connection.

4:4 Now to the one who works, his wage is not credited as a favor, but as what is due.

An employer owes "one who works" wages for their work. If salvation is works based, then God would owe a person salvation based on their works. But God is never obligated by His creatures. There is no synergy between faith and works with regard to salvation. Grace is not the end point—it is the beginning.

4:5 But to the one who does not work, but believes in Him who justifies the ungodly, his faith is credited as righteousness, ...

This verse transitions from the general illustrative principal of verse 4 to the theological principle. The expression "one who does not work" represents the person who does not try to depend on works for their standing with God.

"Him who justifies the ungodly"—God justifies us. He does it; we don't deserve it. We renounce our sins and we renounce any claim that our works make us deserving. We surrender, and by the grace of God our "faith is credited [by God] as righteousness." This passage does not advocate Christian laziness or Christian complacency. This passage does not free us from our obligation to let the Spirit work through us.

4:6 . . . just as David also speaks of the blessing on the man to whom God credits righteousness apart from works: . . .

Paul has been building a case from the Pentateuch using Abraham as his primary proof. Now he furthers the case by appealing to the prophets and writings using David as his secondary proof. The central theme being proven is that "God credits righteousness apart from works."

4:7-8 "Blessed are those whose lawless deeds have been forgiven, and whose sins have been covered. Blessed is the man whose sin the Lord will not take into account."

The words of David are from Psalm 32:1-2. The key word: "account." God does not take our good works into account when He forgives and saves us. What is more important is that God does not take the quality and/or quantity of our bad works—our sins—into account when He forgives and saves us. It is God's act in *not* taking our "lawless deeds" into account that establishes forgiveness.

The moment of justification has nothing to do with moral transformation. We don't deserve to be justified, but if we repent under the conviction of the Spirit, God changes the status of our relationship with Him from *condemned* to *forgiven*.

God is both just and the Justifier. God saves us.

4:9-10 Is this blessing then on the circumcised, or on the uncircumcised also? For we say, "Faith was credited to Abraham as righteousness." How then was it credited? While he was circumcised, or uncircumcised? Not while circumcised, but while uncircumcised; . . .

Abraham's justification took place in Genesis 15, about thirty years before he was circumcised in Genesis 17. Therefore, faith alone is sufficient for gaining membership into Abraham's spiritual family.

4:11 . . . and he received the sign of circumcision, a seal of the righteousness of the faith which he had while uncircumcised, so that he might be the father of all who believe without being circumcised, that righteousness might be credited to them, . . .

Circumcision was never intended to have any independent value. Abraham's later circumcision added nothing to his justification. The sign of circumcision was just a visible seal that confirmed his justification.

Apart from justification, no ritual or sacramental work makes a person a part of God's family. It was always through faith that a person became part of Abraham's spiritual family. No ritual or sacramental work can cause justification.

4:12 . . . and the father of circumcision to those who not only are of the circumcision, but who also follow in the steps of the faith of our father Abraham which he had while uncircumcised.

Because he believed, Abraham was qualified by God to be the spiritual father of "all who follow in the steps of the faith." When he was later circumcised, Abraham was specifically qualified by God to be the father of the Jewish nation and all Jewish believers. He is thus the spiritual father of all believers whether or not they are circumcised.

The Jews believed that right standing with God could only come through membership in the Jewish tradition. Paul has turned what they thought to be the *macro* into a *micro*. Circumcision was never a guarantee that would ensure entrance into heaven. Circumcision was always a time-bound mark of a relationship built on sovereign justification through faith.

Paul shows that Abraham was always more than the spiritual father of the Jews and expands Abraham's role to spiritual father of all who believe in Jesus Christ.

Engaging in mechanical ritual and/or sacramental activity, including being born into or incorporated into the nation of Israel, has never made anyone individually right with God.

4:13 For the promise to Abraham or to his descendants that he would be heir of the world was not through the Law, but through the righteousness of faith.

The "righteousness of faith" agreement between God and Abraham occurred four hundred and thirty years before the Law was given. God's promises to Abraham could not have been based on Abraham keeping the Law.

4:14 For if those who are of the Law are heirs, faith is made void and the promise is nullified.

> **Paraphrase:** *If only those who keep the Law are heirs to God's promise, then there will be no heirs because no fallen human can keep the Law.*

> *Faith would then be futile and useless, and the promise of God would have no human use or value.*

The Law does not secure the promise.

4:15 . . . for the Law brings about wrath.

The Law does not rescue anyone from condemnation. By clearly defining what God requires of humanity, the Law amplifies sin, produces more wrath, and confirms judgment to condemnation.

God's wrath existed before the Mosaic Law and exists outside of the Mosaic Law (Romans 1:18, 2:12, 3:23). No one gets a pass on sin.

4:15b . . . but where there is no law, there is also no violation.

> **Paraphrase:** *But where there is no command to obey a specific law, there cannot be a deliberate violation of that law.*

Everyone sins; ignorance of the Law is no excuse. But a person who knows the Law and willfully, mindfully violates it is even more accountable to God than those without the Law.

4:16-17a For this reason it is by faith, in order that it may be in accordance with grace, so that the promise will be guaranteed to all the descendants, not only to those who are of the Law, but also to those who are of the faith of Abraham, who is the father of us all, (as it is written, "A father of many nations have I made you") in the presence of Him whom he believed, . . .

God's grace guarantees God's promise. The only way to access the unmerited favor of God's grace is by faith. This puts all of humanity on the same spiritual level before God. The "many nations" verse from Genesis 17:5 reinforces the inclusion of the Gentiles.

4:17b . . . even God, who gives life to the dead and calls into being that which does not exist.

God exists beyond created time. He is timeless in His divine sovereignty. In the Old and New Testaments, sovereign God authoritatively speaks of promised, future time-bound things that do not exist yet as if they already exist.

4:18 In hope against hope he believed that he might become a father of many nations according to that which had been spoken, "So shall your descendants be."

Amplification: *In hope [born of faith in sovereign God] against hope [born out of time-bound logical reasoning or sensory evidence] he believed [the divine prophecy from Genesis 15:5] . . .*

4:19a Without becoming weak in faith he contemplated his own body . . .

TIMELESS	TIME-BOUND
heaven things	earth things
without becoming weak in faith	He contemplated His own body
"In hope" (4:18a)	"against hope" (4:18a)
"I do believe" (Mark 9:24b)	"help my unbelief" (Mark 9:24b)

4:19b . . . now as good as dead since he was about a hundred years old, and the deadness of Sarah's womb.

TIME-BOUND: despite the "deadness of Sarah's womb"

TIMELESS: Abraham had faith in the "God who gives life to the dead" (4:17b).

Abraham continued to believe sovereign God's promise despite the time-bound evidence confronting his senses.

4:20 . . . yet, with respect to the promise of God, he did not waver in unbelief but grew strong in faith, giving glory to God, . . .

This does not imply that Abraham's faith was perfect. Abraham was a sinner. But despite the evidence of his senses, his understandings in the world, and how he wrestled with those things (Genesis 17:17), Abraham never "wavered in unbelief"—he never lost his faith. Abraham did not create a

55

crisis of faith for himself between the apparent physical evidence in time and the sovereign promise of God.

4:21 . . . and being fully assured that what God had promised, He was able also to perform.

Through continued trusting in God, Abraham's faith grew as he waited. The strengthening faith of Abraham gave glory to God while giving assurance to Abraham.

4:22 Therefore it was also credited to him as righteousness.

"Therefore," Paul reasserts his argument that Abraham's faith was credited to him as righteousness. Verse 22 closes the exposition of Genesis 15:6 that began in Romans 4:3.

4:23-25 The Faith of Abraham—The Faith of Christians

4:23-24 Now not for his sake only was it written that it was credited to him, but for our sake also, to whom it will be credited, as those who believe in Him who raised Jesus our Lord from the dead.

Christians are "those who believe in Him who raised Jesus our Lord from the dead." It is Christians "to whom it will be credited." It was "for our sakes also."

Verse 24 emphasizes God as the one who raised Jesus from the dead. This is to emphasize the relationship between Abraham's faith and Christian faith. The Old Testament is directly connected with the New Testament and speaks directly to Christians. Christians and Abraham share the same faith-based justification, and while Abraham did not know Jesus Christ as the specific content of the promise, the object of faith is the same.

Our faith has the same nature as Abraham's and the same object: God.

4:25 . . . He who was delivered over because of our transgressions, and was raised because of our justification.

The phrase "delivered over" is a divine passive with God as the implied object of the action. Jesus was delivered over by God because we are sinners, and was raised from the dead to secure the possibility of our justification.

Jesus's death on the cross provides the necessary basis for God's justifying action. Jesus's resurrection is a demonstration that God accepted Jesus's suffering and death as full payment for sin. The Father's wrath is satisfied, and, in the resurrection, His favor was directed toward Christ and through Christ to those who believe. God's approval of Christ's sacrifice results in God's justification of anyone united with Christ.

[Jesus Christ]	was delivered over	because of	our transgressions,
[Jesus Christ]	was raised	for the sake of	our justification.

Isaiah 53:12b:

[Jesus Christ]	was numbered	with	the transgressors;
[Jesus Christ]	bore the sin	of	many,
[Jesus Christ]	interceded	for	the transgressors.

Exposition of faith in chapter 4:

- 4:3-8, faith contrasted against works
- 4:9-12, faith contrasted against ritual
- 4:13-16, faith contrasted against Law
- 4:17-21, faith contrasted against time-bound evidence

Chapter 4 makes it clear that faith is credited as righteousness only by the grace of God.

5:1-7:25 THE HOPE OF SALVATION

5:1-11 The Blessings of Justification

5:1a Therefore, having been justified by faith...

This sums up the central teaching of Romans 1–4.

5:1b ... we have peace with God through our Lord Jesus Christ, ...

The Old Testament prophets used the term *peace* to express the salvation that God would bring His people in the last days (Ezekiel 34:25; Isaiah 54:10;

Jeremiah 37:26). In Isaiah 52:7 peace is equivalent to salvation. Peace with God goes beyond just a cessation of hostilities; it also means reconciliation and salvation. If we have real, saving faith, then we are justified, and "we have peace with God through our Lord Jesus Christ." We are no longer God's enemy, and He Is no longer our enemy.

Too often we still behave as if we are God's enemy, and then we worry and fret and pray in strange ways to counterbalance the friction that we are causing. Paul tells us that if we are justified, we do not have to go through all of that. We are at peace with the God who is now at peace with us.

5:2 . . . through whom also we have obtained our introduction by faith into this grace in which we stand; and we exult in hope of the glory of God.

> "grace"—unearned, undeserved favor that God extends to humanity
>
> "grace"—the state into which God's saving work transfers the believer

Now that we are at peace with God, we can have access to Him any time, any place, to deal with anything we need to deal with. This grace goes beyond the moment of justification and encompasses everything coming our way from God through Christ. We can now confidently "exult in hope of the glory of God."

5:3-4 And not only this, but we also exult in our tribulations, knowing that tribulation brings about perseverance; and perseverance, proven character; and proven character, hope; . . .

Believers live in the hope of our faith contrasted against the fallen world we walk in. We live in the tension between this age of Satan and the age of Christ to come. Sufferings of any kind are then pressure tests that are meant to refine our faith as we subjugate them to our hope in Christ. That is why we are not only to "exult in [the midst of] our tribulations," we are to "exult in our [specific] tribulations."

Suffering subordinated to our hope and peace in Christ yields the spiritual qualities Paul lists. We transcend tribulations by "knowing" (the word is causal). We persevere, and in so doing we prove out our Christian character in time, and our hope in Christ strengthens. This process of patient perseverance yields a spiritual *knowing* wherein we realize that the tribulation is more than just getting randomly crushed.

Before we were at peace with God, any suffering-pressure applied to our lives was felt as hurt, pain, discomfort, discontent, etc., that existed without purpose or direction. For those of us at peace with God, we realize that suffering has direction and purpose and that tribulations exist for spiritually shaping and refining reasons.

If suffering causes doubt in God's promise, bitterness, despair, unbelief, etc., then the enemy has dragged the believer back into the world and is winning battles in time. Staring down the apparent hopelessness of Satan's time-bound world with the timeless peace and hope we get by the grace of sovereign God builds conviction-muscle, a *knowing* that fuels our certainty of that for which we hope.

5:5 . . . and hope does not disappoint, because the love of God has been poured out within our hearts through the Holy Spirit who was given to us.

This is the first time in Romans that Paul speaks of God's love. Any time God's love is referenced in the Bible, mentally insert the word *holy* before it. This creates the appropriate contrast between God's holy love and human standards of love.

> "the love of God"—the subject of the verb "pouring out"
>
> "the love of God"—"[holy] love of God for us," *not* "our love for God"
>
> "poured out within our hearts"—God's holy love is conveyed to our senses by the indwelling Holy Spirit.

The deeper we move into the reality of our salvation, the more of God's holy love we can feel in times of tribulation. Hope fortifies and strengthens in this dynamic in a way that it never would without trials and tribulations. We surrender in faith to the Christian reality that even though we do not know why something is happening, the God we are at peace with does know, and He tells us to be at peace —He has got this.

Our hope should manifest as an inner subjective, emotionally sensory certainty that God loves us. This internal sensation within the believer, made vital in the objective actions of God on our behalf, gives us assurance that "hope does not disappoint."

5:6-8 For while we were still helpless, at the right time Christ died for the ungodly. For one will hardly die for a righteous man; though perhaps for the good

man someone would dare even to die. But God demonstrates His own love toward us, in that while we were yet sinners, Christ died for us.

> **Paraphrase:** (verse 6) *At the time God had always intended it to happen, while humanity was still helplessly fumbling and bumbling along in sin, Jesus Christ died for a world of rebellious and underserving, Godless sinners.* (verse 7) *Human love at its best might motivate a person to die for a truly good person or close personal acquaintance, but not for an enemy.* (verse 8) *When Christ died for sinful humanity, God demonstrated that His holy love is far greater than any expression or manifestation of human love.*

5:9 Much more then, having now been justified by His blood, we shall be saved from the wrath of God through Him.

Assurance: Since God has already done the most difficult task of sacrificing Jesus and allowing us to be justified by His blood, "much more then" God can be depended on to do the easier thing of saving those He justifies from end-times wrath.

5:10 For if while we were enemies we were reconciled to God through the death of His Son, much more, having been reconciled, we shall be saved by His life.

The justification language of verse 9 is legal courtroom language. The reconciliation language of verse 10 is the language of personal relationship. We all started out as enemies of God, and, as we were hostile to God, God was hostile toward us (see 1:18). Through the sacrifice of Christ, believers are reconciled to God in the present and protected by Christ at the final judgment.

5:11 And not only this, but we also exult in God through our Lord Jesus Christ, through whom we have now received the reconciliation.

Anyone who is stumbling and/or struggling with their day-to-day faith should contemplate what they have in Christ: justification and reconciliation resulting in peace with God. Reflecting on these things should cause a believer to rejoice in a peace that has the power to overcome all present tribulations while providing assurance for both the immediate and the distant future.

5:12-21 Christ's Obedience Overcomes Adam's Disobedience

Verses 12 and 18 of chapter 5 track the main theme of this paragraph: the power of Christ's obedience to overcome Adam's act of disobedience. Verses 13-17 form a supportive excursus.

The ongoing parallels between Adam as "one man" and Jesus Christ as "one man" affirm Adam as a historical person, not a fictional or mythological construct.

5:12 Therefore, just as through one man sin entered into the world, and death through sin, and so death spread to all men, because all sinned– . . .

Death was not a natural part of human existence at first. Adam brought death to humanity through sin. The spiritual death and disease of sinful separation from God exposed humanity to physical disease and physical death.

"[S]in" is singular here, meaning an essence condition, not the plural manifestation of sinful actions. The plural "men" in "death spread to all men" refers to people of both sexes. It translates as "men" here and in verse 18 to show the connection to Jesus Christ as the singular "man," "one Man," or "One" in verses 5:15, 17, 18, and 19.

We see that "all sinned"—sin is pervasive in the universe and endemic to humanity. No one can avoid sinning. Sin (5:12a) produces death (5:12b), and all humans die (5:12c) because all sin (5:12d).

God is telling us the *why* and not the *how*. We do not know the spiritual or physical mechanics of how Adam's sin resulted in death for everyone. We do not know the exact nature of the connection between Adam's sin and the sin of all of humanity. What we are told is that the sin and death phenomena inevitably repeats itself in every human being.

This verse in no way implies that Adam's guilt is transmitted. A baby is not born guilty; a baby is born into a sin-poisoned universe. All die because all sin—all die because Adam sinned. No one escapes the power of sin.

5:13a . . . for until the Law sin was in the world, . . .

Sin was corrupting humanity before the Mosaic Law was given to Israel.

5:13b-14a . . . but sin is not imputed when there is no law. Nevertheless death reigned from Adam until Moses.

Even though people were not accountable by the details of God's later revealed Law, they were still subject to the provisions of Romans 1.

5:14 . . . even over those who had not sinned in the likeness of the offense of Adam, who is a type of Him who was to come.

Even though people before the time of the Law were not mindfully transgressing against God's explicit command as Adam did, they still sinned against God and were still subject to the universal death penalty.

---

typology: *noun*

Old Testament people, institutions, or events intended to be an early indication of the end times age introduced by Jesus Christ. Adam's act of sin prefigures Christ's act of obedience, making Adam a "type of Christ."

Adam and Christ are both covenantal heads of humanity, so all people are either *in Adam* or *in-Christ*. Everyone is in Adam at birth and can only be in Christ through the new birth of salvation.

5:15a But the free gift is not like the transgression.

"But" signifies Paul qualifying the typological relationship between Adam and Christ introduced in verse 14. Verses 15-17 show three contrasts between the work of Adam and the work of Christ: a contrast of degree (5:15b), a contrast of consequence (5:16), and a contrast of activity (5:17).

5:15b For if by the transgression of the one the many died, much more did the grace of God and the gift by the grace of the one Man, Jesus Christ, abound to the many.

Due to Adam's transgression "many" died. The "all sinned" of verse 12 makes it clear that the first "many" of verse 15 refers to all of humanity. Verse 15 shows a *contrast of degree*: the work of Christ is a manifestation of the grace of God, making it greater in every way than the sin of Adam.

5:16 The gift is not like that which came through the one who sinned; for on the one hand the judgment arose from one transgression resulting in condemnation, but on the other hand the free gift arose from many transgressions resulting in justification.

Here is a window into God's miraculous grace. One transgression from Adam was serious enough to institute judgment resulting in condemnation through Adam. But the gift that leads to justification through Christ came after the many and varied transgressions of all humanity. Verse 16 shows a *contrast of consequence*: Adam's act of disobedience brought condemnation and death. Christ's act of obedience, His gift, brought the possibility of justification.

5:17 For if by the transgression of the one, death reigned through the one, much more those who receive the abundance of grace and of the gift of righteousness will reign in life through the One, Jesus Christ.

The "those who receive" in 5:17 makes it clear that the second "many" in 5:15b refers to "those who receive . . . the gift of righteousness." Verse 17 shows a *contrast of activity*: Adam's transgression caused death to reign, making it the perfect example of all sinful human activity. God's "gift of righteousness" comes through His "abundance of grace," making it "much more" to "those who receive the abundance of grace" through Christ.

5:18 So then as through one transgression there resulted condemnation to all men, even so through one act of righteousness there resulted justification of life to all men.

"So then" in 5:18 completes the "just as" of 5:12. Verse 5:18 summarizes the basic argument started in 5:12, developed in 5:13 and 5:14, and fleshed out in 5:15-17—all people are in Adam, but only those who receive the gift of righteousness are in Christ.

The use of "as" and "so" shows the focus to be on the method of sin and righteousness being passed from the leader to the receiving group, not the number of people in each group.

Some people use the parallelism in this verse as a proof-text to support universalism: "all" were made sinners, "all" will be saved. The immediate context of verses 5:17 and 5:19, and the overall context provided by verses 1:16–4:25, make this interpretation an impossibility.

5:19 For as through the one man's disobedience the many were made sinners, even so through the obedience of the One the many will be made righteous.

> **Personal contrast:** the personal disobedience of Adam vs. the personal obedience of Christ
>
> **Personal results:** "many [people] were made sinners—many [people] will be made righteous."

The "all men" from verse 18 is restated as "the many" in verse 19, further invalidating a universalist interpretation of verse 18.

5:20-21 The Law came in so that the transgression would increase; but where sin increased, grace abounded all the more, so that, as sin reigned in death, even so grace would reign through righteousness to eternal life through Jesus Christ our Lord.

The Law was not given to fix sin; its purpose was to amplify and expose sin. Sins of conscience against God's natural law became willful transgressions against God's revealed Law. But the power and provision of God's grace, manifested in Christ, far outstrips the power of sin.

EXCURSUS: SIN

Sin is the default human condition of separation from God.

- *Imputed sin* is what we receive from what Adam did in the Garden. The result of what Adam did is that every human will die physically.
- *Imparted sin* is our sin nature. Because of the sin-poisoned condition we find ourselves in, we are affected even as children as our sin nature develops.
- *Intentional sin* occurs when our imparted sin nature manifests consciously and sinful actions become intentional—we begin to willfully and mindfully sin. When we cross that spiritual threshold— and only God knows exactly when that is—we become accountable to God for our sins.

6:1-14 Dead to Sin, Alive with Christ—Subduing the Power of Sin

6:1 What shall we say then? Are we to continue in sin so that grace may increase?

This question is in response to the assertion in 5:20 that, "where sin increased, grace abounded all the more." Is God somehow bound to give more grace in response to willful sin on the part of believers? Since God forgave all of our sins at salvation, can't we then indulge in as much sin as we want and enjoy even more grace as God's automatic response? Doesn't this "free grace" destroy the foundations of morality and encourage more sinning?

6:2 May it never be! How shall we who died to sin still live in it?

How shall we who died to sin [still live in the lifestyle of sinful transgressions]?

How shall we who died to sin [still live in the habitual practice of sinful actions]?

A believer who has "died to sin" goes through a fundamental, supernatural change in state of being at conversion. This is not about the penalty of sin removed by justification; it is about our new relationship to the power of sin by way of regeneration—the indwelling of the Holy Spirit. Sin did not die—the believer dies in Christ. Sin remains, but it does not reign.

Even though sin pollution is still the condition of the world and a real threat, believers are not to indulge in sinful living. For a justified, regenerate believer, sin's power has been broken. This fact will be evidenced during sanctification by Spirit-led, authentic works. The apostles James and John insist that justification must be evidenced in time.

6:3 Or do you not know that all of us who have been baptized into Christ Jesus have been baptized into His death?

Conversion is a real, supernatural event joining us with Christ and is therefore a real joining with the death of Christ. We die to the power of sin, and we are raised by the power of the Holy Spirit to new life.

EXCURSUS: BAPTISM

Faith is mentioned in every chapter of Romans, while baptism is only mentioned in two verses. If water baptism is essential to salvation as some Christians believe, then why doesn't Paul directly address the matter in a letter that clearly spells out how we get saved? Considering that by the time this letter was written the use of "baptism" without an accompanying modifier would have immediately brought water baptism to the minds of the Christians, the omission at this point in the letter would be even more glaring.

The early church thought of justification, regeneration, and water baptism as the complete expression of the supernatural conversion—community initiation experience. But while faith was always assumed to lead to baptism, and baptism always assumed faith, salvation was not held to be contingent upon water baptism. The matter was straightforward: If you are a Christian, you get baptized. If you are calling yourself a Christian, and you aren't baptized, why didn't you get baptized?

If God's justifying decree of "not guilty" is what establishes and secures our salvation, then water baptism can only be a symbol of our union with Christ—it cannot contribute to it. Water baptism is a matter of witness, testimony, and surrendered obedience that takes place after salvation. The work of justification is all of God.

6:4 Therefore we have been buried with Him through baptism into death, so that as Christ was raised from the dead through the glory of the Father, so we too might walk in newness of life.

"buried with [Christ]"

TIME-BOUND: the physical events of the death, burial, and resurrection of Christ

TIMELESS: the spiritual realities of the death, burial, and resurrection of Christ

"buried with [Christ] through baptism into death"—Baptism here does not explain *how* we were buried with Christ at conversion; it illustrates *that* we were buried with Christ at conversion.

"as Christ was raised . . . so we too"

TIME-BOUND: The events of the death, burial, and resurrection of Christ caused a shift in time from the old age of Adam to the new age of Jesus Christ.

TIMELESS: The spiritual effects of the death, burial, and resurrection that occur at conversion transfer across time to every individual who is with Christ.

The focus here is not on the individual details. Our conversion serves to both empower us and call us so that "we might walk in the newness of life" with Christ.

> **6:5** For if we have become united with Him in the likeness of His death, certainly we shall also be in the likeness of His resurrection, . . .

> **TIME-BOUND:** If we have been joined with Christ in repentance and justification "in the likeness of His death," so then we will also be conformed with Christ in regeneration and sanctification "in the likeness of His resurrection."

> **TIMELESS:** If saved "in the likeness of His death," always saved "in the likeness of His resurrection."

If saved (united with Him in justification and regeneration), always saved (resulting in glorification).

> **6:6** . . . knowing this, that our old self was crucified with Him, in order that our body of sin might be done away with, so that we would no longer be slaves to sin; . . .

Our old self in Adam was "crucified with [Christ]" by the combination of Christ's death and the spiritual death at our conversion. By God's act of justification, we are transferred from the old age of sin and death to the new age of righteousness and life.

"[B]ody of sin" is not referring to the physical body in isolation as being inherently sinful. This refers to the whole person with an emphasis on points of interaction with the world. Believers are no longer part of the body of Adam; believers are part of the body of Christ.

The temptation for a Christian to engage in sinful actions still remains, but the power of sin to totally and completely rule and dominate has been defeated. A Christian should be progressively growing in sanctification and should display increasing spiritual maturity and obedience to biblical precepts.

6:7 . . . for he who has died is freed from sin.

Death with Christ (repentance-justification-regeneration) breaks the hold of sin on a person.

6:8 Now if we have died with Christ, we believe that we shall also live with Him, . . .

> **TIME-BOUND:** If we have died with Christ, we can enjoy new life with Christ right now.

6:9 . . . knowing that Christ, having been raised from the dead, is never to die again; death no longer is master over Him.

> **TIMELESS:** If we have died with Christ, we will be with Christ after physical death or at the second coming (whichever comes first).

Through the incarnation, Christ came into the world under the influence of the power of sin and death—the old age of Adam. Because "death no longer is master over [Christ]," then "if we have died with Christ, we believe that we shall also live with Him." Our assurance is the hope of faith that comes through spiritual *knowing*.

6:10 For the death that He died, He died to sin once for all; but the life that He lives, He lives to God.

Jesus fully identified with sinful humanity in the old age, resulting in death having authority over Him—Jesus physically died. Jesus was subjected to the power of sin, but He never gave in to its power and actually sinned.

> "He died to sin"—Death is the product of sin. Christ's separation from the power of sin shows that death cannot rule over Him, thus affecting the power of sin.
>
> "once for all"—Christ's transfer into a new state of being was final and definitive. Christ's death took on the penalty of all of the sins of humanity past, present, and future.
>
> "[Christ] lives to God"—Christ's death is the gateway to life.

6:11 Even so consider yourselves to be dead to sin, but alive to God in Christ Jesus.

"dead to sin"—free from the ruling power of sin and free from inevitably surrendering to sin

"alive to God"—able to be blessed while moving through the world

"in Christ Jesus"—It's all about the relationship: grace and faith.

6:10	even so	6:11
Jesus "died to sin"	so that we can be	"dead to sin"
Jesus "lives to God"	so that we can be	"alive to God in Christ Jesus"

6:12-13 Therefore do not let sin reign in your mortal body so that you obey its lusts, and do not go on presenting the members of your body to sin as instruments of unrighteousness; but present yourselves to God as those alive from the dead, and your members as instruments of righteousness to God.

Here is the tension for a believer between what sovereign God has already and forever accomplished and the sanctifying walk of obedience in time.

Prohibition 1: "do not let sin reign in your mortal body." Make it your practice to avoid sinful actions. The battle is spiritual, but it plays out in mortal bodies. The believer is no longer a "body of sin," but the "mortal body" remains. We still participate in the weakness of this age, so we must engage mental and spiritual discipline and soundly manage our emotions, energies, and faculties.

Prohibition 2: "do not go on presenting the members of your body to sin as instruments of unrighteousness." "Instruments" translates a military term in the original language that means "weapons." Our skills, abilities, and giftings are weapons that must no longer be made available to the enemy. We must constantly avoid using our abilities and resources in the service of sin.

Command: "present yourselves to God as those alive from the dead." We must constantly and mindfully present ourselves to God for service. Only those who are "alive from the dead" (i.e., supernaturally converted) can do this.

6:14 For sin shall not be master over you, for you are not under law but under grace.

Promise: "sin shall not be master over you."

TIME-BOUND: the confidence to wage war against sin

TIMELESS: the hope we have for the future

Provision: "you are not under law but under grace."

"under law"—subject to the powers of the old age and the Law

"under grace"—subject to the new age and freedom from the power of sin

Christians live under grace in the new age of Christ and not under Law in the old age of Adam. Before Christ, sinners could escape from the powers of the old age and the condemning power of the Law by embracing God through faith by way of the Law and the Prophets and looking forward in hope to the coming of the Messiah. Christians are no longer under the Law of Moses in the manner of theocratic Israel before the death of Christ. But the moral aspects of the Law were reinforced by Christ, are still in effect, and are to be obediently adhered to.

TIMELESS: justification, regeneration, redemption (what God has done for us)

TIME-BOUND: sanctifying obedience (what we are supposed to do)

Separating what God has done for us from what we are supposed to do creates an aggressive works-based attitude—an imbalance toward time-bound-ness. This can lead to the moralist and/or legalist mistake of thinking that individual effort, elaborate programs, or extra-biblical rules and rituals can lead to sanctified holiness.

Joining what God has done for us to what we are supposed to do, with no distinction, creates a lack of Christian responsibility in time—an imbalance toward timelessness. This can lead to an apathetic neglect of the commands of Christ and holiness and the belief that sanctification will happen automatically in a state of spiritual osmosis.

Our timeless spiritual state in context of the sovereignty of God is to become our time-bound, day-to-day reality. We are supposed to become, in time, what we are becoming beyond time. Sanctification requires active immersion in surrendered living.

6:15-23 Freed from Sin—Enslaved to Righteousness

6:15 What then? Shall we sin because we are not under law but under grace? May it never be!

According to 6:14, those who are justified "are not under law but under grace."

> **Human logic question:** Since sin's condemning power over us is broken at justification, can't we take advantage of God's grace by continuing to willfully, mindfully sin?
>
> **Answer:** God's grace should be a constraining power as well as a liberating power. Christian freedom *from* sin is not a freedom *to* sin.

6:16 Do you not know that when you present yourselves to someone as slaves for obedience, you are slaves of the one whom you obey, either of sin resulting in death, or of obedience resulting in righteousness?

"Do you not know" is Paul's way of saying, "This is something you already know." Habitually giving oneself over to something or someone makes a person a slave to that something or someone. Christians who constantly give in to temptation, in effect, become slaves to sin again. God's declaration of "not guilty" should manifest as living experience. Christians who are no longer legally bound as slaves to sin must no longer live as if they are slaves of sin.

Every day we are "either of sin . . . or of obedience." There is no neutral ground. Lost people who think they are free to make their own way in the world are surrendered to an illusion created and sustained by Satan. Christians who think they are free to make their own way in the world are living under an illusion created and sustained by Satan.

There is no such thing as human autonomy. We are under the power and authority of sin, or we are under the power and authority of God. Some lost people think, *Should I keep my freedom or surrender to God?* The reality is, *Should I serve sin or should I serve God?* Too many Christians think, *How much sin can I get away with while serving God?* Faithful obedience to the biblical precepts should be central to Christian life.

> **TIME-BOUND:** Willful sin in a Christian life leads the believer away from Christ, "resulting in [a condition of spiritual] death." Obedience leads to conduct pleasing to God, "resulting in [moral] righteousness."

> **TIMELESS:** Lost people can either remain a slave to Satan, "resulting in [eternal] death," or surrender to obedience to Christ, "resulting in [eternal] righteousness."

---

essence idolatry: *noun phrase*

any worldly thought or mental wave of worldly thoughts, that you cannot turn off at will, becomes an idol. The time and energy that you invest in it unchecked becomes idol worship.

6:17-18 But thanks be to God that though you were slaves of sin, you became obedient from the heart to that form of teaching to which you were committed, and having been freed from sin, you became slaves of righteousness.

> *. . . obedient from the heart . . . to that [word] to which you were [handed over].*

> **Paraphrase:** *You got saved, your heart wants to follow Jesus, and even though you aren't under the Law, you are still bound by an authoritative form of teaching.*

Obedience to the Word is an outgrowth of God handing us over to the Word at conversion. Saving faith and ongoing commitment from the heart are inseparable. The only way to become freed from sin is to become a slave to God.

6:19a I am speaking in human terms because of the weakness of your flesh.

> **Paraphrase:** *I am using this limited, imperfect human slavery analogy to make a spiritual point because of the difficulty you have in understanding spiritual things.*

6:19b For just as you presented your members as slaves to impurity and to lawlessness, resulting in further lawlessness, so now present your members as slaves to righteousness, resulting in sanctification.

Comparison: "just as you presented . . . so now present."

> **Paraphrase:** *Just as you were once single-mindedly dedicated to idols like lust, power, and money resulting in ever-increasing sinful actions, so now pursue holiness with that same single-minded zeal, resulting in ever-increasing conformity to Christ.*

6:20 For when you were slaves of sin, you were free in regard to righteousness.

Lost people celebrate and revel in their apparent freedom "in regard to righteousness." The only thing they are really free from is the ability to live in a way that pleases God.

6:21 Therefore what benefit were you then deriving from the things of which you are now ashamed? For the outcome of those things is death.

An attitude of shame is a spiritually healthy reaction toward the things we did while lost. There is never any spiritual benefit in sinful living. The only result of the freedom that lost people indulge in by rejecting God is spiritual death.

6:22 But now having been freed from sin and enslaved to God, you derive your benefit, resulting in sanctification, and the outcome, eternal life.

	Status	Condition	Time-bound Result	Outcome Beyond Time
6:20	lost	slave of sin	free from righteousness	separation from God
6:21	lost	indulging sin	things to be ashamed of	eternal death
6:22	justified	slave of God	ongoing sanctification	eternal life

6:23 For the wages of sin is death, but the free gift of God is eternal life in Christ Jesus our Lord.

"[W]ages" is plural; "sin" is singular. A wage is something that someone has earned and deserves. The wages of both physical and eternal death will be paid by God to those who remain surrendered to sin.

A free gift is the opposite of what someone deserves, but it must be paid for by someone. The "free gift of God is eternal life" paid for by "Christ Jesus our Lord."

	The Master	The Means	The Outcome
6:23a	sin	a wage earned	eternal death
6:23b	God	a gift received	eternal life

The release from the power of the Law is not to be perverted into an excuse for sinning. Being under grace carries with it obligations of obedience. The question is not whether a human has a master, but which master the human is serving.

7:1-6 RELEASED FROM THE LAW—JOINED TO CHRIST

In verses 1, 2, and 3, small *l* "law" refers to Roman law and Mosaic Law.

7:1 Or do you not know, brethren (for I am speaking to those who know the law), that the law has jurisdiction over a person as long as he lives?

"Or do you not know" introduces an idea that Paul assumes his reader already knows. Rabbinical tradition taught, "if a person is dead, he is free from the Torah and the fulfilling of the commandments" (*Shabbat* 30a and 151b).

7:2-3 For the married woman is bound by law to her husband while he is living; but if her husband dies, she is released from the law concerning the husband. So then, if while her husband is living she is joined to another man, she shall be called an adulteress; but if her husband dies, she is free from the law, so that she is not an adulteress though she is joined to another man.

Verses 2 and 3 illustrate the general principle just put forward in 7:1.

Point 1 (looking back to verse 1): Death breaks all relationship to any time-bound law and God's Law as it exists in time.

Point 2 (looking forward to verse 4): By breaking the relationship with all law, death enables a person to enter into a new relationship.

Some people use these verses to prove that all remarriage outside the death of a spouse is adulterous. But this illustration is not a comprehensive treatise on remarriage, nor does it have anything to do with divorce; it is an example cited to prove the points of verses 1 and 4. Paul is talking to those who know the Law of Moses and Roman law, and he is representing the New Testament law of faith. Both the Old Testament Law and Roman law (and the New Testament under certain circumstances) allow for remarriage on grounds other than the death of a spouse.

In this illustration, since the husband is still living and no divorce is mentioned, the joining with another is adulterous.

---

allegory: *noun*

"married woman" = lost person
"husband" = Law
"another man" = Jesus Christ

Paraphrase: (7:2) *For a lost person is bound by the law of sin to the penalty of the Law manifesting in that person. But if a lost person is justified, then that person is released from the law of sin with regard to being condemned under the Law. (7:3) So then, if a lost person attempts to join Christ without being justified, that person is still guilty before God and is living in a state of sinful spiritual adultery. But if a lost person genuinely repents—if they are justified by God—they are free from the penalty of sin and joined with Jesus Christ.*

7:4 Therefore, my brethren, you also were made to die to the Law through the body of Christ, so that you might be joined to another, to Him who was raised from the dead, in order that we might bear fruit for God.

Since death breaks a person's bondage to the Law (7:2), so then, like the woman in the illustration (7:3), a believer has been through a death that severs them from bondage to the Law, enabling them to be joined to Christ (7:4).

In chapter 6 the believer dies to sin in order to live for God. In chapter 7 the believer is "made to die to the Law" in order to be joined with Christ. Therefore, you were delivered from the Law's condemning power through the body of Christ. When you are justified, you don't—you can't— divorce yourself from the law of sin or the Law. You were "made to die to the Law" by the grace of God. Being dead to the condemning power of the Law means that once you are justified, "sin shall not be a master over you, for you are not under law but under grace" (6:14).

This does not mean that a believer has nothing more to do with the Law of Moses. The Law also teaches about God's holiness and what God expects from His people morally and ethically and is still binding in those ways.

"[T]hrough the body of Christ [you have died] . . . so that you may be joined to another." Paul is referring to the physical body of Christ Himself. Some traditions have read this to mean, "through the [corporate] body of Christ," as a reference to the visible church. But this interpretation violates the context even in this verse alone.

In this verse, the "another" who we are joined to is "Him who was raised from the dead." Why does God do this for us? "[I]n order that we might bear fruit for God."

TIME-BOUND: Our witness and testimony evidenced in the world through our Christian works.

TIMELESS: Our Christian works giving witness and testimony to the glory of God.

7:5 For while we were in the flesh, the sinful passions, which were aroused by the Law, were at work in the members of our body to bear fruit for death.

"while we were in the flesh"—while we were lost

"In the flesh" does not refer to a physical part of a person. It also does not translate well as "sinful nature" in the manner of a personal impulse within a person. The "flesh" is the power of the old age. The non-believer is enveloped in sin and controlled by sinful, worldly principles and values.

The "flesh" is the sin-power sphere in which a lost person lives. This usage of "flesh" represents an objective constant that all of humanity is subject to.

In 3:20 the Law reveals sin. In 5:20 the Law turns sin into transgression. In this passage, sinful passions are awakened by the Law. The Law lays out God's standard, stimulates a human's innate rebelliousness against God, and thus arouses sinful passions. The term *sinful passions* represents sin itself as an active, impersonal force. This force is at work in the "members of our bodies"—our physical, emotional, and cognitive faculties. The power of sinful passions, at work in our physical, emotional, and cognitive faculties, "bear fruit for death." Three powers of the old age: sin, Law, death.

7:6 But now we have been released from the Law, having died to that by which we were bound, so that we serve in newness of the Spirit and not in oldness of the letter.

> "now that we have been released from the Law"—now that we are Christians

This is the second time in Romans that Paul contrasts the letter of the Law against the Spirit (see 2:27-29). The essence of the old covenant is the Law as an external, written demand of God. With or without faith, the presence of the Law stimulated sin. A Jew trying to keep the Law without faith would inevitably bear spiritual fruit for death.

The essence of the new covenant is the potential for a new spiritual condition created by God's Spirit. A Christian has been released from the bondage of the Law. A Christian can now "serve in the newness of the Spirit."

The contrast is between the old covenant and the new covenant—the old age of Adam and the new age of Christ. The contrast is not between an old life living mechanically under the Law and a new life in Christ with no rules or restrictions.

7:7-13 Is the Law Sinful?

7:7 What shall we say then? Is the Law sin? May it never be! On the contrary, I would not have come to know sin except through the Law; for I would not have known about coveting if the Law had not said, "You shall not covet."

Paul responds to a criticism of the gospel: if the Law increases transgression (5:20) and arouses sinful passions (7:5), is the Law by its nature sinful?

Many Jews accused Paul of putting Moses at odds with Christ and of destroying any continuity between the Law of Moses (Old Testament) and the gospel of Jesus Christ (New Testament).

> "to know sin"—What kind of *knowing* is this? Through the Law we can come to know the real nature and power of sin; we can understand the sinfulness of sin (see 3:20).
>
> "You shall not covet"—Jewish writers before Paul tended to view coveting as the root of all sins. Due to its position as the last commandment, they viewed it as a summation of all the commandments.

The tenth commandment deals with inner attitude. Paul's usage here illustrates failure to live by the Law at the deepest level.

7:8a-b But sin, taking opportunity through the commandment, produced in me coveting of every kind.

Through the Law we can know sin as actual experience; we can intrinsically experience sin for what it really is. Sin is a power that works with purpose (see Genesis 4:7). Sin takes advantage of the commandment to produce exactly what the commandment prohibits.

The tenth commandment brings us to see the true nature of coveting, but it is sin that uses the commandment as a starting point to produce manifestations of coveting in detail.

> "coveting of every kind"

TIME-BOUND: fame, wealth, power, possessions (control over things)

TIMELESS: the desire to be one's own god (control over God)

7:8c-9 . . . for apart from the Law sin is dead. I was once alive apart from the Law; but when the commandment came, sin became alive and I died.

Three plug-ins for the personal pronouns *I* and *me*:

1. Paul (as every sinner)

> **Paraphrase:** *I was once alive apart from the Law as a little child who did not understand the power of sin, but when I became old enough to be responsible for the commandment, sin became alive to me and I spiritually died in Adam.*

2. Israel (as God's people)

> **Paraphrase:** *Israel once lived apart from the Law as God's people while not understanding the power of sin, but when the commandment came at Sinai, sin took the opportunity to create transgression and deepened the spiritual lostness of Israel.*

3. Adam (as the originator)

> **Paraphrase:** *Adam was once spiritually alive apart from the Law, but when the commandment not to eat from the tree came, sin became alive through the serpent and brought spiritual condemnation to Adam.*

The Law is not sin, but sin has a definite relationship to the Law.

7:10 . . . and this commandment, which was to result in life, proved to result in death for me.

Many Jews believed that the Law had life-giving power. But the Law, and the command in the Garden, only had the potential for life if perfectly obeyed. The commandment in the Garden was proved to result in death for Adam, and the Law was proved to result in death for Israel, for Paul, and for every human.

7:11 . . . for sin, taking an opportunity through the commandment, deceived me and through it killed me.

In 7:8 the Law defined sin, causing it to create and amplify sinful impulses. Verse 7:10 develops the opportunistic nature of sin. Verse 7:11 restates 7:8 with an intensified focus.

1. Adam: Sin used the commandment in the Garden to deceive the first human pair, resulting in spiritual death.
2. Israel: Sin used the Law to deceive Israel into thinking it could attain spiritual life by keeping the Law, resulting in spiritual death.

3. Paul (as every sinner): Sin uses the Law's power to amplify sin to deceive humanity with regard to the true nature of sin, resulting in the embracing of sin and spiritual death.

7:12 So then, the Law is holy, and the commandment is holy and righteous and good.

"Law" refers to the entire body of Mosaic Law. "[C]ommandment" refers to the specific commandment on coveting used as a representative of the whole in this paragraph. The Law is holy by its origin. It was given by Holy God.

Since the Law is holy, it is righteous. The Law demands what is right. The Law prescribes righteous conduct. The Law cannot be declared guilty of any wrongdoing.

Since the Law is holy, it is good. Only God is perfect in holiness. Since the Law is created by God, and is called good by God's standard, then the nature of the Law itself is good.

What shall we say then? Is the Law sin? May it never be! (7:7a)

Adam could not sustain his relationship with God in the Garden by keeping one commandment. Israel could not earn salvation by keeping the Law. Therefore, Paul (as every sinner) cannot earn salvation by works of the Law. We must rely completely on the grace and mercy of God through Jesus Christ.

7:13 Therefore did that which is good become a cause of death for me? May it never be! Rather it was sin, in order that it might be shown to be sin by effecting my death through that which is good so that through the commandment sin would become utterly sinful.

Verse 7:13 is a transitional bridge:

- A summary of 7:7-12: The Law is from God. It is good. The Law defines sin in detail, turning sin into conscious, willful rebellion against God. Sin then manifests through the Law.
- An introduction for 7:14-25: Does the Law cause death? No. Sin works through the Law to produce death.

The power of sin is amplified, and the presence of sin is exposed as the intentional violation of God's will, "so that through the commandment sin would become utterly sinful."

7:14-25 Living with the Law

Paul is reflecting on being unregenerate and regenerate.

7:14 For we know that the Law is spiritual, but I am of flesh, sold into bondage to sin.

Lost Saul: I know that the Law is holy and of God, but I am of the world and unable to keep the Law. I was sold into sin, and I remain in bondage to sin despite knowing the Law. I can't live up to all of the rules and regulations I put on myself and everyone around me.

Saved Paul: I am still human, and I am deeply scarred by my years of bondage. I will never overcome all of the influence of sin in this lifetime. I understand the Scriptures better than ever, and I know that, although saved, I can't live up to God's standard under my own power.

7:15 For what I am doing, I do not understand; for I am not practicing what I would like to do, but I am doing the very thing I hate.

Lost Saul: I am in conflict with the Law. It doesn't make logical sense to me. I do what I claim I don't like. I am under the power of the very thing I claim to hate and am unable to do the thing I claim to love. The Law is in my face, and God seems to be a million miles away.

Saved Paul: I still stumble into conflict with the Law. It doesn't make logical sense to me. I do what I know I don't like. I have the Holy Spirit indwelling me, and yet the very thing that originally separated me from God keeps manifesting in the things that I do.

7:16-17 But if I do the very thing I do not want to do, I agree with the Law, confessing that the Law is good. So now, no longer am I the one doing it, but sin which dwells in me.

Lost Saul: The fact that I have a conscious will that comes under some degree of conviction when I sin is a confession to myself that the Law of God is true. I realize this, but why do I keep sinning? There is more going on here than just my will. Because sin is dwelling in me with power, I am unable to resist, even though the Law clearly tells me what God wants of me.

Saved Paul: I recognize my remaining connection to sin and the internal friction that my sinning causes. The Law isn't the problem; I am the problem. And so I confess that the Law of God is true and good. I don't want to sin; my heart isn't in it anymore. I am accountable for my sins, but they are no longer a fair representation of my soul.

7:18 For I know that nothing good dwells in me, that is, in my flesh; for the willing is present in me, but the doing of the good is not.

Lost Saul: Despite my knowledge of the Law, nothing good dwells in me by God's standard. I am a lost person alienated from God, trying to earn my own salvation. The Law has divided me against myself. Despite my best efforts, I cannot effectively do God's Law.

Saved Paul: Nothing good dwells in the flesh; it is utterly sinful. It is sold into bondage to sin. The flesh wants me to do things that my regenerated will doesn't want to do. My spiritual will is at war with worldly want.

7:19 For the good that I want, I do not do, but I practice the very evil that I do not want.

Lost Saul: I am under the power of the evil I claim to not want and am unable to live out the good I claim to know all about.

Saved Paul: The evil that I do not want keeps manifesting in things that I do. The evil that I do in the world keeps getting in the way of the good that I now want from my heart.

7:20 But if I am doing the very thing I do not want, I am no longer the one doing it, but sin which dwells in me.

Lost Saul knew: I am unable to do what God requires of me even though the Law clearly tells me what God requires of me.

Saved Paul learned the hard way: The Law isn't the problem; I am the problem. I don't want to sin, my heart isn't in it anymore, and yet sinfulness keeps manifesting.

7:21 I find then the principle that evil is present in me, the one who wants to do good.

Lost Saul: The power of evil is present and ruling in me even when I want to do good. I have a pretty good theological understanding of this principle;

COMMENTARY: THE LETTER TO THE ROMANS

I've been a Pharisee to the best of my ability for a long time—and yet, here I am . . . lost.

Saved Paul: The presence of evil still finds its way into me even though I want to do good by the Spirit. I'm surrendered, focused, and armed to the teeth theologically; I've been discipled by the risen Jesus Christ, and . . . the flesh won't get on board. The presence of sin is still finding ways to undermine my sanctification.

7:22-23 For I joyfully concur with the law of God in the inner man, but I see a different law in the members of my body, waging war against the law of my mind and making me a prisoner of the law of sin which is in my members.

Lost Saul: In my reasoning mind, I can take joy in the law of God even though I can plainly see the power of sin waging war against my will by way of the flesh. Despite my understandings, I am held captive by the power of sin working in me.

Saved Paul: In my heart, with my new nature, I can take joy in the law of God even though I can plainly see the presence of sin still waging war against my spirit by way of the flesh. Deep inside myself, I can find joy in the walking spiritual paradox I have become. I am at peace with God, and yet, despite my salvation, my flesh can still be taken captive by the presence of sin.

7:24 Wretched man that I am! Who will set me free from the body of this death?

Lost Saul cries out in despair: I am a wretched sinner. Who will set me free from this nightmare of spiritual frustration and condemnation?

Saved Paul reflects on all of this and still cries out: I am a wretched sinner. Who will set me free from the sinful condition of my flesh? "*Who* will set me free," not "*what*" or "*how.*" "*Who*"—it's all about Jesus.

Lost Saul came to realize that Jesus Christ provides deliverance from sin and death. Praise God, there is a way out! He repented, He gave the entirety of his life to Jesus. And now as *Saved Paul*, he says this:

83

7:25 Thanks be to God through Jesus Christ our Lord! So then, on the one hand I myself with my mind am serving the law of God, but on the other, with my flesh the law of sin.

In both conditions there is the conflict between mental assent to the Law and ongoing practical failure to keep the Law. It's the same sin problem viewed from both sides of salvation with the same solution in either case: Who will set us free? Jesus Christ our Lord.

How can Paul (and you and I) claim a Christian victory over this thoroughly rotten state of affairs? Paul asks how from verse 18 to verse 24. But after wrestling with *how*, Paul finally realizes that it's *who*. Without a real experiential relationship with Christ, there will be no joy, peace, self-control, discipline, love, meekness, faith, etc. Those things only come from Jesus.

Paul understands this better than any other disciple because even though they spent actual time-bound time with Jesus on this earth, Paul was the only one who was discipled by the risen Jesus Christ in the course of a timeless/time-bound, mystical, direct transmission. The apostles experienced the supernatural; Paul experienced the mystic. This is the key to understanding Paul. But theologians stay so busy being dazzled by Paul's intellectual skills that we miss the mystic connection.

Who will deliver me? It will not be an intellectually grasped theological principle. It will be Christ the Lord. That's who!

Paul's words bear the tinge of the mystical. Mystics regularly speak from their own journey and their own arrival point at the same time. Paul thinks and writes and teaches as someone who was fortunate enough to have the ultimate mystical experience, while being artistic and talented enough to communicate what he experienced in the mystic—all planned by God, of course. Most commentators seem to ignore this as they cling to the ghost of Aristotle and the Greek pure reason fallacy. I do not believe you can fully understand Paul without acknowledging his lived supernatural and mystical worldview.

So then, are we to view these verses in light of verse 5? Is Paul writing about what lost people go through when they are exposed to the Bible, coming under conviction but not yet saved? Or, should we view these verses in light of verse 6? Is Paul writing an introduction to chapter 8 about how we wrestle with sin in the process of sanctification?

In verse 25, Paul has just told us that union with Christ Jesus is the only way, the only truth, the only life, and the only goal. Staring that in its face renders the other theological stuff to be significantly less important.

In this case, the answer to whether Paul was reflecting on Lost Saul or Saved Paul could best be answered by, "Yes, and. . . ."

8:1-39 ASSURANCE

Chapter 8 restates themes from chapters 6 and 7 while emphasizing the blessings and privileges conferred on believers by the Holy Spirit. Romans 8:1-17 elaborates on Romans 5:12-21. Romans 8:18-39 elaborates on Romans 5:1-11.

8:1-11 Life Through the Holy Spirit

8:1 Therefore there is now no condemnation for those who are in Christ Jesus.

"[C]ondemnation" is the state of separation from God that every lost person will experience for eternity. Anyone "in Christ Jesus" is removed from the state of condemnation. For anyone "in Christ Jesus," there is "no condemnation"—justification is forever.

8:2 For the law of the Spirit of life in Christ Jesus has set you free from the law of sin and of death.

The Holy Spirit comes to the believer with power and authority and sets us free from the power and authority of sin. The message is polarized and polarizing. The only thing that can free us from the "law of sin and death" is the "law of the Spirit of life," which is only available "in Christ Jesus." It is the Holy Spirit who transfers us from one realm to the other. There is no middle ground alluded to or allowed for anywhere in the Bible.

8:3 For what the Law could not do, weak as it was through the flesh, God did: sending His own Son in the likeness of sinful flesh and as an offering for sin, He condemned sin in the flesh.

The Law has been proven to be unable to rescue people from sin and death (3:19; 3:28; 4:13-15; 7:7-25). This is not the fault of the Law, as it was never given as a means to secure righteousness and was therefore weakened "through the flesh."

The Law is a standard for holiness and a diagnostic for sin, not a cure for sin. The Law condemns sin but could not break sin's power. The Spirit will only transfer the believer out of the realm of sin and death because, in Christ Jesus and His cross, "in the likeness of sinful flesh and as an offering for sin," God has already condemned sin.

Christ fully entered into the human condition "in the likeness of sinful flesh" and was directly exposed to the power of sin, but Christ was not "in the flesh" in the sense of verses 7:5 or 8:8. God condemned sin by executing His judgment on sin through the atoning sacrifice of Jesus ("an offering for sin").

8:4 . . . so that the requirement of the Law might be fulfilled in us, who do not walk according to the flesh but according to the Spirit.

God didn't condemn sin just to satisfy some sense of mechanical justice or to restore cosmic balance regardless of humanity. He did it "so that the requirement of the Law might be fulfilled in us"—so that He could offer us a way home. Those of us who have accepted Christ will no longer have our lives determined and directed by rebellion against God; we will give evidence of our salvation by living in obedience "according to the Spirit."

8:5 For those who are according to the flesh set their minds on the things of the flesh, but those who are according to the Spirit, the things of the Spirit.

In chapter 7, verses 14-25 are positional and behavioral, with each one addressing Paul both as an unconverted Jew and as a Christian. The verses in chapter 8 are oppositional, contrasting the saved condition against the lost condition.

> "mind"—not just mental processes; all the attributes of the human psyche/soul

8:6 For the mind set on the flesh is death, but the mind set on the Spirit is life and peace.

Objective reality: the "death" status of those "set on the flesh" is contrasted against "life" in the Spirit and "peace" with God through justification. In this verse, "peace" and "life" are not subjective (as in, peace of mind or quality of life).

8:7-8 . . . because the mind set on the flesh is hostile toward God; for it does not subject itself to the law of God, for it is not even able to do so, and those who are in the flesh cannot please God.

The "mind set on the flesh" is the psyche of a lost person. It is not possible to be neutral because the psyche of a lost person "is hostile toward God." Even though not everyone is as evil as they possibly could be, and even though not all people commit every possible sinful action, every person apart from Christ is totally in the grip of sin, the result being "those who are in the flesh cannot please God."

> "in the flesh"—destructive, self-centered rebellion against God regardless of the life details

Without the Holy Spirit, the human psyche will not and cannot align itself with God. Left to ourselves, we cannot rescue ourselves from this condition. We "cannot please God."

8:9 However, you are not in the flesh but in the Spirit, if indeed the Spirit of God dwells in you. But if anyone does not have the Spirit of Christ, he does not belong to Him.

To be a Christian means to have the indwelling of the Holy Spirit. There is no Christianity in a person if there is no indwelling of the Holy Spirit. A Christian is *of* the flesh of Adam, but a Christian is no longer *in* the flesh of Adam.

The Spirit enters into the new believer. The believer now lives in the Spirit— in the realm of the Spirit. The Spirit now rules and guides.

8:10 If Christ is in you, though the body is dead because of sin, yet the spirit is alive because of righteousness.

Your (small *s*) spirit is totally dependent on the (big *S*) Holy Spirit of God. "If Christ is in you," your (small *s*) spirit is alive. Even with the Spirit indwelling, "the body is dead because of sin." You will experience physical death. The indwelling Spirit and the indwelling Christ are distinct but inseparable.

> 8:11 But if the Spirit of Him who raised Jesus from the dead dwells in you, He who raised Christ Jesus from the dead will also give life to your mortal bodies through His Spirit who dwells in you.

Assurance: The power of the Spirit raised Jesus from the dead. The same Spirit will raise believers from the dead, giving "life to your mortal bodies." If you are saved, the Spirit of God indwells you. Your (small *s*) spirit has been regenerated.

Do you have the Spirit of God indwelling you? Only you and God know for sure.

EXCURSUS: TRINITY

The word *Trinity* is not found in the Bible. It is a time-bound theological term that points at a timeless, mystical truth that defies human logic. God presents as Trinity throughout the Bible. In a few New Testament places, the presentation is very clear and obvious. In the Old Testament you have to find the puzzle pieces and put them together. In places like Romans 8, you just have to pay attention to what you are reading:

> *Spirit of God [the Father] (8:9a), Spirit of Christ (8:9b), Spirit of Him (8:11)*

TIME-BOUND: The Bible tells us God is Father / God is Son / God is Holy Spirit.

TIME-BOUND: The Bible tells us Father is not Son—Father is not Spirit / Son is not Father—Son is not Spirit / Spirit is not Father—Spirit is not Son.

TIME-BOUND / TIMELESS: God is who God is.

Time-bound logic is next to useless here. The best that time-bound language can do is point at the Godhead by way of God's attributes. God exists beyond time-bound structures and cannot be fully understood by way of any theological presentation. We use the term *Trinity* to express in a simple way that which cannot be logically expressed. The term *Trinity* allows us to talk about that which cannot be logically talked about more succinctly.

8:12-13 Living by the Spirit

8:12 So then, brethren, we are under obligation, not to the flesh, to live according to the flesh...

The word *flesh* sums up all of this world that is characteristic of life in rebellion against God. Believers have not been removed from the presence or influence of the flesh but are no longer obligated to live under the flesh as their master.

8:13 . . . for if you are living according to the flesh, you must die; but if by the Spirit you are putting to death the deeds of the body, you will live.

Eternal separation from God is the penalty for "living according to the flesh." Regenerate believers are in the process of sanctification. There must be clear indication that a believer is invested in "putting to death the deeds of the body."

Life in the Spirit cannot be achieved by human effort apart from the Spirit (moralism or legalism). There must be surrender to the touch of the Holy Spirit. Life in the Spirit is not about mindless surrender, leading to dissolution of the self (yielding a Spirit-controlled bio-robot). There must be ongoing human response taking place in time.

> **TIME-BOUND:** Human activity and participation in the process of sanctification is an obligation and must be present in some form. No one can make legitimate claim to salvation while living in ongoing, open rebellion against God's word.

> **TIMELESS:** Sanctifying activity is completely dependent on the power and presence of the Spirit. Sanctification can only take place "by the Spirit." No one can go it alone.

8:14-17 Adoption

8:14 For all who are being led by the Spirit of God, these are sons of God.

In the Old Testament, Yahweh is pictured as Israel's father. The phrases "sons of God" and "son of God" are used to indicate the people of Israel God has called to be His own. Anyone who has been justified and regenerated is now led by the Spirit of God and is part of God's family.

8:15 For you have not received a spirit of slavery leading to fear again, but you have received a spirit of adoption as sons by which we cry out, "Abba! Father!"

The fear inherent in being a slave to sin is replaced by the joy of adoption into God's family. The phrase "we cry out" is the language of emotion. Believers cry out to God because the truth of salvation can be deeply felt and intensely experienced. The experience of assurance is based on feeling as well as fact.

Abba is the intimate Aramaic term for "father" and carries a meaning similar to the English word *daddy* that a little child uses. Christians have a familial relationship with God.

8:16 The Spirit Himself testifies with our spirit that we are children of God.

The presence of the (big *S*) Holy Spirit indwelling us produces an awareness in our (small *s*) spirit that not only are we legally adopted into God's family, we are supernaturally realigned with God in a way more profound, yet similar to, the time-bound relationship between parent and child.

8:17 . . . and if children, heirs also, heirs of God and fellow heirs with Christ, if indeed we suffer with Him so that we may also be glorified with Him.

> **Paraphrase:** *. . . and if we are justified/regenerated, we have full legal status as adopted children in our new family and are already promised our inheritance with God and Christ, if indeed we are saved and in the process of sanctification, so that we may also be glorified with Him later.*

8:18-27 Future Glory

This paragraph develops verse 17b, continues the theme of assurance, and ties back into the major theme of this section of the letter, beginning in 5:1-

11. Since "there is now no condemnation for those who are in Christ Jesus" (8:1), and since we are "free from the law of sin and death" (8:2), how do we maintain hope in the face of suffering and death? If we are free from the law of sin and death, why do we suffer and die?

8:18 For I consider that the sufferings of this present time are not worthy to be compared with the glory that is to be revealed to us.

> **TIME-BOUND:** There is no comparison to the limited things that can happen to us when we are time-bound, and what we will experience when we go beyond time.

> **TIMELESS:** What we are experiencing now in Christ is just scratching the surface of "the glory that is to be revealed to us."

Verses 8:19-25 develop the "to be revealed" from verse 8:18.

8:19 For the anxious longing of the creation waits eagerly for the revealing of the sons of God.

The plan of salvation has been revealed and put into motion. While Christians are already sons and daughters of God, we don't always look or act like sons and daughters of God. Creation here refers to the sub-human world. Paul personifies sub-human creation in the same way as Psalm 65:12-13, Isaiah 24:4a, Jeremiah 4:28a, and Jeremiah 12:4a. The personified creation is waiting for the full manifestation of Christianity.

8:20-21 For the creation was subjected to futility, not willingly, but because of Him who subjected it, in hope that the creation itself also will be set free from its slavery to corruption into the freedom of the glory of the children of God.

Sub-human creation is not what God originally intended it to be. Because of sin, creation cannot be what it was intended to be. But Adam did not have the power to subject all of creation, and Satan does not have the power to subject all of creation. God alone has the power and the right to condemn all of creation to futility because of sin. Creation was subjected to condemnation "in hope" of being set free from sin. The ultimate destiny of creation is not annihilation but transformation.

8:22 For we know that the whole creation groans and suffers the pains of childbirth together until now.

The personified creation "groans and suffers" under the presence of sin—that's why things in creation are the way they are. Childbirth is varying degrees of difficult. But once the child is delivered, the pain of childbirth is replaced with hope and joy (see John 16:20b-22 for a parallel).

8:23 And not only this, but also we ourselves, having the first fruits of the Spirit, even we ourselves groan within ourselves, waiting eagerly for our adoption as sons, the redemption of our body.

> "the first fruits of the Spirit"—everything the Holy Spirit has done since the raising of Christ
>
> "the first fruits [of] the Spirit"—the first fruits [which is] the Spirit
>
> "we . . . groan within ourselves"—an inward, non-verbal attitude of frustration and longing (but not weakness or doubt) due to the indwelling of the Spirit

Christians are moving in the place between justification/regeneration and glorification. Living as God's adopted in the "Already-Not Yet" is not easy.

8:24 For in hope we have been saved, but hope that is seen is not hope; for who hopes for what he already sees?

Hope is an outgrowth of Christian faith. The sanctifying walk is forward looking to the place beyond death. It's natural for Christians, hoping for things that cannot be seen, to experience frustration with the incompleteness of our faith playing out in the world.

8:25 But if we hope for what we do not see, with perseverance we wait eagerly for it.

If we stay focused on eternal things, the hope that our faith engenders will drive our perseverance, and we will faithfully and eagerly wait out our time on earth.

8:26-27 In the same way the Spirit also helps our weakness; for we do not know how to pray as we should, but the Spirit Himself intercedes for us with groanings

too deep for words; and He who searches the hearts knows what the mind of the Spirit is, because He intercedes for the saints according to the will of God.

> "In the same way"—Connects back to hope in verse 25.
>
> "helps our weakness"—Joins with us to help our weakness and bears the burden of our weakness.
>
> "we do not know how to pray as we should"—The Spirit's intercession makes the prayer of a believer powerful and effective even though we cannot clearly discern God's will as we pray.
>
> "the Spirit Himself intercedes [on our behalf] with groanings too deep for words"—the Spirit's language of intercessory prayer that takes place between the Spirit and God when we pray; the Holy Spirit intercedes on our behalf by aligning our prayers with the will of God despite our inability to pray as we should

This passage is often mistakenly connected with speaking in tongues. There are several reasons why this is not the case:

1. The means of intercession referred to here comes to the aid of all believers. First Corinthians 12:30 states that not all believers will, can, or should speak in tongues.

2. The single Greek word translated here as "too deep for words" means "unspoken" or "unutterable" in the non-audible sense of "can't be spoken." It cannot mean "ineffable" in the sense of not being able to be expressed by human language.

3. The groans are attributed to the Spirit. But there is no linguistic connection present to suggest that Paul could be identifying the groans as coming from the Spirit and being expressed through the believer. All attention here is focused on the Spirit's intercession: God and the Spirit are in perfect harmony as the Spirit intercedes for us.

> **Paraphrase:** *In the same way that faith-driven hope sustains us, the Spirit joins with us to help our weakness; for we are unable to clearly discern God's will in the things we pray for, and our wills aren't perfectly in alignment with the will of God, but the Spirit Himself intervenes on our behalf in an unspeakable way that perfectly matches the will of God; and God, who knows the innermost hearts of humans, perfectly knows the mind of the Spirit because the Spirit prays on behalf of believers in perfect alignment with God's will.*

8:28-30 The Sovereignty of God

8:28 And we know that God causes all things to work together for good to those who love God, to those who are called according to His purpose.

> "those who love God"—God's people: Christians
>
> "those who are called"—those whom God has justified: Christians
>
> "those who love God"—"those who are called"
>
> "according to God's purpose"—"God loved the world in this way" (John 3:16-18)

The context of chapter 8 is assurance of salvation. God is causing all things to work for the ultimate good of His faithful, regardless of how things appear to us in the "sufferings of this present time" (8:18-25). This verse in no way promises material wealth, physical well-being, or an easy cultural or social situation.

The "good" that results when God is "causing all things to work together" is the higher good of a stronger faith and a more certain hope. Everything that God allows to happen in this world is intentional to His ultimate ends.

8:29 For those whom He foreknew, He also predestined to become conformed to the image of His Son, so that He would be the firstborn among many brethren.

> "foreknew"—divine initiative
>
> "predestined"—the destination toward which believers are set in motion
>
> "For those whom He foreknew"

TIMELESS: God knew us from before the existence of the time-bound universe.

TIME-BOUND: . . . and He knew us in time before we came to know Him.

"predestined to be conformed to the image of [Jesus]"

TIME-BOUND: Our inevitable conforming to God's will in our sanctifying walks through following the example of Christ (see 8:17b).

TIMELESS: Our inevitable transformation into the image that Christ already enjoys.

"so that [Jesus] would be the firstborn among many brethren"

TIME-BOUND: As the first born-again, Jesus's sacrifice in time opened the path to glory.

TIMELESS: Our inevitable destination in the glory that Christ already enjoys.

8:30 . . . and these whom He predestined, He also called; and these whom He called, He also justified; and these whom He justified, He also glorified.

TIMELESS: God predestined, God called, God justified, God glorified—all are in the same tense. If God predestines, calls, and justifies in the past tense, then glorification is a done deal.

TIME-BOUND: Individual believers are assured that God is working for their ultimate good in time and will glorify them beyond time. God is in control.

None of this diminishes the importance or reality of the human response of faith. The tension of time-bound humanity existing within timeless sovereignty places our limited and skewed time-anchored perception in proper context within sovereign God's timeless and actual reality. Meditating on the paradoxical and illogical intermix of that which is time-bound in context of that which is timeless points us into the mystery of Christianity and encourages deeper immersion in the Bible.

8:31-39 The Believer's Security

8:31 What then shall we say to these things? If God is for us, who is against us?

> **Amplification:** *What then shall we say [in response to verses 29 and 30]? If God is for us [by predestining, calling, and justifying us,] who is [capable of being] against us [as a threat to our glorification]?*

8:32 He who did not spare His own Son, but delivered Him over for us all, how will He not also with Him freely give us all things?

> **Amplification:** *[God] who did not spare His own Son, but delivered [Jesus] over for us all, how will [God] not also with [Jesus] freely give us all things?*

This develops the idea presented at Romans 5:8-9. The sign that God is for us is that He gave Jesus for us. There is no room for doubting God's commitment to our salvation.

Abraham, out of obedience, was willing to sacrifice his beloved son, Isaac, to God, but God spared Isaac (Genesis 22). God, out of holy love, delivered Jesus over to be crucified. The same God who spared Isaac's son did not spare His own Son.

8:33-34a Who will bring a charge against God's elect? God is the one who justifies; who is the one who condemns?

Satan will accuse us. Enemies of God will accuse us. Our own consciences will accuse us because of our sins. These are the ones who condemn. Since "God is the one who justifies," none of these accusations can override or overrule God's "not-guilty" verdict.

8:34b Christ Jesus is He who died, yes, rather who was raised, who is at the right hand of God, who also intercedes for us.

The language of Psalm 110:1 ("who is at the right hand of God") is used in this verse and also in Matthew 22:42-45; Matthew 26:64; Acts 2:33-35, 5:31, 7:55-56; Ephesians 1:20; Colossians 3:1; Hebrews 1:3, 1:13, 8:1, 10:12, 12:2; and 1 Peter 3:22. Jesus Christ died to secure our justification, was raised from the dead, ascended to God to sit at His right hand, and so is able to intercede for us as our High Priest before God.

8:35-37 Who will separate us from the love of Christ? Will tribulation, or distress, or persecution, or famine, or nakedness, or peril, or sword? Just as it is written, "For Your sake we are being put to death all day long; we were considered as sheep to be slaughtered." But in all these things we overwhelmingly conquer through Him who loved us.

The sum of all the world's trials, temptations, and ills are contrasted against the love of Christ. The quote from Psalm 44:22 in verse 36 shows that trials and bad things of all sorts have always been part of following God and that these things can and will happen to Christians. There is no Christian perfection or perfect Christian circumstances in this life.

> "But in all these things we overwhelmingly conquer"—Everything, including suffering and death, works toward God's ultimate good for those living in the love of Christ (see 8:28).

8:38-39 For I am convinced that neither death, nor life, nor angels, nor principalities, nor things present, nor things to come, nor powers, nor height, nor depth, nor any other created thing, will be able to separate us from the love of God, which is in Christ Jesus our Lord.

"death . . . life"—the two possible states of existence

"angels . . . principalities"—the spirit realms of angels and demons

"things present . . . things to come"—all of time and timelessness

"powers"—any and all forces of humanity or the enemy

"height . . . depth"—heavens and earth; the entire created universe

"any other created thing"—a catch-all for any other thing you might think up (including yourself)

TIMELESS: Eternal security means that once you are justified by God, it is impossible to become un-justified. If God could get it wrong, or if you are capable of undoing what God has decreed, then God would be something much less than sovereign.

TIME-BOUND: The expression "Once saved, always saved" doesn't sufficiently dial in the timeless aspect of justification for me. I like "If saved, always saved" better. Holding it this way also clearly illustrates what is—and isn't—happening in the case of a false conversion.

9:1-11:36 THE PROBLEM OF ISRAEL'S UNBELIEF

Paul has previously defined Christians as Abraham's heirs (chapter 4), heirs of God's glory (5:2; 8:18-30), possessors of the Holy Spirit (chapter 8), and God's adopted children (8:14-17).

What had been promised to Israel now belongs to Christians, whether Jew or Gentile. But the Israelites were told that "you are a holy people to the LORD your God: the LORD your God has chosen you to be a people for His own possession out of all the peoples who are on the face of the earth" (Deuteronomy 7:6).

The Roman Christians, and many others, were trying to figure out how much of Jewish heritage should be part of their Christian faith:

- If the Gospel is "to the Jew first" (1:16), why have the majority of Jews rejected it?
- What has become of Israel's Old Testament status as God's chosen people?
- Where is the continuity between the Old Testament and the gospel?
- Does the New Testament gospel stand as the completion and fulfillment of the Old Testament?
- Does the New Testament gospel betray the Old Testament promises to Israel and mark an abandonment of Israel by God?
- Is Israel on its own salvation path running parallel to Christianity?

Almost one third of the Old Testament quotations in Romans are found in chapters 9–11. Paul will show where Old Testament Israel stands in relation to the gospel of Jesus Christ and that there is nothing in the gospel that is inconsistent with God's promises to Israel when those promises are properly understood.

Summary:

- 9:1-5—Introduction: Paul's lament
- 9:6-29—The word of God has not failed; it was misunderstood and held improperly. Salvation was always a gift and never a birthright.
- 9:30–10:21—What shall we say then about this abrupt turn in salvation history?
- 11:1-10—the situation Israel now finds itself in

- 11:11-32—God is using Israel's rejection of the gospel to reach out to the Gentile world. One day a remnant of Israel will be included again.
- 11:33-36—Doxology

9:1-5 Introduction

9:1-3 I am telling the truth in Christ, I am not lying, my conscience testifies with me in the Holy Spirit, that I have great sorrow and unceasing grief in my heart.

The biblical requirement for lawful testimony is two or three witnesses (Deuteronomy 17:6; 19:15). Paul claims that Jesus Christ and the Holy Spirit are direct witnesses to the truth of his teaching.

9:3 For I could wish that I myself were accursed, separated from Christ for the sake of my brethren, my kinsmen according to the flesh.

The majority of Jews have rejected the gospel. Paul is heartbroken over the fate of his Jewish kinsmen. He is so upset about the way things have turned out that he muses over trading his salvation for the salvation of all Israel (note the parallel to Exodus 32:30-32).

9:4-5 . . . who are Israelites, to whom belongs the adoption as sons, and the glory and the covenants and the giving of the Law and the temple service and the promises, whose are the fathers, and from whom is the Christ according to the flesh, who is over all God, blessed forever. Amen.

TIME-BOUND: "Christ according to the flesh."

TIMELESS: "Christ . . . who is over all God, blessed forever."

Paul's shift from "Jew" to "Israelite" is significant. The name "Jew" was politically and nationally oriented. At first, a Jew was a member of the tribe of Judah. After the Exile, Judah was all that was left of historical Israel, and the name "Jew" began to be used for any member of the Israelite nation. The name "Israelite" indicated the special religious position of the Jewish people and the distinctness of Israel from all other nations.

Verses 4 and 5 list eight privileges associated with the name "Israelite":

1. *Adoption:* In 8:15 and 8:23, adoption is the status conferred on believers by the Spirit at justification. It cannot mean the same thing here with reference to Israel because of 2:1-29; 3:9-20; 9:6b-13; 9:30-10:8; and 9:2-3. Also, the term is never used in the Old Testament or in Judaism. In this verse, *adoption* is used to sum up Old Testament teaching about Israel as God's son. God's adoption of Israel conveys to the nation all the rights and privileges of the old covenant. Despite the unbelief of individual Jews moving through time, Israel has a timeless place in God's plan. Paul predicts this later in Romans 11:25-28.

2. *The glory:*

TIME-BOUND: God's presence with the people of Israel in the Old Testament.

TIMELESS: The continuation of God's presence into the end times.

3. *The covenants:* Noah, Abraham, Israel at Sinai, David in 2 Samuel 7:1-17, Jeremiah 31:31-34.
4. *The Law:* Given directly to Israel by God.
5. *The temple service:* The sacrificial system and associated worship.
6. *The promises:* Given to the patriarchs Abraham, Isaac, and Jacob.
7. *The fathers:* "Israelites . . . whose are the fathers"—the patriarchs of Israel belong to the Israelite family, thus the promises to the patriarchs are for all of Israel.
8. *The Christ:* "Israelites . . . from whom is the Christ according to the flesh"—The Christ, the Messiah, does not belong to Israel, but is from Israel by way of the incarnation. Despite all of the privileges corporate Israel enjoys, individual Jews are not guaranteed a saving relationship with Jesus Christ.

If the Old Testament teaches that being a physical member of Israel automatically makes a person a spiritual member of God's family, then Jesus Christ would not be the only path to God. The New Testament gospel of Jesus Christ would then be in conflict with the Old Testament. If God voided His promises to Israel and the patriarchs, then God's promises in the Old Testament cannot be trusted. If His Old Testament promises cannot be trusted, then how can we trust His New Testament promises?

9:6-13 They Are Not All Israel

9:6 But it is not as though the word of God has failed. For they are not all Israel who are descended from Israel; . . .

In context of verses 4 and 5, "the word of God" is referring specifically to God's promises to Israel in the Old Testament. Paul clarifies where ethnic Israel stands in relation to both the Old Testament and the New Testament.

The Jews believed that anyone in the physical lineage of Israel was an Israelite spiritually and would automatically benefit from the promises made to corporate Israel. There was no concern in Judaism over not receiving salvation; the only way to not receive the promises was to renounce the faith.

Some argue that Paul is only writing about the corporate inclusion of the Gentiles alongside corporate Israel in this verse. But Paul doesn't write, "For they are not all Israel who are *only* from Israel." Paul does write, "For they are not all Israel who are *descended* from Israel."

> **Amplification:** *For they are not all Israel [in the spiritual sense] who are descended from Israel [in the physical sense].*

9:7 . . . nor are they all children because they are Abraham's descendants, but: "Through Isaac your descendants will be named."

Paul's first argument in support of verse 6 is this: Jews looked to their descent from Abraham as the source of their spiritual standing with God. Abraham had two sons, Ishmael and Isaac. Both were promised many descendants, but only Isaac was promised the covenant. The case of Ishmael and Isaac shows that not everyone who is descended from Abraham is part of covenant Israel.

9:8 That is, it is not the children of the flesh who are children of God, but the children of the promise are regarded as descendants.

> **TIME-BOUND:** "children of the flesh"—children of Ishmael; "children of the promise"—children of Isaac. Both are natural descendants of Abraham. Only children who belong to the promise are the covenantal descendants of Abraham.

> **TIMELESS:** "children of God" is always used by Paul to reference salvation (contrasted against the general salvation-historical "adoption" from verse 4). People who belong to the flesh are not "children of God."

The spiritual standard for being Old Testament "children of God" is the promise is Genesis 15:6. The spiritual standard for being New Testament "children of God" is still rooted in the promise of Genesis 15:6—Abraham believed.

9:9 For this is the word of promise: "At this time I will come, and Sarah shall have a son."

Ishmael was born in normal circumstances through a fertile woman. Isaac was born through a barren woman who was over ninety years old.

"I will come"—God intervening directly in a situation

The promise to Abraham in Genesis 17:15-16, reiterated in Genesis 18:10 and 18:14, was fulfilled by God's supernatural intervention not by what could be regarded as normal circumstance.

9:10, 9:12 And not only this, but there was Rebekah also, when she had conceived twins by one man, our father Isaac; . . . it was said to her, "The older will serve the younger."

Paul's second argument in support of verse 6 is this: God chose Jacob over Esau. God promised that Jacob would be the inheritor even though Jacob was the younger brother. Therefore, God makes His own choices and is no respecter of human preferences or traditions.

> **TIMELESS:** God promised that Jacob would be the inheritor before Jacob and Esau were born. Omniscient God's will alone determines human destiny despite time-bound appearances.

9:11 . . . for though the twins were not yet born and had not done anything good or bad, so that God's purpose according to His choice would stand, not because of works but because of Him who calls.

> **TIME-BOUND:** The prophetic word was spoken to Rebekah before Jacob and Esau were born. There were no works by Jacob or Esau playing out in time for God to base His decision on. Isaac was chosen; Ishmael was

not. Jacob was chosen; Esau was not. All so that "God's purpose . . . would stand." If the word of God depended in any way on the vagaries of sin-poisoned humanity, it would have failed long ago. God's ultimate purpose is not subject to our works. God's purpose in time is only fulfilled "because of Him who calls."

> **TIMELESS:** "God's purpose according to His choice" is all that ever really matters. God makes the choices from beyond time that then play out in time. We make choices in time that are either consonant or dissonant with the timeless sovereign will of God.

Our movements in time are real and meaningful, and God already knows every move we will make. This is the mysterious, unsolvable, illogical paradox that the Bible presents us with.

9:13 Just as it is written, "Jacob I loved, but Esau I hated."

Holy love and holy hate in this verse are not emotions that God feels but actions that God carries out: "Jacob I [accepted], but Esau I [rejected]."

> **TIME-BOUND:** When we look back in time, we can see that Jacob was a follower of God and Esau was not. From our perspective, looking back in time, it appears that each man made choices and that their decisions in time justify God's verdict whenever it was rendered.

Consider: Both Jacob and Esau experienced time. They both thought and believed that they were making real and meaningful choices in time.

> **TIMELESS:** God exists beyond time. He knows the end from the beginning. He knew that Jacob would be a follower of God and Esau would not. From our limited view of God's timeless sovereignty, each man's choices and decisions in time were already known by God, and God's verdict had already been rendered "though the twins were not yet been born."

Consider: Both Jacob and Esau experienced time. Whatever they thought and believed back then, they are now no longer here making choices in time.

103

9:14-24 God Is Sovereign—Dealing with the Paradox

Argument summary:

> **Question:** verse 14—Is God unjust?
>
> **Answer:** verse 15—No, "for He says to Moses. . . ."
>
> **Conclusion:** verse 16—"So then. . . ."
>
> **Question:** verse 14—Is God unjust?
>
> **Answer:** verse 17—No, "for the Scripture says to Pharaoh. . . ."
>
> **Conclusion:** verse 18—"So then. . . ."

9:14 What shall we say then? There is no injustice with God, is there?

God chose Jacob over Esau before they were born (9:13). If God is making judgments from beyond time (9:12), before the people being judged are alive in time to have done anything good or bad (9:11), is God just? By time-bound human standards of justice, God can be accused of injustice.

9:15 For He says to Moses, "I will have mercy on whom I have mercy, and I will have compassion on whom I have compassion."

Paul rejects the argument from the time-bound sense of justice. God's decision to choose Jacob and reject Esau was not an isolated incident; it reflects the very nature of sovereign God. Paul uses God's own words to make his case.

9:16 So then it does not depend on the man who wills or the man who runs, but on God who has mercy.

> "it"—God's justice; salvation or condemnation
>
> "the man who wills"—inner desire; purpose; readiness to move forward in time
>
> "the man who runs"—expressed desire and/or purpose executed in time
>
> "the man who wills . . . the man who runs"—the totality of human ability and capacity

104

TIME-BOUND: The human will is bound in time and only exists in context of timeless sovereignty. It is not free in the sense that God's will is free.

TIMELESS: Salvation is not based on human will or works. Salvation depends on the mercy of sovereign God.

9:17 For the Scripture says to Pharaoh, "For this very purpose I raised you up, to demonstrate My power in you, and that My name might be proclaimed throughout the whole earth."

> "For this very purpose..."—to show that God is sovereign over all, whether they are evil or good

Even God's actions that appear to us to have a negative purpose serve the ultimate purpose of demonstrating the power of God and glorifying God (Exodus 7:5). God made Pharaoh ruler of Egypt and sovereignly hardened his heart to cause the name of God to spread throughout the time-bound world (see Exodus 7:3).

TIME-BOUND: Pharaoh sinned and hardened his heart (Exodus 9:34).

TIMELESS: Pharaoh's heart was hardened by God (Exodus 9:35).

9:18 So then He has mercy on whom He desires, and He hardens whom He desires.

> "hardens"—makes spiritually insensitive; renders a person unresponsive to God

Everyone unsaved is, in essence, hardened against God, even though individual sinfulness expresses in varying ways (3:23). The human will has never been free.

If God hardens your heart, it's hardened . . . unless He un-hardens it and you place faith in the person and work of Jesus . . . unless you place faith in the person and work of Jesus and He un-hardens it . . . until un-hardening

. . . and God already knows whether or not you will . . . and you don't . . . until you do . . . and it's already done . . . even though it seemed to you that it wasn't yet . . . even though it seems to you that. . . .

How a time-bound creature can make meaningful decisions in context of timeless sovereignty cannot be penetrated with logic. The whole idea violates human logic. The best pure-reason-style thinking can do is render the mystery as an either/or problem to be solved: either God is sovereign, or humans have free will. God is not the author of this kind of time-bound confusion; we are.

The existence of time-bound reality surrounded and encompassed by timeless God creates a paradox in time that is fundamentally illogical by Aristotelian-based time-bound thinking yet spiritually reasonable upon Spirit-led contemplation.

EXCURSUS: DIVINE SOVEREIGNTY AND HUMAN RESPONSIBILITY

Early Judaism was split into three groups over the relationship between divine sovereignty (timelessness) and willful human activity (time-bound-ness).

Pharisees: Only certain events are fated by God; the rest depend on the actions of humanity.

Essenes: Everything is fated by God. Everything that happens to humanity is predetermined.

Sadducees: There is no such thing as fate. Human conduct is the direct cause of any positive or negative effects in the world.

The Pharisee position is similar in essence to Arminian thought processes and raises the following questions:

- If humans have some measure of control over their destinies, is God only partially sovereign and only somewhat all-knowing?
- If God is only conditionally sovereign, if His omniscience is in any way limited, can His promises and prophecies in the Bible be trusted?

The Essene position is similar in essence to Calvinist thought processes and raises the following questions:

- If God is sovereign, and everything is foreknown and predetermined from the beginning of the universe until its end, how can human decision-making mean anything? How can there be any human moral agency?
- If God is sovereign, and everything is foreknown and predetermined from before Creation, doesn't that make God responsible for sin?

The Sadducee position has the same root as most liberal thought processes and asserts that whatever God is, God is not sovereign. In this intentionally time-bound-limited way of thinking, God created the universe and turned it loose to run its course with no sovereign foreknowledge of how things will play out. God has been watching from the beginning, but His awareness is bound by time, and His consciousness is constrained to move through time from past to future, limited in this sense in much the same way as His human creations.

9:19 You will say to me then, "Why does He still find fault? For who resists His will?"

In Romans 1:18-23, it appears as if God's judgment is in response to people who resist Him, making humans responsible for sin. Romans 9:18 says that sovereign God "hardens whom He desires," implying that God is the causal agent for human sin. Paul's objector asks,

- If what you say in verse 18 is true, then how can God still find fault in someone who resists His will?
- If everything in time is playing out exactly as God has already foreseen it, how is it just for God to judge us for doing what He already knew we would do?
- Doesn't sovereignty as you present it make God responsible for sin?

TIME-BOUND: In some places, the Bible puts forward clear teachings about human moral agency, free will, and time-bound responsibility.

TIMELESS: In some places, the Bible puts forward clear teachings about divine sovereignty.

NOTE: No biblical writer offers a logical solution to the tension between human responsibility existing in context of divine sovereignty. Throughout the Bible, truths regarding both viewpoints or positions are presented, and no attempt is made to reconcile them.

9:20 On the contrary, who are you, O man, who answers back to God? The thing molded will not say to the molder, "Why did you make me like this," will it?

The rebuking tone is not taken because of the nature of the question; God wants us to dig into the mystery. In the original language, "answers back" suggests a contentious stance. The tone is taken in response to the attitude of the questioner who is judging the ways of God. Isaiah 29:16 and Isaiah 45:9b are paraphrased to emphasize where we stand in relationship to God.

9:21 Or does not the potter have a right over the clay, to make from the same lump one vessel for honorable use and another for common use?

What we can understand about God's sovereign knowledge is likened to what a pot can understand about the potter who created it.

> **TIME-BOUND** (focusing on what God makes): God has the right to use people as He sees fit to complete His plan of salvation. Jews, like anyone else, can be hardened to fulfill some purpose of God, but the Bible also presents the possibility of renewal by repentance (see Jeremiah 18:1-6).

> **TIMELESS** (focusing on the act of making): God has the right to create some persons who He destines for salvation and some who are destined for condemnation (see Isaiah 29:16; 45:9b).

9:22 What if God, although willing to demonstrate His wrath and to make His power known, endured with much patience vessels of wrath prepared for destruction?

What if God, who is willing and able to demonstrate His wrath and power at any time, has indeed let certain people live out their unrepentant destinies in time while sovereignly knowing that they were "vessels of wrath prepared for destruction"?

9:23 And He did so to make known the riches of His glory upon vessels of mercy, which He prepared beforehand for glory.

And what if He allowed all of that sinful history to unfold just to amplify the contrast between sin and His glory, so that repentant "vessels of mercy, which He prepared beforehand for glory" would be able to deeply know "the riches of His glory" that they have received in salvation?

9:24 . . . even us, whom He also called, not from among Jews only, but also from among Gentiles.

And what if He extended "the riches of His glory" to certain Gentiles as well? What if He did? What if He does?

> **TIMELESS:** Who are you to contentiously answer back to God just because you can't handle the tension of the time-bound human condition in context of God's timeless sovereignty?

> **TIME-BOUND:** If you are saved, contemplating these paradoxical understandings while living a life of prayer and worship should drive you into a deeper state of surrender as you consider where you stand as a human vase in relation to God the Potter.

9:25-33 Israel and the Gentiles

9:25-26 As He says also in Hosea, "I will call those who were not My people, 'My people,' and her who was not beloved, 'beloved.' And it shall be that in the place where it was said to them, 'you are not My people,' there they shall be called sons of the living God."

Paul paraphrases Hosea 2:23b-c and Hosea 1:10b. In Hosea 1:6-9, the Hebrew names for Hosea's children translate as "not-my-people" and "not beloved." The prophet Hosea predicted a renewal of God's mercy toward the rebellious northern tribes of Israel that God had rejected. Paul interprets and applies the Hosea text in context of Christ.

The boundaries between Jew and Gentile have been broken down. Old Testament predictions for a renewed Israel are fulfilled in the body of Christ at this point in salvation history.

9:27-28 Isaiah cries out concerning Israel, "Though the number of the sons of Israel be like the sand of the sea, it is the remnant that will be saved; for the Lord will execute His word on the earth, thoroughly and quickly."

Isaiah 10:22-23 is quoted to show that the New Testament teaching that only a remnant of Israel will be saved was also the Old Testament teaching. It has always been the case that "they are not all Israel who are descended from Israel."

Many Jews did not or would not listen to the prophets. Many Jews misunderstood the prophecies. Many Jews throughout the ages refused to search the Scriptures. Regardless, ignorance of the Law was not, and is not, an excuse.

9:29 And just as Isaiah foretold, "Unless the Lord of Sabaoth had left to us a posterity, we would have become like Sodom, and would have resembled Gomorrah."

Without the promises of God, Israel deserved the same treatment as Sodom and Gomorrah. It was always the promises of God, not the actions of the people, that allowed anyone to have any future with God. God doesn't owe anyone anything. It's always been about grace and faith.

9:30-31 What shall we say then? That Gentiles, who did not pursue righteousness, attained righteousness, even the righteousness which is by faith; but Israel, pursuing a law of righteousness, did not arrive at that law.

In chapters 6–8, "righteousness" was used in the sense of morality. Here, Paul uses "righteousness" as the believer in right standing with God by way of His justifying work, returning to the forensic meaning established in chapters 1–4.

"[T]he righteousness which is by faith" is contrasted against "pursuing a law of righteousness." Gentile believers attained righteous status with God by way of faith, even though they had not been pursuing the righteousness that the Law demanded. Due to their lack of faith, works-based Jews were pursuing a (small *l*) law of righteousness. Even though they had God's Law, they failed to attain righteous standing with God.

9:32a Why? Because they did not pursue it by faith, but as though it were by works.

> *For we maintain that a man is justified by faith apart from works of the Law. (Romans 3:28)*

> *So then it does not depend on the man who wills or the mans who runs, but on God who has mercy. (Romans 9:16)*

9:32b-33 They stumbled over the stumbling stone, just as it is written, "Behold, I lay in Zion a stone of stumbling and a rock of offense, and he who believes in Him will not be disappointed."

"a stone of stumbling"—Jesus Christ (see Isaiah 28:16 and 8:14)

Inappropriate focus on the Law caused many Jews to miss Christ. Instead of putting their faith in Jesus as the keystone in the plan of salvation, the gospel became an obstacle for many Jews.

"a rock of offense"—Christ confronting the Jews; Jews offended by Christ

10:1-4 The Righteousness of God vs. Their Own Righteousness

10:1 Brethren, my heart's desire and my prayer to God for them is for their salvation.

Paul makes it clear that he finds no comfort in the fall of the Jews. He cared *deeply*. A deeper understanding of timeless, divine sovereignty should not cause us to become numb to the reality of the time-bound lost people around us. We should care *deeply*.

10:2 For I testify about them that they have a zeal for God, but not in accordance with knowledge.

Many Jews were zealous in their pursuit of God. But religious or spiritual zeal for God does not automatically lead to salvation. Many sincerely religious people are wrong in their beliefs. Religious or spiritual zeal for God, without revealed biblical knowledge (practical biblical wisdom) is next to worthless.

10:3 For not knowing about God's righteousness and seeking to establish their own, they did not subject themselves to the righteousness of God.

"the righteousness of God"

TIMELESS: God's dynamic activity of declaring right.

TIME-BOUND: The human status of being right by way of humble and obedient surrender.

"God's righteousness" is contrasted against "seeking to establish their own [righteousness]"—self-righteousness; seeking to establish a relationship with God by personal effort and works

The long-term spiritual ignorance of Jewish self-righteousness set the stage for their failure to recognize Jesus Christ as the Messiah. God's plan for Israel was never about what a good job the Israelites were doing. Self-righteousness was always getting in the way of faith (see Deuteronomy 9:4-6).

10:4 For Christ is the end of the law for righteousness to everyone who believes.

This verse carries the same theme as Matthew 5:17. Our relationship with God comes through Jesus Christ, not through the Law. The period of time where the Mosaic Law is the central element in God's dealings with humanity has come to an end. A Christian's relationship to God is mediated in and through Christ.

But Jesus did not abolish the Law—He fulfilled it. The Mosaic Law in its entirety is still part of the revealed word of God and should be studied in context of the New Testament and responded to by the mature believer (see 2 Timothy 3:16).

Some parts of the Law, like the Ten Commandments, are still binding on Christians (although they must be understood and applied in a New Testament context).

Amplification: *For Christ is the [culmination, consummation, climax] of the Law [with the purpose that there might be] righteousness to everyone who believes.*

Jesus Christ consummates one era of salvation history and inaugurates a new one.

10:5-13 The Message of Salvation

10:5-6a For Moses writes that the man who practices the righteousness which is based on law shall live by that righteousness. But the righteousness based on faith speaks as follows:

Here, "righteousness . . . based on law" (obedience) is contrasted against "righteousness based on faith" (belief). Leviticus 18:1-30 warns the Israelites to live by God's statutes and ordinances, not those of Egypt where they have come from and not those of Canaan where they are going. Leviticus 18:5 is quoted here to show the essence of following the Law: sanctifying blessing from God is contingent on obedience.

> **TIME-BOUND:** The only way to "live by that [sanctifying] righteousness" is to "[obediently] practice the righteousness which is based [in time] on law." Throughout the Bible, faith and practice—belief and doing—run side by side. Neither should be ignored, but they do not serve the same purpose. Gospel faith is about salvation. Living obediently is about sanctification. When the two are mixed improperly, the result can be eternally fatal.

> **TIMELESS:** "the righteousness based on faith speaks"—Faith is alive because it is about the righteousness of God. There is no sanctifying obedience in time without saving faith.

10:6b "Do not say in your heart. . . ."

This is quoted from Deuteronomy 9:4. In Deuteronomy 9:4-6, Moses warns Israel that they did not earn the land because of their righteousness.

10:6c "'Who will ascend into heaven?' (that is, to bring Christ down)."

No Israelite needed to ascend into heaven to bring the Old Testament down by super-spiritual human effort. In the same way, no Christian needs to exert some sort of super-spiritual human effort to "bring Christ down."

10:7 "or 'Who will descend into the abyss?' (that is, to bring Christ up from the dead)."

Here is an amplification of 6c: God didn't need any help from us with the incarnation or the resurrection. Our only contribution to the work of God is obedience.

"Who will ascend . . . who will descend" represents tasks impossible for a human. Only God could bring Christ down, and only God could raise Christ up.

10:8 But what does it say? "The word is near you, in your mouth and in your heart" —that is, the word of faith which we are preaching.

> **Amplification:** *But what does [Deuteronomy 30:14] say [about the righteousness based on faith]?*

God brought His word "near" to Israel so that they could know Him by faith and obey Him in time. God brings His word "near" to us so that we can know Him by faith and obey Him in time.

Salvation, the righteousness based on faith—"the word of faith"—is both accessible ("mouth") and understandable ("heart"). When we are saved, how near is God's word to us? It is written on our hearts.

The three quotes in verses 6c, 7, and 8 are from Deuteronomy 30:11-14 where Moses is warning the Israelites that God has made His Law clear to them; they cannot claim ignorance as an excuse for disobedience. It is the grace of God that establishes a relationship with His people. The grace of God driving the Mosaic Covenant is the same grace of God working now in the new covenant.

Just as Israel could not plead ignorance of God's will back then, neither Jew nor Gentile can plead ignorance of God's revelation in Jesus Christ now.

10:9 . . . that if you confess with your mouth Jesus as Lord, and believe in your heart that God raised Him from the dead, you will be saved.

Verse 9 is a development of verse 8:

> "confess with your mouth"—Give outward evidence of your inward faith.

"Jesus as Lord"—Jesus Christ, the Son of God, as Master with total power and authority over your life

"and believe in your heart"—Intellectual agreement by itself is a human work. Heart belief is a deep, inward trust and all-in surrender of the totality of your being. God judges the heart. You can't fool—or fool with—God.

"and believe . . . that God raised Him from the dead"—You must have an understanding of the meaning and significance of the resurrection as it relates to sin and salvation.

If you meet the above requirements, "you will be saved."

10:10 . . . for with the heart a person believes, resulting in righteousness, and with the mouth he confesses, resulting in salvation.

heart belief—righteousness—salvation: the central theme of Romans

Paul is not presenting verbal confession as a second requirement for salvation after heart belief. Confession is the outward, mental expression and evidence of the inner response of heart belief. The righteousness of justification is conferred in this life, and the end times deliverance of salvation is promised in the next life.

10:11 For the Scripture says, "Whoever believes in Him will not be disappointed."

Isaiah 28:16 is quoted to support the connection of faith and salvation.

"Whoever believes"—Salvation is open to all who believe by God's standard of belief (see 10:9-10).

TIME-BOUND: Our actions in time have real meaning and effect.

10:12 For there is no distinction between Jew and Greek; for the same Lord is Lord of all, abounding in riches for all who call on Him.

As there is no distinction between Jew and Gentile in sin and judgment (see verse 3:23), there is also no distinction in how the Lord dispenses grace. "The Lord is Lord of all," whether saved or lost. But salvation is limited to "all who call on Him."

115

10:13 . . . for "Whoever will call on the name of the Lord will be saved."

Joel 2:32 is quoted to support verses 10:11 and 10:12. In the Old Testament, the Israelites called on Yahweh for salvation while looking forward to the Messiah (the cross). In the New Testament and beyond, Christians call on Jesus Christ the Messiah for salvation while looking back to the cross.

> **TIME-BOUND/TIMELESS:** While our actions in time have real meaning and effect, remember everything Paul has previously written when contemplating 10:11-13.

10:14-21 Accountability

10:14-15a How then will they call on Him in whom they have not believed? How will they believe in Him whom they have not heard? And how will they hear without a preacher? How will they preach unless they are sent?

The four rhetorical questions related to verse 13 yield four assertions regarding salvation:

> **1. TIME-BOUND:** People cannot call on Jesus Christ if they do not believe in Jesus Christ.

> **2. TIME-BOUND:** People cannot believe in Jesus Christ if they do not have knowledge about Jesus Christ.

> **3. TIME-BOUND:** People cannot have knowledge about Jesus Christ unless someone disciples them with biblical preaching.

> **4. TIMELESS:** Jesus Christ won't be proclaimed unless preachers are "sent" (called, empowered) by God. Implicit in this assertion is that God sends called preachers into the world.

10:15b Just as it is written, "How beautiful are the feet of those who bring good news of good things!"

Isaiah 52:7 is quoted to provide scriptural confirmation as to the necessary role of preaching and spreading the gospel and to affirm that God does send called preachers into the world (meeting the fourth condition of the previous verse). "Beautiful" can also be rendered as "timely," increasing the end times focus.

10:16 However, they did not all heed the good news; for Isaiah says, "Lord, who has believed our report?"

The quote from Isaiah 53:1 places the context in terms of those who have heard the good news. Even when God-called preachers preach the good news and people hear it, "not all heed the good news"—many will not believe and therefore cannot call on the Lord.

> **TIME-BOUND:** If someone has heard the gospel of Jesus Christ and rejected it, remaining lost is not a matter of passive unbelief; remaining lost indicates a mindful and accountable refusal to believe.

10:17 So faith comes from hearing, and hearing by the word of Christ.

Faith comes from hearing the message that Christ is the crucified and risen Lord and Savior.

10:18 But I say, surely they have never heard, have they? Indeed they have; "Their voice has gone out into all the earth, and their words to the ends of the world."

> "to the ends of the world"—the Gentile world

The quote from Psalm 19:4 in its original context states that God's general revelation has been proclaimed all over the world from the beginning of time. Paul uses this quote as an analogy to God's special revelation now being spread "to the ends of the world" as he knew it. This verse asserts that no Jew back then could claim that they had not heard the gospel.

10:19-20 But I say, surely Israel did not know, did they? First Moses says, "I will make you jealous by that which is not a nation, by a nation without understanding

will I anger you." And Isaiah is very bold and says, "I was found by those who did not seek Me, I became manifest to those who did not ask for Me."

Corporate Israel should have "found" Jesus Christ through correct understanding of the Scriptures. But they didn't, so God sent the gospel to the Gentiles—"a foolish nation." Prophetic result: jealous and angry Jews in fulfillment of Isaiah 65:1.

10:21 But as for Israel He says, "All the day long I have stretched out My hands to a disobedient and obstinate people."

Isaiah 65:2a:

> **TIMELESS:** "I have spread out My hands all day long." God's extension of grace remains constant across time; He keeps His word.

Isaiah 65:2b:

> **TIMELESS / TIME-BOUND:** "to a rebellious people"—predestined to rebel, choosing to rebel (see Romans 9:17-18)

Isaiah 65:2c:

> **TIME-BOUND:** "who walk in the way which is not good, following their own thoughts." Israel was, for the most part, "a disobedient and obstinate people."

11:1-10 And the Rest Were Hardened

11:1 I say then, God has not rejected His people, has He? May it never be! For I too am an Israelite, a descendant of Abraham, of the tribe of Benjamin.

Even though Israel, for the most part, refused to acknowledge Jesus Christ, the transition in salvation history that takes place at the cross of Christ does not mean that God has pulled the rug out from under corporate Israel. Paul, as a Jewish Christian, is himself evidence that God has not abandoned corporate Israel. Many other Jews became Christians (even though most did not).

11:2a God has not rejected His people whom He foreknew.

TIME-BOUND: "God has not rejected His People" (see 1 Samuel 12:22 and Psalm 94:14). Individual Israelite disobedience does not cancel God's promises to corporate Israel.

TIMELESS: "God has not rejected His People whom He foreknew." God's promises were made with divine foreknowledge of how individual sinfulness would manifest in time. Israel was elected as a corporate entity, but there was never a guarantee of salvation for each individual Israelite.

11:2b-4 Or do you not know what the Scripture says in the passage about Elijah, how he pleads with God against Israel? "Lord, they have killed Your prophets, they have torn down Your altars, and I alone am left, and they are seeking my life." But what is the divine response to him? "I have kept for Myself seven thousand men who have not bowed the knee to Baal."

In 1 Kings 19, Israel is in full-blown apostasy. Elijah is the only prophet of God still alive, and as he flees for his life, He pleads his situation to God. Elijah is assured that God has preserved a remnant of faithful Israelites to serve Him.

11:5 In the same way then, there has also come to be at the present time a remnant according to God's gracious choice.

Both Paul and Elijah were confronted with what appeared to be the end of spiritual Israel. In each case, even when the majority of individual Israelites go apostate, God keeps His covenant with corporate Israel by preserving a remnant of faithful believers. The end of verse 5 emphasizes that this preservation is "according to God's gracious choice," not according to any intrinsic merit on the part of Israel.

The difference between Paul and Elijah's situations is that now individual Jews are no different than individual Gentiles in terms of salvation.

119

11:6 But if it is by grace, it is no longer on the basis of works, otherwise grace is no longer grace.

"[W]orks" here refers to anything that humans do, not just works of the Law. A fundamental tenet of grace is that Holy God is perfectly free to bestow it when, where, and how He sees fit. If human works could secure salvation, then grace would not be grace. Where time-bound and timeless meet, human faith is the *result* of God's grace, not its *basis*.

11:7 What then? What Israel is seeking, it has not obtained, but those who were chosen obtained it, and the rest were hardened.

(See verse 9:31.)

> **Amplification:** *What [corporate] Israel is seeking [right standing with God] it has not obtained, but those [individuals] who were chosen [by election] obtained it.*

TIME-BOUND: "and the rest were hardened [by personal choice]."

TIMELESS: "and the rest were hardened [by God]."

11:8-10 . . . just as it is written, "God gave them a spirit of stupor, eyes to see not and ears to hear not, down to this very day." And David says, "Let their table become a snare and a trap, and a stumbling block and a retribution to them. Let their eyes be darkened to see not, and bend their backs forever."

All of this happened "just as it is written." (See Deuteronomy 29:1-4; Isaiah 29:9-14; Psalm 69:20-28.)

11:11-15 God's Purpose in Israel's Current Rejection

11:11 I say then, they did not stumble so as to fall, did they? May it never be! But by their transgression salvation has come to the Gentiles, to make them jealous.

> "stumble"—corporate Israel's rejection of the righteousness of God manifesting through Christ
>
> "fall"—irretrievable spiritual ruin

Does the current era of stumbling mean that corporate Israel has permanently fallen from God's grace? Paul has already told us that the gospel of Jesus Christ has divided Israel into two parts: a remnant that has and will attain the righteousness of God through salvation, and the rest who were and will be hardened in their sin and excluded. The purpose of Israel's current corporate condition was and is twofold:

1. Time-bound corporate Israel's overall rejection of Jesus has brought the gospel to all of humanity in a way the Jews would never have allowed for.

TIME-BOUND: The jealousy motif emphasizes the importance of human action and response.

2. The prophecy of Deuteronomy 32:21 is being fulfilled in time.

TIMELESS: God keeps all of His promises to corporate Israel and to the world.

11:12 Now if their transgression is riches for the world and their failure is riches for the Gentiles, how much more will their fulfillment be!

Israel's transgression in rejecting Christ and subsequent spiritual defeat resulted in spiritual blessings for the Gentile world at large. If Israel's stumbling has resulted in this much blessing on the world, how much more will future Israel be blessed at the fulfillment of all this?

11:13a But I am speaking to you who are Gentiles.

This suggests that the majority of Christians in Rome were Gentile converts.

11:13b-14 Inasmuch then as I am an apostle of Gentiles, I magnify my ministry, if somehow I might move to jealousy my fellow countrymen and save some of them.

The sovereign hardening of corporate Israel against Jesus Christ has always resulted in a time-bound hardening of Christians against Jews and even against Jewish Christians. Paul makes it clear that his special focus as "apostle of Gentiles" has not led him to give up on reaching out to his "fellow countrymen." He has no disdain for Jews as individuals.

> **TIME-BOUND:** Regardless of corporate institutional conditions, individuals within those institutions can respond to the gospel.

11:15 For if their rejection is the reconciliation of the world, what will their acceptance be but life from the dead?

> "rejection"—rejection by God (see 11:8)
>
> "acceptance"—corporate restoration of Israel by God

Israel's corporate transgression (verse 11) and failure (verse 12) resulted in rejection by God (verse 15) in this stage of salvation history. Israel's "fulfillment" (verse 12) in time will be when their "acceptance" (verse 15) triggers the end of salvation history, resulting in "life from the dead" (verse 15).

> **TIMELESS:** The conclusion of "life from the dead" emphasizes God's ultimacy in all of this.

> **TIME-BOUND / TIMELESS:** God keeps all of His promises to corporate Israel and the world.

11:16-24 A Warning to Gentile Believers

Paul now explains the relationship of Gentile Christians to the current and future state of corporate Israel that he introduced in verses 11-15.

The Olive Tree Illustration

In many ancient Jewish texts, Abraham and the patriarchs are called the root of Israel.

> "root"—God's promises to the patriarchs (Abraham, Isaac, and Jacob)
>
> "branches"—ethnic Israel

"wild olive"—Gentile

"wild olive tree"—the lost people of the world

"cultivated olive tree"—the people of God on both sides of the cross

See especially Jeremiah 2:21, 6:9, 8:13, 11:16; Hosea 14:5-8; Psalm 80:8-15; John 15:1-6.

Contrast with Judges 9:8-15; Ezekiel 6:13; 1 Kings 14:22-23; Isaiah 2:12-13, 10:33-34; Amos 2:9; Zechariah 11:1-2; Matthew 3:9-10; Jude 12.

A healthy, well-tended olive tree was very productive and was the most widely cultivated fruit tree in the Mediterranean area. The untended wild olive tree was notoriously unfruitful. In ancient agriculture, a branch from a cultivated tree would be grafted onto a wild tree to cause the wild tree to become cultivated and produce better fruit.

The image in this passage reverses the natural process. Contrary to the usual nature of grafting, wild Gentile branches are being grafted into the already cultivated olive tree of Israel. By nature, the grafting in of Gentiles should ruin the cultivated tree of Israel, but by the supernatural process of grace, the wild branches are transformed by the root.

11:16 If the first piece of dough is holy, the lump is also; and if the root is holy, the branches are too.

"first piece [first fruits] of dough" and "lump"—See Numbers 15:21 and 1 Corinthians 5:6, 15:20, and 15:23.

Paul uses this parallel first fruits illustration to remind us that ultimately Israel has always been all about Jesus the Messiah. If the origin of Israel—based in Christ—is holy by God's promise to the patriarchs, then corporate Israel is holy too; and if the promise to Abraham is holy looking forward, then ethnic Israel as a corporate entity remains holy looking forward too.

11:17-18 But if some of the branches were broken off, and you, being a wild olive, were grafted in among them and became partaker with them of the rich root of

the olive tree, do not be arrogant toward the branches; but if you are arrogant, remember that it is not you who supports the root, but the root supports you.

> **Amplification:** . . . *grafted in among [the remaining Jews] and became partaker with [the remaining Jews]. (Not "grafted in [to replace the Jews].")*

> **Paraphrase:** *If some of the Israelites, due to lack of saving faith, were hardened by God, and you, a lost Gentile, were accepted by faith in among the remnant and now share in the promise of God to the patriarchs, do not be arrogant to either the remaining Jewish Christians or to the unbelieving Jews; remember that you are not keeping God's word alive—God the Word is keeping you alive.*

11:19 You will say then, "Branches were broken off so that I might be grafted in."

> **Paraphrase:** *You will say to me then, "Many Jews have been removed from the people of God so that I could become one of God's people."*

11:20 Quite right, they were broken off for their unbelief, but you stand by your faith. Do not be conceited, but fear.

> **Paraphrase:** *It's true, many Jews have been separated from God by their unbelief while you have been established only because you believe. So then, do not be proud and conceited about your new status, but rather stand in awe and reverentially fear God.*

Gentile Christians have a long history of presenting themselves as the completion and full manifestation of God's plan for salvation as a replacement for Israel. But the end of the story includes the full restoration of corporate Israel. You and I are not the story; we are a part of the story.

11:21 . . . for if God did not spare the natural branches, He will not spare you, either.

> **Paraphrase:** *For if God judged many of His own people to condemnation because of unbelief, He will judge you to condemnation as well if you are guilty of the same offense.*

Reverential fear of God is the appropriate response to all of this.

11:22 Behold then the kindness and severity of God; to those who fell, severity, but to you, God's kindness, if you continue in His kindness; otherwise you also will be cut off.

> **Paraphrase:** *Observe in reverential fear the nature of God's judgment— the holy kindness and the holy severity of God: severe judgment to condemnation on those who do not believe; but to you who believe, the kindness of judgment to salvation—provided your faith is proved to be true; otherwise, if you are presuming on God's kindness in the same way as a lost Jew, you too will be cut off from the people of God and under condemnation.*

TIME-BOUND: Timeless saving faith will endure and prove itself out in time.

11:23 And they also, if they do not continue in their unbelief, will be grafted in, for God is able to graft them in again.

> **Paraphrase:** *Even Jews who appear to you to be under condemnation can be saved if their unbelief becomes belief, because salvation is all of God, and God is all-powerful.*

TIME-BOUND: Do not presume to understand all of the implications of timeless divine sovereignty. No matter how much theological skill you achieve, God is sovereign, and you are not.

11:24 For if you were cut off from what is by nature a wild olive tree, and were grafted contrary to nature into a cultivated olive tree, how much more will these who are the natural branches be grafted into their own olive tree?

The church of justified believers is the fulfillment and continuation of Israel and the current focus of God's work in the world. The church of justified believers is not the new Israel—it is the true Israel.

The gospel of Jesus Christ makes an exclusive truth claim about salvation. In this sense, the gospel is anti-Judaic; salvation cannot come through Torah, only through Christ. But the New Testament is not anti-Semitic; the gospel is not hostile toward ethnic Israel. Christ's church is rooted in the patriarchs, and Gentiles have been grafted into that root.

There is and always has been only one cultivated olive tree, and its healthy branches are all of the true people of God. The gospel boundary is faith in Jesus Christ, not ethnicity or institution.

11:25-32 The Salvation of "All Israel"

11:25 For I do not want you, brethren, to be uninformed of this mystery—so that you will not be wise in your own estimation—that a partial hardening has happened to Israel until the fullness of the Gentiles has come in.

In Jewish apocalyptic literature, "mystery" usually refers to an end times event that is known by God and revealed to a prophet for the strengthening and encouragement of Israel. Paul uses "mystery" as something that is hidden from time-bound humanity in the past and is now revealed in the gospel. The language here insists that Paul is claiming divine revelation as to the meaning of the prophecy recorded in Isaiah 27:9 and 59:20-21, partially quoted here.

> "so that you will not be wise in your own estimation"—a further admonishment in continuation of the warnings from 11:17-21. Gentile Christians are not to boast in their assumptions regarding their status relative to Jews and Jewish Christians.
>
> "a partial hardening has happened to [corporate] Israel"—Room is made for Gentiles to "come in" to the promise through a partial hardening of Israel. The majority of Jews have been set aside by God while a number of Gentiles known only to God are grafted in (see Luke 21:20-24).

There is no indication here, or anywhere else in Scripture, of a total, complete, and final hardening of Israel, resulting in abandonment or replacement. (See also Jeremiah 31:33-34.)

11:26a . . . and so all Israel will be saved; just as it is written.

Paul has already made it clear that God is saving a certain number of Jews as we move toward the second coming. Now he looks through that movement to the end. An amplification looking across time: "and so [in this manner] all [the elected remnant of] Israel [across time] will be saved." An amplification looking to the end: "and so [when the fullness of the Gentiles has come in] all [elect] Israel [at that time] will be saved."

God has fulfilled His covenant with Abraham by sending the Messiah, and the covenant still awaits its final completion.

11:26b-27 "The Deliverer will come from Zion, He will remove ungodliness from Jacob. This is My covenant with them, when I take away their sins."

The Old Testament text translates as "A Redeemer will come *to* Zion" (Isaiah 59:20). In Hebrews 12:22, Zion is associated with the heavenly Jerusalem. Paul alters the Isaiah quote to make it clear that the final deliverance of Israel is accomplished by Christ at the second coming ("The Deliverer will come from Zion [to Zion]").

The Old Testament text translates as "Therefore through this [hardening] Jacob's iniquity will be removed" (Isaiah 27:9a). The judgment of Israel in Isaiah 27 is both temporary and restorative. The prophecy looks forward to the time when "the full price of the pardoning of his sin" (Isaiah 27:9b) will be paid and Israel will be restored. Paul parallels the temporary/restorative model in Romans and ties the message to the cross by focusing Isaiah 59:21a on the forgiveness of sins.

Israel's corporate "fulfillment" (Romans 11:12) in time will be when their "acceptance" (Romans 11:15) triggers the end of salvation history, resulting in "life from the dead" (Romans 11:15). "These who are the natural branches [will] be grafted into their own olive tree" (Romans 11:24) when "the fullness of the Gentiles has come in" (Romans 11:25).

> **Amplification:** *"This is My covenant with [Israel] when [by their acceptance of the Gospel of Jesus Christ] I take away their sins." (Romans 11:27; see Romans 3:21-26)*

11:28 From the standpoint of the gospel they are enemies for your sake, but from the standpoint of God's choice they are beloved for the sake of the fathers.

> "for your sake"—During this phase in history lots of Gentiles are getting saved.

From the standpoint of the gospel, a lost Jew is no different than a lost Gentile; they are both enemies of God (see Romans 5:10; 1 Corinthians 15:25; Philippians 3:18; James 4:4; Hebrews 1:13; Job 13:24; Micah 2:8; Nahum 1:2). From the standpoint of God's election, corporate Israel is beloved for the sake of the promise made to Abraham, Isaac, and Jacob.

11:29 ... for the gifts and the calling of God are irrevocable.

> "gift"—In the Bible, a gift is something freely given by God. In this verse, "gift" refers to the unique blessings given to Israel (see 9:4-5).
>
> "calling"—election to salvation

The saving promises made to corporate Israel will happen because God keeps His word.

11:30-31 For just as you once were disobedient to God, but now have been shown mercy because of their disobedience, so these also now have been disobedient, that because of the mercy shown to you they also may now be shown mercy.

God allowed the Jewish rejection to lead to the Gentiles' ability to experience God's mercy. The Gentile experience of God will eventually lead to Israel's renewed experience of God's mercy.

The final "now" in verse 31 means that the promise of Jewish salvation could be fulfilled at any time (see Matthew 24:36-39; Mark 13:32-37).

11:32 For God has shut up all in disobedience so that He may show mercy to all.

> "shut up"—imprisoned

The gospel has shown the world that all of humanity is imprisoned together in sin. All of humanity, each individual Jew and Gentile, has been shown to be disobedient without distinction. There is no promise of universal salvation here, nor would such a promise stand in context of the letter as a whole. The holy mercy that God has shown to all is the sending of Jesus Christ.

TIME-BOUND: God's holy mercy doesn't negate His holy justice. The biblical expression of God's holy attributes, taken together, clarify the gospel expression of His holy love from the perspective of time. The only way to take advantage of God's holy mercy is by placing saving faith in the person and work of Jesus Christ. Some people will; many won't.

TIMELESS: Nothing in time can force God's hand. If you are saved, regardless of how it seems to you in time, God saved you.

11:33-36 A Hymn of Praise

11:33-36 Oh, the depth of the riches both of the wisdom and knowledge of God! How unsearchable are His judgments and unfathomable His ways! For who has known the mind of the Lord, or who became His counselor? Or who has first given to Him that it might be paid back to him again? For from Him and through Him and to Him are all things. To Him be the glory forever. Amen.

The gospel is straightforward in its complexity and ultimately simple. We exist in God's paradoxical intermix of sovereignty and time-bound-ness. We are responsible for what God makes us responsible for, and God is absolutely sovereign—both at the same time.

No expression of systematic theology can solve God's sovereignty paradox. Applying time-bound Aristotelian logic as an attempt to solve the paradox can only distort the relationship of divine sovereignty and human responsibility by inevitably defaulting to one or the other with a limited human viewpoint from time dominating in either case. Attempting to solve the paradox of time-bound humanity making meaningful decisions in time in context of divine sovereignty always results in the logical binding of one in favor of the other and the dismissal or dishonoring of the mystical, paradoxical design nature of the Bible.

12:1-15:13 LIVING LIFE IN CHRIST

12:1-2 Total Dedication to God

Chapters 1–11 proclaim the gospel of Jesus Christ and are presented mainly in the indicative—believers are instructed about sin and righteousness and told what God has done for them in Christ. Chapters 12 through the thirteenth verse of chapter 15 are presented mainly in the imperative. Based on the authority of the gospel, believers are now exhorted to obey certain specifics of Christian living in time.

12:1 Therefore I urge you, brethren, by the mercies of God, to present your bodies a living and holy sacrifice, acceptable to God, which is your spiritual service of worship.

In light of all of the arguments from chapters 1–11 ("Therefore"), verses 1 and 2 summarize what the Christian response to the gospel should look like while at the same time providing a heading for this entire section moving forward.

Paul is *the* ambassador of Christ and His authoritative representative; God is speaking through Paul's writings. Paul does not command us on his own personal authority; he authoritatively "urges" us to respond appropriately to the experience of God's mercy and the authority of the gospel.

The Greek word translated as the plural "mercies" is itself a translation of a Hebrew word that has a singular meaning. All the things in the letter about what God has done are summed up singularly as the plural "by the mercies of God," which could be rendered as a singular summation of the plural: in view of the mercy of God in action.

God doesn't just ask for what we give through our Christian lives; God commands that we "present [our] bodies a living and holy sacrifice." We are to offer all of ourselves and our lives as an ongoing "living and holy sacrifice" to God. The sacrifice is "living" because it continues until the person offering it dies. The sacrifice is "acceptable to God" because it is "holy"—because the believer has been set apart and dedicated to the Lord.

The Jewish temple is no longer the center of worship. Every Christian is a priest, and every Christian body is a temple of the Holy Spirit ("which is your spiritual service of worship"). Christian worship is not confined to any one place or time; Christian worship involves all places and times.

> "spiritual service of worship"—appropriate worship that gives God what He wants as opposed to the irrational worship of Romans 1:23-25
>
> "[inner] service of worship"—authentic worship that comes from the heart and mind and doesn't just mechanically go through the motions
>
> "[reasonable] service of worship"—sensible worship that fits the circumstances as the appropriately reasoned response to God by the renewed Christian mind

> **Paraphrase:** *Therefore, in light of all you have learned about the righteousness of God, on my authority as God's ambassador I urge you, in view of the mercy of God in action, to present the entirety of yourselves as continuous, ongoing sacrifices set apart as holy and acceptable to God, which is your true worship.*

Romans 12:1 echoes forward the imperatives from Romans 6:12-13, 19, and reverses the downward spiral of the "therefore" in Romans 1:24 (taken with 1:25 and 1:28).

12:2 And do not be conformed to this world, but be transformed by the renewing of your mind, so that you may prove what the will of God is, that which is good and acceptable and perfect.

For followers of Christ, the power of sin to dominate has been broken in us, but the presence of sin remains. Christians are not to live in unbiblical patterns of behavior. Christians are not to passively or actively endorse unbiblical behaviors in an effort to appease or get along with the lost world. The command is direct and present: do not conform.

> "this world" / "this age"—this period of time where the world is dominated by sin and Satan
>
> "mind"—human moral consciousness and human practical reason
>
> "be transformed"—apply yourself to progressing in spiritual change at the deepest level
>
> "by the renewing of your mind"—Spirit-driven reprogramming of your mind
>
> "prove"—discover so as to carry out
>
> "God gave [lost humanity] over to a depraved mind" (Romans 1:28)—a spiritually worthless, spiritually unqualified mind incapable of renewing itself through practical reasoning

When you were saved, the regenerating power of the Holy Spirit changed your relationship to sin. You are now able to "be transformed by the [ongoing] renewing of your mind" that takes place in the process of sanctification. For the converted, the state of Romans 1:28 has been reversed. Because of the power and presence of the Holy Spirit, "you [are able to discover so as to carry out] what the will of God is." And the will of God for you in sanctification is for you to discover and live out "that which is good and acceptable [to God] and perfect."

> **Paraphrase:** *And do not immerse in or go along with this age where the world is dominated by sin and Satan, but apply yourself to progressing in spiritual change at the deepest level by the ongoing, Spirit-driven reprogramming of your moral consciousness and practical reasoning, so that you may discover so as to carry out what the will of God is, that which is good, acceptable to God, and perfect.*

Paul does not divide the human body (12:1) from the human mind (12:2). There is always a relationship between thinking and action. Christians not only possess a biblical worldview, but we are told that we are now able to discover so as to carry out the will of God. Because of our regeneration, we are able to recognize and understand what is acceptable to God as well as effectively apply ourselves to obedience. In this living, moving process of sanctification, we do not do away with God's Law; we live in the dynamic spiritual relationship of the law of Christ, a place beyond mere application of the Law wherein we become further conformed to Christ by the ongoing spiritual renewing of our minds.

The vision of verses 1 and 2: a place beyond external commands where the Spirit-driven Christian mind is able to respond instinctively and intuitively to any life situation in a way that pleases God.

12:3-8 Humility and Service

12:3 For through the grace given to me I say to everyone among you not to think more highly of himself than he ought to think; but to think so as to have sound judgment, as God has allotted to each a measure of faith.

> "the grace given to me"—Paul's authoritative apostolic calling, not the grace of salvation
>
> "a measure of faith"—Part of the sound judgment of the renewed mind is the humility to understand where we stand in relation to God. Our understanding of faith is only a measure of God's understanding. This humility provides the foundation for sober and sound self-assessment.

> **TIME-BOUND:** Saving faith is the common standard for all Christians—you either have a faith that saves or you don't. This applies equally to everyone who is saved.

> **TIMELESS:** If you have a "measure of faith," it's because God allotted it to you. Do not think more highly of yourself than you ought to think.

12:4-5 For just as we have many members in one body and all the members do not have the same function, so we, who are many, are one body in Christ, and individually members one of another.

> "one body in Christ"—Salvation is personal, but Christian existence is corporate.

TIME-BOUND: The visible church of institutions and denominations creates the illusion of isolated groups of Christians at odds with each other in their diversity.

TIMELESS: The real body of Christ is the invisible church made up of all of the justified, regenerate believers past, present, and future.

Everyone who is saved is a member of the body of Christ. It is impossible for a believer to exist as an isolated spiritual entity. Even though our personal attributes and experiences shape us into diverse individuals, our regenerated spirits are "individually members one of another."

12:6-8 Since we have gifts that differ according to the grace given to us, each of us is to exercise them accordingly: if prophecy, according to the proportion of his faith; if service, in his serving; or he who teaches, in his teaching; or he who exhorts, in his exhortation; he who gives, with liberality; he who leads, with diligence; he who shows mercy, with cheerfulness.

Fact: "we have gifts that differ."

Standard: "according to the grace given to us [by God]."

Condition: We are to assess our gifts soberly and humbly and "exercise them accordingly."

The list of gifts is not exhaustive; it is representative and instructional. Gifts are not given for self-indulgent use or for elevating the self over others.

Outward expressions: "prophecy," "service," "teaching," "exhortation"

"prophecy"—Avoid speculative fantasizing beyond what God clearly gives; watch out for self-fulfilling motivations. Real prophecy will always align with the Bible.

Prophecy is always open to scrutiny (1 Corinthians 14:29-33). When serving, teaching, and/or exhorting others, be "in" the activity, be authentic, and be surrendered.

Inner attitudes: "giving," "leading," "mercifulness"

"giving"—simple, prayerful, in the moment; no sense of "what's in it for me?"

133

"leading"—eager, persistent, determined effort; avoid laziness or doing just enough to get by

"mercifulness"—real inner joy, real gladness; never begrudgingly or with a bad attitude

12:9-21 Holy Love and Christian Ethics

12:9a Let love be without hypocrisy.

Jesus answered, "The foremost is, 'Hear, O Israel! The Lord our God is one Lord; and you shall love the Lord your God with all your heart, and with all your soul, and with all your mind, and with all your strength.'" (Matthew 12:29-30)

Holy love is the model. Love patterned on holiness is sincere and conforms to the nature of God.

12:9b Abhor what is evil.

Holy love hates sin. A regenerate spirit should be disgusted by sinful activities. It is not loving to tell someone that sinful activities aren't sinful.

12:9c . . . cling to what is good.

Holy love will not lead a person to do something the Bible says is wrong. Holy love will not encourage someone to avoid doing what is right. The result of being transformed by the renewing of the mind is a spirit that conforms to the Bible. We are to abhor what God abhors and cling to what God loves.

12:10 Be devoted to one another in brotherly love, give preference to one another in honor.

"The second is this, 'You shall love your neighbor as yourself.' There is no other commandment greater than these." (Matthew 12:31)

Holy love is the standard.

"A new commandment I give to you, that you love one another, even as I have loved you, that you also love one another. By this all men will know that you are My disciples, if you have love for one another." (John 13:34-35)

Jesus Christ is the model. Christians are bound together by the Spirit as members of God's family. We are to recognize, respect, and honor each other's importance and defer to one another.

12:11a ... not lagging behind in diligence.

Don't become spiritually lazy or complacent.

12:11b ... fervent in spirit.

Let the Holy Spirit set you on fire; be open to the Spirit.

12:11c ... serving the Lord.

We serve the Lord in obedience. The Holy Spirit will not tell you to do anything that is out of alignment with the Scriptures. We are made fervent in spirit for the purpose of serving the Lord.

12:12 ... rejoicing in hope, persevering in tribulation, devoted to prayer.

Looking forward in the hope of glory helps us to persevere in times of suffering. A life devoted to prayer fuels our rejoicing and strengthens our ability to persevere.

12:13 ... contributing to the needs of the saints, practicing hospitality.

The early church in any given locality pooled its resources in an effort to provide for everyone who had material needs. Christian love and concern must have a practical expression in time to be authentic.

In the world of Paul's time, there were few hotels. Christians were expected to take care of traveling Christian missionaries and workers. We are to go out of our way to be friendly and welcoming to members of the body of Christ, wherever we find them.

12:14 Bless those who persecute you; bless and do not curse.

Blessings can move through people, but they come from God. Take pity on those who persecute you, and ask God to work on their hearts.

> "But I say to you, love your enemies and pray for those who persecute you."
> (Matthew 5:44)

"But I say to you who hear, love your enemies, do good to those who hate you, bless those who curse you, pray for those who mistreat you." (Luke 6:27-28)

Extend forgiveness as a method; be merciful as your default stance.

12:15 Rejoice with those who rejoice, and weep with those who weep.

All of us with the indwelling of the Spirit are connected together by and in the Spirit. Holy love will respond with genuine joy when blessings pour out on fellow believers. Holy love will authentically identify with the sufferings of our brothers and sisters.

12:16a Be of the same mind toward one another.

Followers of Christ share the same indwelling Spirit. We are in Christ, and Christ is in us; we are all in the body together. We are not called to think the exact same things about all of the details of life, but we are all undergoing the Spirit-driven renewing of our minds. We are to do our best to live in the mindset shown to us by Christ.

12:16b ... do not be haughty in mind.

Personal pride destroys Christian unity and fellowship. We are all members of one body, and Jesus Christ is the Head. Individual Christians possess a wide range of gifts and abilities, but with Jesus as the standard, no one has anything personal to boast about.

12:16c ... but associate with the lowly.

No one in the body of Christ is to be exalted over anyone else. We are all called to be bondservants of Jesus, and we share in the same salvation. All Christians' works are to be approached with humility. The quality of surrendered engagement is more important than the perception of the importance of the work.

12:16d Do not be wise in your own estimation.

The standard by which you judge your level of wisdom should never be your own.

COMMENTARY: THE LETTER TO THE ROMANS

12:17a Never pay back evil for evil to anyone.

Retaliation is not the Christian way.

> *"You have heard that it was said, 'An eye for an eye, and a tooth for a tooth.' But I say to you, do not resist an evil person; but whoever slaps you on your right cheek, turn the other to him also." (Matthew 5:38-39)*

In context of the Bible as a whole, this cannot be a call for Christian pacifism.

12:17b Respect what is right in the sight of all men.

> "Respect"—take thought; reflect in your mind

Take thought for what is honest and proper, striving to be above reproach in the sight of everyone.

> *[F]or we have regard for what is honorable, not only in the sight of the Lord, but also in the sight of men. (2 Corinthians 8:21)*

12:18 If possible, so far as it depends on you, be at peace with all men.

Live in the renewed mind of 12:1-2. It's not always possible to be at peace with other people, but we should default to making the effort while maintaining our Christian witness.

> *"Have salt in yourselves, and be at peace with one another." (Mark 9:50b)*

> *"These things I have spoken to you, so that in Me you may have peace. In the world you have tribulation, but take courage; I have overcome the world." (John 16:33)*

Conflict with the lost world is inevitable, but so far as it depends on you personally, don't use the conflict to justify personal behaviors that needlessly increase the conflict.

12:19 Never take your own revenge, beloved, but leave room for the wrath of God, for it is written, "Vengeance is Mine, I will repay," says the Lord.

> "beloved"—loved by God; member of the body of Christ

> **TIME-BOUND:** Remember where you stand—and where you used to stand—with God. Never hold an attitude of seeking revenge regardless of the circumstances.

TIMELESS: God is holy. All of His holy attributes are in play. God, in His wrath, will retaliate against all of those who are against Christ. In the end, God will settle all accounts.

12:20 "But if your enemy is hungry, feed him, and if he is thirsty, give him a drink; for in so doing you will heap burning coals on his head."

Quoted from Proverbs 25:21-22, the metaphors of "fire" and "coals" represent God's presence and judgment in the Old Testament. Do what is right by God's standard, and leave the burning coals for God to sort out (either through conviction to repentance or at the Final Judgment).

> *"You have heard that it was said, 'You shall love your neighbor and hate your enemy.' But I say to you, love your enemies and pray for those who persecute you." (Mark 5:43-44)*

12:21 Do not be overcome by evil, but overcome evil with good.

Resist the temptation to conform to the world. Default to kindness and mercy whenever possible. Overcome the evil of others by living in the renewed mind of Romans 12:1-2.

> *"These things I have spoken to you, so that in Me you may have peace. In the world you have tribulation, but take courage; I have overcome the world." (John 16:33)*

Show the character of Christ to the lost world.

13:1-7 The Christian and Secular Government

13:1 Every person is to be in subjection to the governing authorities. For there is no authority except from God, and those which exist are established by God.

To "be in subjection" is to be generally obedient and to recognize and be accepting of authority. This applies to "every person" but should be deeply understood and accepted by Christians.

TIMELESS: God is sovereign. As difficult as the thought can be to hold and contemplate, everything that is happening is happening because God not

COMMENTARY: THE LETTER TO THE ROMANS

only allows it to happen—He ordains it. God has His own purposes, and His hand is everywhere.

TIME-BOUND: Good authorities seem to be a blessing. Evil and/or corrupt authorities seem to be instituted to bring about trials or judgment. Regardless, humanity did not create the idea of government—God did.

13:2 Therefore whoever resists authority has opposed the ordinance of God; and they who have opposed will receive condemnation upon themselves.

Rebelling against reasonable authority for the sake of self-righteousness, covetous self-interest, or to create anarchy is opposed to the "ordinance of God." To rebel against reasonably functioning authority is to rebel against God. To make a habit out of rejecting any authority ultimately leads to the rejection of all authority.

13:3a For rulers are not a cause of fear for good behavior, but for evil.

This is how things should be but not how things always are. Good authorities stabilize a society and prevent anarchy and the tyranny of the masses. Good authorities establish reasonable and necessary limitations as part of God's plan for humanity.

13:3b-13:4a Do you want to have no fear of authority? Do what is good and you will have praise from the same; for it is a minister of God to you for good.

Ideally, individuals and authorities are to work together for the common good. Whenever and wherever possible, Christians are to do good. Reasonable authorities will recognize that Christians are good for a society.

13:4b But if you do what is evil, be afraid; for it does not bear the sword for nothing; for it is a minister of God, an avenger who brings wrath on the one who practices evil.

While individual Christians are not to take individual revenge against wrong-doers, civil authorities have the right and responsibility to punish evil using "the sword" of justice up to and including capital punishment. A reasonably functioning government has the right to punish those who violate its laws.

TIME-BOUND: The vengeance that Christians are prohibited from engaging with is administered in time by God's chosen secular authorities.

13:5 Therefore it is necessary to be in subjection, not only because of wrath, but also for conscience' sake.

TIME-BOUND: Fear of suffering wrath will motivate submission to reasonable authority. The Christian conscience goes beyond this and senses in it God's providential plan for humanity. The Christian view of society should always be grounded in authority and order.

TIMELESS: God established the principle of governing authorities. Civilization subjected to governing authority is God's model. Sin hardwires us to rebel against authority. The judgment and wrath of a reasonable government against evil foreshadows God's final judgment and wrath against all evil.

13:6 For because of this you also pay taxes, for rulers are servants of God, devoting themselves to this very thing.

We pay taxes because we know we have to. There is an implicit recognition of the authority of government in our actions. Ideally, our consciences should lead us to embrace paying taxes because we know that we should support reasonable governing authority.

TIMELESS: "[R]ulers are servants of God"—a reminder of the sovereignty of God. Everyone and everything ultimately serves God's purposes. Secular rulers may think that they have some degree of ultimate authority when they collect taxes or enforce a country's laws, but everything in time is playing out in context of timeless divine sovereignty.

TIMELESS: "[D]evoting themselves to this very thing"—Whether they know it or not, every knee will bow to God.

13:7 Render to all what is due them: tax to whom tax is due; custom to whom custom; fear to whom fear; honor to whom honor.

"Render to all what is due them"—the practical application of verses 1–6.

"tax to whom tax is due"—direct taxes

"custom to whom custom"—indirect taxes

"fear to whom fear"—Be respectful of legal limitations.

"honor to whom honor"—Honor the authority even when you can't honor the person with the authority.

What is due to secular authorities is to be rendered in the context of submission. There is no call here for absolute, blind obedience to all things government. When evaluating government, we are to be mindful of its place in God's ordering of things. We acknowledge the absolute divine ordination of leadership structures, and we observantly submit to biblically reasonable governance.

For the most part, we are to be obedient as citizens. We are not to refuse to obey just because some things are unjustly handled. Governments always fall short of God's standards. But we draw the line when government attempts to displace or replace God. Our ultimate allegiance is to God, and all biblical instructions pertaining to government and civilization must be interpreted in that context.

We acknowledge the rightful existence of governmental authority, and we submit to secular rules and regulations as long as they do not directly violate, or ask us to violate, the biblical tenets of our faith.

"Render to Caeser the things that are Caeser's and to God the things that are God's." (Mark 12:17)

Government is not to be elevated to a place of authority equal to or greater than God; government should be submitted to in context of God.

13:8-10 Holy Love and God's Law

13:8a Owe nothing to anyone except to love one another.

The clause in 8a transitions from verse 7. The things listed in the previous verse should be handled with integrity and timeliness. When doing business,

Christians should adhere to the terms of the contract. Debts of this nature have an end point. The contract is fulfilled, the debt no longer exists.

> "one another"—The sharing of holy love can only be fully realized between Christians. But we are also commended here to extend Christian love to "anyone."

Bless those who persecute you; bless and do not curse. (Romans 12:14)

If possible, so far as it depends on you, be at peace with all men. (Romans 12:18)

13:8b . . . for he who loves his neighbor has fulfilled the law.

The clause in 8b interprets holy love as an obligation under the Law that has no end date. The only way to pay back the obligation of holy love is to keep extending the love of Christ out into the world. The love referenced here is not sentimental. It is based in the objective content of God's Law. Jesus did not come to abolish the Law—He came to fulfill it.

And [Jesus] said to him, "'You shall love the Lord your God with all your heart, and with all your soul, and with all your mind.' This is the great and foremost commandment. The second is like it, 'You shall love your neighbor as yourself.' On these two commandments depend the whole Law and the Prophets." (Matthew 22:37-40)

13:9 For this, "You shall not commit adultery, You shall not murder, You shall not steal, You shall not covet."

Murder is an expression of absolute elevation of the individual over God. Adultery is self-absorbed lust and is opposed to the quality of faithfulness God demands. Stealing is rebellion against blessing. Covetousness manifests as wanting what someone else has and not being content with what God has provided. The adulterer uses the life of another. The murderer takes the life of another. The thief violates the life of another.

13:9b . . . and if there is any other commandment, it is summed up in this saying, "You shall love your neighbor as yourself."

There is no room here for self-absorbed interpretation such as, *I love 'this' about myself, so I'll love 'this' about you as well.* The second command is like the first; the second can't manifest without the first. We are obligated to extend the love of Christ because Christ extended His love to us. We owe this to Christ, and it's a debt we can't finish repaying.

13:10 Love does no wrong to a neighbor; therefore love is the fulfillment of the law.

A Christian authentically extending the love of Christ is fulfilling the second foundational point of the Law while giving evidence of fulfilling the first foundational point. The highest human expression of holy love is the ongoing fulfillment of these two commandments in the sanctifying walk of a Christian.

13:11-14 Living In the Light

13:11-12a Do this, knowing the time, that it is already the hour for you to awaken from sleep; for now salvation is nearer to us than when we believed. The night is almost gone, and the day is near.

"do this"—all of this. Everything we have been learning about sanctification. Do it.

"knowing the time"—understanding the time

1. "it is already the hour for you to awaken from sleep"—For saved people, it is time to walk faithfully regardless of what the lost world is doing. Don't walk around spiritually asleep. Reject spiritual laziness and indifference. Do not conform to the present age.
2. "now salvation is nearer to us than when we believed"—"[S]alvation" here is God's completion of salvation history at the second coming. Every day, the final salvation of Christ's return is nearer to us than when we first were saved, and nobody, from Paul's time to now, knows how much nearer.
3. "the night is almost gone, and the day is near"—The spiritual darkness of this present evil age is passing, and the day of the Lord is near.

13:12b Therefore let us lay aside the deeds of darkness and put on the armor of light.

"darkness"—the realm of evil; the present evil age

"deeds of darkness"—sinful activities; immersion in sin

143

"light"—the light of Christ; the realm of the Spirit

"armor of light"—weapons of light; gifts and blessings; both defensive and offensive

We are to defend ourselves against the deeds of darkness while actively extending the gospel into the world.

13:13 Let us behave properly as in the day, not in carousing and drunkenness, not in sexual promiscuity and sensuality, not in strife and jealousy.

We are to behave in a manner appropriate to our calling. We have been released from the darkness and brought into the light. We are not to retreat to the darkness and engage in sinful and un-Christian conduct.

"strife and jealousy"—divisiveness in the body of Christ

13:14 But put on the Lord Jesus Christ, and make no provision for the flesh in regard to its lusts.

Present tense.

The conscious act of conforming to the image of Christ on a daily basis is the counter to the sinful tendency to make provisions for the flesh in regard to its lusts.

Amplification: *And do not [go along with or] be conformed to this [age of darkness], but be [changed] by the [ongoing] renewing of your mind [in Christ], so that you may prove [in time] what the will of God is [for you]—that which is good and acceptable and perfect. (Romans 12:2)*

14:1-12 The Strong Christian and the Weak Christian

14:1 Now accept the one who is weak in faith, but not for the purpose of passing judgment on his opinions.

A contrast is established between the weak in faith and the strong in faith. Both categories of believer are trusting in Jesus as Savior and Lord.

This section is dealing with the practical implications of saving faith playing out in time in context of the Roman Gentile and Jewish Christians. The strong and the weak are dealing with convictions about what faith in Jesus Christ allows and prohibits in their lives. The presentation insists that the best sanctifying result is to move from weak in practical faith to strong in practical faith.

There will always be weaker and stronger Christians. Stronger Christians must work with the errant opinions of weaker Christians without judging them to condemnation or being too quick to judge them to separation. Given the call for unity, the type of weakness described here cannot refer to core issues of salvation.

14:2 One person has faith that he may eat all things, but he who is weak eats vegetables only.

The "weak in faith" Jewish Christians in Rome likely had trouble obtaining kosher meat. They felt obligated by Old Testament Law to abstain from meat that might not be kosher. The majority of the Gentile Christian population had a better understanding of new covenant Christianity and were mentally free from Old Testament dietary rules and regulations.

> **Paraphrase:** *A Christian with a strong understanding of the faith knows that he may eat all things, but a Christian with a weak understanding of the faith still follows Jewish dietary rules.*

14:3 The one who eats is not to regard with contempt the one who does not eat, and the one who does not eat is not to judge the one who eats, for God has accepted him.

> "for God has accepted him"—Paul is writing about justified believers in both cases.

Stronger Christians with more depth of understanding regarding sanctification are not to pridefully look down on weaker Christians wrestling with biblical misunderstandings or biblical ignorance. Weaker Christians are not to pridefully entrench in their misunderstandings and ignorance while judging stronger Christians to condemnation over sanctifying details.

Christians have no right to reject from fellowship anyone whom God has accepted (and there must be solid testimonial evidence by the biblical standard of salvation that God has indeed accepted them).

14:4a Who are you to judge the servant of another?

> **Amplification:** *Who are you [weaker Christian] to judge the servant of [Christ]?*

> **Amplification:** *Who are you [Christian] to [look down on] the servant of [Christ]?*

No Christian has the authority to pass ultimate judgment to condemnation on another believer.

14:4b To his own master he stands or falls; . . .

All believers have times of standing in favor with and falling out of favor with Jesus in terms of the sanctifying details.

14:4c . . . and he will stand, for the Lord is able to make him stand.

In the end, all justified believers will stand in glory by the power and grace of God.

14:5 One person regards one day above another, another regards every day alike. Each person must be fully convinced in his own mind.

The keeping of festival days, days of fasting, and the Sabbath were integral to Old Testament Judaism. Along with dietary law, keeping of days—especially the Sabbath—was a point of tension and disagreement wherever Gentile and Jewish Christians mixed.

Paul does not command either group to do what the other is doing. Many ritual issues are matters of preference and left to the discretion of the individual believer as to their spiritual efficacy and personal value.

14:6 He who observes the day, observes it for the Lord, and he who eats, does so for the Lord, for he gives thanks to God; and he who eats not, for the Lord he does not eat, and gives thanks to God.

A real believer, who feels obligated by Old Testament days, observes them for the Lord and is glorifying God. A real believer, who eats an unrestricted diet, offers the meal to the Lord and is glorifying God. A real believer, who eats a restricted diet, offers the meal to the Lord and is glorifying God.

In each case, same salvation, same motivation, same end result.

14:7 For not one of us lives for himself, and not one dies for himself; . . .

Nothing a Christian does can reference the self alone. For the regenerate, alone is an illusion. Christians are always in Christ. It is spiritually impossible for a Christian to be separated from Christ.

14:8 . . . for if we live, we live for the Lord, or if we die, we die for the Lord; therefore whether we live or die, we are the Lord's.

> **TIME-BOUND:** In this life, up to and including our physical death, everything we do is supposed to be for the Lord and for the glorification of God.

> **TIMELESS:** In this life and after physical death, we belong to Jesus Christ, and we will be glorified. Everything is ultimately for the Lord and for the glorification of God.

14:9 For to this end Christ died and lived again, that He might be Lord both of the dead and of the living.

Christ's death and resurrection establish Him as Lord in time and beyond time. Jesus Christ is Lord over all and everything.

14:10 But you, why do you judge your brother? Or you again, why do you regard your brother with contempt? For we will all stand before the judgment seat of God.

No believer has the right to cast doubt on the salvation of a fellow believer over non-salvific issues. Only God judges to condemnation, and only God has the right to hold us in contempt.

14:11 For it is written, "As I live, says the Lord, every knee shall bow to Me, and every tongue shall give praise to God."

The strong believer and the weak believer are reminded that God and God alone will judge all people and all actions on the last day.

14:12 So then each one of us will give an account of himself to God.

Both the strong believer and the weak believer are reminded that neither is exempt from accounting for their behaviors in time. Each one of us will have to give an account of our lives directly to God.

14:13-23 Do Not Cause Other Believers to Stumble

14:13a Therefore let us not judge one another anymore, . . .

> **Amplification:** *Therefore, [in context of 14:1-6,] let us not judge one another anymore [in regard to non-essentials], . . .*

Both strong and weak believers are to be careful how they are holding nonessentials of the faith.

14:13b . . . but rather determine this—not to put an obstacle or a stumbling block in a brother's way.

Strong believers must have a heightened awareness of the effect non-essential investments can have on weak believers. Pushing a weak believer too far, too fast can cause a spiritual crisis and become an obstacle to growth.

14:14 I know and am convinced in the Lord Jesus that nothing is unclean in itself; but to him who thinks anything to be unclean, to him it is unclean.

Paul speaks and writes with the authority of Jesus's bondservant. Christians are no longer subject to ritual defilement as defined in the Old Testament Law. Categories of clean and unclean no longer apply to foods.

Weak believers either cannot assimilate truth at the same rate as strong believers or need more time to deal with deeper understandings in the Scriptures. In either case, they need to be handled carefully and respectfully.

14:15a For if because of food your brother is hurt, you are no longer walking according to love.

When a neutral practice is forced on weak believers wrestling with that practice, the resulting violation of conscience causes weak believers to feel separated from strong believers. When coupled with an attitude of superiority or scorn, Christian love is diminished.

148

14:15b Do not destroy with your food him for whom Christ died.

Christ paid the ultimate price for both weak and strong believers. Don't destroy each other spiritually over non-essentials.

14:16 Therefore do not let what is for you a good thing be spoken of as evil; . . .

Do not let your intentional actions as a strong believer cause a weak believer to speak about legitimate Christian freedoms as evil.

14:17a . . . for the kingdom of God is not eating and drinking, . . .

> **Amplification:** *[T]he [manifested] kingdom of God is not [ritual behavior].*

14:17b . . . but "righteousness and peace and joy" . . .

> *Therefore, having been justified by faith, we have peace with God through our Lord Jesus Christ . . . and we exult in hope of the glory of God. (Romans 5:1-2b)*

14:17c " . . . in the Holy Spirit."

All three blessings in 17b come as a result of the indwelling of the Holy Spirit.

14:18 For he who in this way serves Christ is acceptable to God and approved by men.

The one who serves Christ by focusing on kingdom essentials is in alignment with God's will. The strong Christian, serving Christ in the Spirit, places righteousness, peace, and joy ahead of ritual non-essentials and creates the potential for approval from the weak.

14:19 So then we pursue the things which make for peace and the building up of one another.

> **Amplification:** *So then [the strong] pursue the things which make for peace [with other justified believers] and the building up of [the body of Christ as a whole].*

14:20 Do not tear down the work of God for the sake of food. All things indeed are clean, but they are evil for the man who eats and gives offense.

Even though "all things indeed are [now] clean," the strong are not to destroy the unity of the church for the sake of ritual non-essentials. Spiritually neutral non-essentials can become a source of evil when strong believers make them hills to die on.

14:21 It is good not to eat meat or to drink wine, or to do anything by which your brother stumbles.

> **Amplification:** *It is good [for strong believers] not to [publicly] eat [non-kosher] meat or to [publicly] drink wine [used in pagan rituals], or do anything else [publicly] by which [a weaker believer] stumbles.*

Strong believers are not to change their actions to those of weak believers; strong believers should have enough discernment to know when to refrain from certain actions. It's a good thing to be careful in this way for the sake of others.

14:22 The faith which you have, have as your own conviction before God. Happy is he who does not condemn himself in what he approves.

> **Amplification:** *The faith which you have [regarding non-essentials], have as your own conviction before God. [Having written that to both the weak and the strong], happy is [the strong believer] who does not [unnecessarily] condemn himself in [the non-essentials] he approves.*

14:23 But he who doubts is condemned if he eats, because his eating is not from faith; and whatever is not from faith is sin.

> **Amplification:** *But [the weak Christian] who [wavers in doubt] is [out of alignment with God] if he [engages in some non-essential against his conscience], because his [engagement] is not from [a conviction of] faith; and whatever is not [an expression of convicted] faith is sin[ful].*

- 14:13 "determine this—not to put an obstacle or a stumbling block in a brother's way."
- 14:14 "nothing is unclean in itself."
- 14:15 "Do not destroy with your food him for whom Christ died."

- 14:20 "Do not tear down the work of God for the sake of food."
- 14:20 "All things indeed are clean."
- 14:21 "It is good not to . . . do anything by which your brother stumbles."

Verses 13-23 focus mainly on strong believers. The strong are not to use the correctness of their position to force their ways on the weak. The strength of right understanding must be governed by love for fellow believers with an eye toward building them up and strengthening them.

15:1-6 Unity According to Christ

15:1 Now we who are strong ought to bear the weaknesses of those without strength and not just please ourselves.

Paul identifies himself with the strong believers from the previous verses. Strong Christians are not to act like martyrs forced to bear with and endure the behaviors and attitudes of weak Christians. There should be a genuine sense of caring and supporting as the strong "bear the weakness of those without strength."

In Paul's presentation, the weak are still justified believers and should be treated with love as befitting Christian fellowship. Strong believers are not to isolate themselves in an effort to create a personally pleasing Christian environment. This does not imply adopting the weak attitudes and behaviors of, or pandering to those who are in direct violation of, Scripture.

15:2 Each of us is to please his neighbor for his good, to his edification.

> **Amplification:** *Each [stronger Christian] is to be [encouraging and supportive] of his [weaker Christian] neighbor for his [ultimate spiritual] good, to his [strengthening and building up in the faith].*

15:3 For even Christ did not please Himself; but as it is written, "The reproaches of those who reproached You fell on Me."

Paul quotes Psalm 69:9 as words of Christ, with "You" as God and "Me" as Jesus. Compared to what Christ endured throughout the time of His crucifixion, taking up some slack for our brothers and sisters shouldn't be held as much of a burden.

151

15:4 For whatever was written in earlier times was written for our instruction, so that through perseverance and the encouragement of the Scriptures we might have hope.

> "whatever was written in earlier times was written for our instruction"—The Old Testament is still relevant, revelatory, and necessary on this side of the cross. It was written with the intention that we study it.

[S]o that through [steadfast and patient] perseverance and the encouragement [and comfort drawn from] the Scriptures we might have [a more secure sense of] hope.

Our hope is based in one people of God: Jewish and Gentile Christians—strong and weak Christians. It's all in the Book.

15:5-6 Now may the God who gives perseverance and encouragement grant you to be of the same mind with one another according to Christ Jesus, so that with one accord you may with one voice glorify the God and Father of our Lord Jesus Christ.

Paul's prayer returns to the main theme of verses 14:1–15:13: unity in the body of Christ. We are to maintain a common perspective and purpose despite non-essential differences. Unity is to be in conformance to the will of Christ and the example of Christ. None of this works without the presence of God.

Divisions in the church over non-essentials waste time and energy that should be devoted to the living and proclaiming of the gospel and the glorifying of God.

15:7-13 Accept One Another

15:7 Therefore, accept one another, just as Christ also accepted us to the glory of God.

"Accept" goes beyond "put up with" or "recognize." Justified Christians are to accept one another as members of the same family of God. Christ accepted us in order that God may be glorified. We are to accept one another in order that God may be glorified.

The barrier between the strong and the weak has been broken by Christ's ministry. Both types of believers are justified, and both exist for the glory of God.

15:8-9a For I say that Christ has become a servant to the circumcision on behalf of the truth of God to confirm the promises given to the fathers, and for the Gentiles to glorify God for His mercy; . . .

"the circumcision"—the Jews

The promise of the Abrahamic covenant has been fulfilled by the coming of the Messiah and the bringing in of the Gentiles. Jewish Christians are reminded that Gentile Christians are full members of the family of God. Gentile Christians are reminded that they have been grafted in (11:17) to the Jewish root (11:18). God has kept His word. God is faithful, and God is merciful.

15:9b . . . as it is written . . .

Four Old Testament quotes from the writings (verse 9c and verse 11), the Law (verse 10), and the prophets (verse 12), prove that the inclusion of the Gentiles has always been a part of God's plan.

15:9c "Therefore I will give praise to You among the Gentiles, and I will sing to Your name." (Psalm 18:49)

David had just conquered the Gentile nations. "A people whom I have not known serve me" (Psalm 18:43c)—the Jewish king brought the Gentiles into submission. The Messiah brings Gentiles into submission.

15:10 Again he says,   "Rejoice, O Gentiles, with His people." (Deuteronomy 32:43)

By the mercy of God in the gospel, both Gentiles and Jews can rejoice together.

15:11 And again, "Praise the Lord all you Gentiles, and let all the peoples praise Him." (Psalm 117:1)

Verse 2 of Psalm 117 gives the reasons for praising the Lord: His mercy (lovingkindness) and His truth.

15:12 Again Isaiah says, "There shall come the root of Jesse, and He who arises to rule over the Gentiles, in Him shall the Gentiles hope." (Isaiah 11:10)

Jesse was the father of King David.

> "the root of Jesse . . . who arises" —the Messiah and the resurrection

15:13 Now may the God of hope fill you with all joy and peace in believing, so that you will abound in hope by the power of the Holy Spirit.

Only God can "fill you with all joy and peace," and only the "power of the Holy Spirit" can cause you to "abound in hope."

Don't get hung up on non-essential matters of Christian liberty. Know the difference between essentials and non-essentials. Stay focused on what's important.

15:14-16:27 THE CLOSING

15:14-21 Paul the Minister

15:14 And concerning you, my brethren, I myself also am convinced that you yourselves are full of goodness, filled with all knowledge and able also to admonish one another.

> "full of goodness"—exhibiting generally upright conduct both personally and toward others

In context of the letter as a whole, there is no indication that Paul is being crafty or insincere here. Ancient writers often expressed confidence in their readers to gain acceptance of their ideas. Paul has received plenty of information from his coworkers about the Christians in Rome. Thus he can say, "I myself also am convinced."

The Roman Christians have enough spiritual goodness that they are "able to [properly] admonish one another."

15:15 But I have written very boldly to you on some points so as to remind you again, because of the grace that was given me from God.

> "to remind you again"—Everyone needs ongoing discipling.

"because of the grace"—In Paul's unique case, on the authority of the specific apostolic grace

15:16 . . . to be a minister of Christ Jesus to the Gentiles, ministering as a priest the gospel of God, so that my offering of the Gentiles may become acceptable, sanctified by the Holy Spirit.

Paul was specifically charged to head the ministry of spreading the gospel to the Gentile world.

"minister"—servant, priest

"my offering of the Gentiles"—See Isaiah 66:19-20.

The sacrificial language here is metaphorical. Paul claims no literal sacramental power. No Gentiles were being roasted by Paul as a burnt offering. Animal sacrifices have been replaced by obedient Christians. But the human spiritual sacrifice must still be sanctified by the Holy Spirit to be acceptable to God.

15:17 Therefore in Christ Jesus I have found reason for boasting in things pertaining to God.

The success of Paul's priestly ministry is the work of God's grace in his life.

15:18 For I will not presume to speak of anything except what Christ has accomplished through me, resulting in the obedience of the Gentiles by word and deed, . . .

The purpose: "obedience of the Gentiles," the salvation of the lost world

The means: "by word and deed," the entirety of Paul's apostolic ministry

The instrument: "through me," through Paul

The reality: "what Christ has accomplished," what divine enablement has accomplished

15:19 . . . in the power of signs and wonders, in the power of the Spirit; so that from Jerusalem and round about as far as Illyricum I have fully preached the gospel of Christ.

"signs and wonders"—amplification of "word and deed" from 15:18

Jerusalem was where Paul started his ministry. Illyricum is the furthest he got geographically.

> **The result:** *I have done my part by firmly planting the gospel of Jesus Christ in those areas.*

15:20 And thus I aspired to preach the gospel, not where Christ was already named, so that I would not build on another man's foundation; . . .

There's nothing wrong with building on the foundational work of someone else; that just wasn't Paul's job.

15:21 . . . but as it is written, "They who had no news of Him shall see, and they who have not heard shall understand."

Paul's church-planting ministry was a fulfillment of the prophecy in Isaiah 52:15. His plan was to visit with the Romans for a while and then keep up his missionary work.

15:22-33 Paul's Travel Plans and a Prayer

15:22-29 For this reason I have often been prevented from coming to you; but now, with no further place for me in these regions, and since I have had for many years a longing to come to you whenever I go to Spain—for I hope to see you in passing, and to be helped on my way there by you, when I have first enjoyed your company for a while—but now, I am going to Jerusalem serving the saints. For Macedonia and Achaia have been pleased to make a contribution for the poor among the saints in Jerusalem. Yes, they were pleased to do so, and they are indebted to them. For if the Gentiles have shared in the spiritual things, they are indebted to minister to them also in material things. Therefore, when I have finished this, and have put my seal on this fruit of theirs, I will go on by way of you to Spain. I know that when I come to you, I will come in the fullness of the blessing of Christ.

> **Amplification:** *[Because I have been busy preaching the gospel], I have often been prevented from coming to you. But now, [because I have fulfilled my purpose] in these regions . . . whenever I go to Spain . . . I hope to see you in passing . . . but [right] now, I am going to Jerusalem serving [God's people]. . . . Macedonia and Achaia. . . . are indebted to them. For if the [converted] Gentiles have shared in the spiritual things [of the converted Jews], [the Gentile Christians] are indebted to minister to the [Jewish Christians] also in material things. Therefore, when I have finished [my trip to Jerusalem], and have [affirmed the proper*

reception and understanding of this freewill offering] of theirs, I will go on by way of you to Spain.

15:30-32 Now I urge you, brethren, by our Lord Jesus Christ and by the love of the Spirit, to strive together with me in your prayers to God for me, that I may be rescued from those who are disobedient in Judea, and that my service for Jerusalem may prove acceptable to the saints; so that I may come to you in joy by the will of God and find refreshing rest in your company.

> **Amplification:** *Now I urge you, brethren, [for the sake of] our Lord Jesus Christ and by the love [given by] the Spirit, to strive together [united] with me in your prayers to God for me, that I may be rescued from those who are [unbelievers] in Judea, and that my service [of relief] for Jerusalem may prove acceptable to the saints; so that I may come to you in joy by the will of God and find refreshing rest in your company.*

15:33 Now the God of peace be with you all. Amen.

And amen.

16:1-2 About Phoebe

16:1 I commend to you our sister Phoebe, who is a servant of the church which is at Cenchrae; . . .

Cenchrae—a city eight miles from Corinth. Paul spent eighteen months in Corinth at one point. Later, he composed the Letter to the Romans from Corinth. Paul would have had many opportunities to interact with Phoebe.

> "commend"—Letters of commendation were a common way to secure assistance when traveling. There were few public accommodations, and a recommendation from a well-known person could make it easier to secure housing and other support.
>
> "our sister"—She is a fellow believer.
>
> "Phoebe"—a name taken from Greek mythology. Phoebe was most likely a Gentile convert.
>
> "servant"—The Greek word *diakonos* can be translated as "servant" or "deacon" and, depending on the context, can refer to Christian workers of all types. Any Christian who is actively engaged in serving Jesus Christ is a *diakonos* in the original sense of the word.

Paul uses the term *diakonos* twenty-one times. In Romans 13:4 it refers to secular rulers. In Romans 15:8 and Galatians 2:17, *diakonos* refers to Christ. In 1 Corinthians 3:5; 2 Corinthians 3:6 and 6:4; Ephesians 3:7 and 6:21; Colossians 1:7, 23, 25, and 4:7; and 1 Timothy 4:6, it refers to Paul and his coworkers.

> "servant of the church"—In the early church, the term *diakonos* was applied to both men and women who provided ongoing non-leadership support. It is likely that Phoebe served in this manner as a deaconess to the church at Cenchrae.

First Timothy 3:8 and 12, and Philippians 1:1 are the only places where *diakonos* denotes a ministry office, and in both places the function of the deacon is clearly separated from that of the overseer. As official church roles became more defined, deacons were officially appointed to non-leadership servant roles providing a wide range of support for the overseers (elders). Whether *diakonos* is translated "deacon" or "servant," this verse in no way connects Phoebe to the office of overseer (elder).

16:2 . . . that you receive her in the Lord in a manner worthy of the saints, and that you help her in whatever matter she may have need of you; for she herself has also been a helper of many, and of myself as well.

Cenchrae was a busy seaport. Phoebe was probably a woman with high social standing and some degree of wealth who regularly applied her time and resources in the service of Paul and other traveling Christians. Paul asks the Roman church to receive Phoebe into Christian fellowship "in a manner worthy of the saints," implying assistance with food, lodging, and any other necessities.

Given what is written about Phoebe in these two verses, all we can know is that she was a well-known member of the church at Cenchrae, that she was active in the ministry of the church, and that she was about to go to Rome. She may have been the person who delivered Paul's letter to the Roman Christians.

16:3-16 Greetings to Roman Christians

Paul had never personally ministered to the Roman church. In these verses, he seems to be listing all, or at least most, of the Christians he has had some acquaintance with in Rome. Part of his purpose is to establish a broader base of Roman support for his planned mission to Spain.

In the ancient world, certain names were routinely given to specific kinds of people depending on their social status. Wealthy, powerful people used certain names for their children. Slaves used certain names—or were forced to use certain names—for their children. The majority of names in this list are Gentile. Ten of the named are definitely from slave families and are either slaves or freed men. Only four are definitely not slaves or freed men.

Despite the best efforts of historians, we only know a little bit of personal information about a few of the people Paul mentions in these verses, next to nothing about a few more, and absolutely nothing about the rest. What we see here, in all of these names lost to time-bound history, is the power of the gospel creating friendships and fellowship bonds where none would, or in some cases even could, exist previously.

There are three, and possibly five, house churches mentioned. Early Christians did not have public meeting places. The church at Rome would have been comprised of many house churches.

16:3-5a Greet Prisca and Aquila, my fellow workers in Christ Jesus, who for my life risked their own necks, to whom not only do I give thanks, but also all the churches of the Gentiles; also greet the church that is in their house.

Prisca and Aquila: Acts 18:2-3; 18:18-19; 18:26; 1 Corinthians 16:19

16:5b Greet Epaenetus, my beloved, who is the first convert to Christ from Asia.

Nothing else is known about Epaenetus.

16:7 Greet Andronicus and Junia[s], my kinsmen and my fellow prisoners, who are outstanding among the apostles, who also were in Christ before me.

The Greek name *Iounian* can be masculine or feminine, depending on how it is accented. But most of the earliest Greek manuscripts have no accent markings. All early church commentators, with the possible exception of Origen, translate *Iounian* as the feminine "Junia." Junia was an extremely common name, while the masculine "Junias" was very rare, almost non-existent.

Commentators from the thirteenth to the early twentieth century defaulted to the masculine because Paul calls the pair "apostles," and they either didn't understand the context or didn't want to have the discussion. Modern commentators who want to justify female elders insist on the feminine name because Paul calls the pair "apostles," and they ignore the context to force their point.

In Paul's writings, "apostle" is often used to denote a messenger or an emissary with a specifically defined commission and not as a reference to the chosen twelve (big *A*) Apostles. Andronicus and Junia were probably a husband and wife traveling missionary team.

16:8-15 Greet Ampliatus, my beloved in the Lord. Greet Urbanus, our fellow worker in Christ, and Stachys my beloved. Greet Apelles, the approved in Christ. Greet those who are of the household of Aristobulus. Greet Herodion, my kinsman. Greet those of the household of Narcissus, who are in the Lord. Greet Tryphaena and Tryphosa, workers in the Lord. Greet Persis the beloved, who has worked hard in the Lord. Greet Rufus, a choice man in the Lord, also his mother and mine. Greet Asyncritus, Phlegon, Hermes, Patrobas, Hermas and the brethren with them. Greet Philologus and Julia, Nereus and his sister, and Olympas, and all the saints who are with them.

Nothing else is known about any of these people.

16:16a Greet one another with a holy kiss.

A kiss was a common form of greeting in the ancient world, especially in Judaism. In Jewish culture, the kiss was always on the forehead or the cheek. This cultural kiss greeting was not a long, drawn-out affair. It had no romantic or sexual overtones to it.

The "kiss of peace" was a documented part of Christian liturgy as early as the second century. What turned the common greeting of a kiss into a holy kiss was the intention of the people employing the greeting, not the mechanical action.

At my current level of ignorance and understanding, I believe this verse is more about the intention than the cultural mechanics of the time. We accomplish the exact same thing, with all of the original implications, when we employ an authentic handshake or hug. In this case, it is all about your intent.

16:16b All the churches of Christ greet you.

Paul did not work alone. Everywhere he went, he had coworkers helping him. Every church he started, he left in the hands of someone else. No one should try to go it alone. No one *can* go it alone. The real Christian church is the church invisible—all of the justified and regenerate believers past, present, and future that make up the body of Christ. We are all in this together.

16:17-19 A Warning

16:17 Now I urge you, brethren, keep your eye on those who cause dissensions and hindrances contrary to the teaching which you learned, and turn away from them.

Paul regularly dealt with false teachers in the churches he engaged, but there is no indication that the Roman church was dealing with heretical or deviant teachings. Paul seems to be putting the Roman church on guard that sooner or later false teachers will show up in Rome.

> "dissensions"—False teachers cause spiritual disunity in Christian communities.
>
> "hindrances" (can also be translated as "stumbling blocks")—spiritual problems that can lead to damnation
>
> "contrary to the teaching which you learned"—false doctrine; anything outside of Scripture; anything that twists or distorts Scripture
>
> "turn away from them"—the proper Christian response

16:18 For such men are slaves, not of our Lord Christ but of their own appetites; and by their smooth and flattering speech they deceive the hearts of the unsuspecting.

> "slaves . . . of their own appetites"—slaves of their own flesh; self-absorption, self-pleasure, self-aggrandizement, self-enrichment
>
> "they deceive" with "smooth and flattering speech"—They conceal the content of what they are saying with smooth sounding, dressed up speech.

> "they deceive the hearts of the unsuspecting"—They deceive the consciences of the biblically and spiritually immature who don't know the Scriptures or just are not paying attention. False teachers are "not of our Lord Jesus Christ."

16:19 For the report of your obedience has reached to all; therefore I am rejoicing over you, but I want you to be wise in what is good and innocent in what is evil.

The simple innocence of freedom from the power of sin that comes with justification is not to be taken as license to be spiritually simple-minded. Mature Christians immerse themselves in Scripture and thus can discern between true and false teaching.

> *"Behold, I send you out as sheep in the midst of wolves; so be shrewd as serpents and innocent as doves." (Matthew 10:16)*

16:20a A Promise

16:20a The God of peace will soon crush Satan under your feet.

TIMELESS: The war is over beyond time.

TIME-BOUND: And God still expects you to do the work in time.

TIME-BOUND / TIMELESS: Be encouraged. Whatever happens in your walk and in your ministry, followers of Jesus Christ ultimately will emerge victorious.

16:20b A Blessing

16:20b The grace of our Lord Jesus be with you.

If you are saved, it is.

16:21-23 Greetings from Paul's Associates

16:21-23 Timothy my fellow worker greets you, and so do Lucius and Jason and Sosipater, my kinsmen. I, Tertius, who write this letter, greet you in the Lord. Gaius, host to me and to the whole church, greets you. Erastus, the city treasurer greets you, and Quartus, the brother.

Tertius was Paul's amanuensis—the person who wrote down what Paul dictated. Paul had reason to believe all of these guys were saved. If so, Timothy, Lucius, Sosipater, Tertius, Gaius, Erastus, and Quartus are in heaven waiting to greet you. Christianity is personal and relational.

16:24 Another Blessing

16:24 [The grace of our Lord Jesus Christ be with you all. Amen.]

16:25-27 Doxology

Paul writes with authority as Jesus's bondservant. When Paul writes "my gospel," he is referencing the teachings that were directly revealed to him by the risen Jesus Christ. Paul's teachings are in alignment with the preaching of Jesus Christ. He invented none of this; he received all of it directly from Christ. No one should accept any other version of the gospel than what is recorded in Scripture.

---

doxology: *noun*

an expression of praise to God

16:25-26 Now to Him who is able to establish you according to my gospel and the preaching of Jesus Christ, according to the revelation of the mystery which has been kept secret for long ages past, but now is manifested, and by the Scriptures of the prophets, according to the commandment of the eternal God, has been made known to all the nations, leading to obedience of faith; . . .

> *For in [the gospel of Jesus Christ] the righteousness of God is revealed from faith to faith; as it is written, "But the righteous man shall live by faith." (Romans 1:17)*

16:27 . . . to the only wise God, through Jesus Christ, be the glory forever. Amen.

Praise God!

REFLECTIONS ON

ROMANS

THE RIGHTEOUSNESS OF GOD (ROMANS 1:16-20)

Since Creation, God's fingerprints are on everything. Study the natural sciences at any depth and you are immediately confronted with incredible order—from the most micro of studies to the most macro. All of it screams intelligence and purpose. Paul calls these things God's invisible attributes. You have to willfully reject the implications of the patterns and order in the universe to deny created purpose. And that is what lots of people do—right in line with Romans chapter 1.

The information available through creation is not enough to save us, but it is enough to show us that we need saving if we are paying attention. When we rebel against that information, we exist in a state of open hostility toward God. That which is known about God is evident in the human conscience and by created instinct. Why it is evident? Verse 20 says that God made it evident. God has made every human intrinsically, intuitively aware of Him and His way of doing things through His external revelation in creation and His internal revelation in our consciences. All cultures and peoples are guilty before God. Nobody gets to claim ignorance.

God is holy. Creation is God's masterpiece, His workmanship. Creation is more than enough to cause anyone to stop and consider what's going on and why we are here. Romans makes the claim that, whatever else our creative God had in mind, our internal and external experience of the universe is designed to do just that.

Romans 1:18-19 makes it clear: God is upset, and His wrath is justified. Everything that is under heaven, and not under the gospel, is under the holy wrath of an all-seeing God. Here is why we desperately need the righteousness of God through His gospel. People willfully and mindfully commit ungodly and unrighteous acts as they suppress whatever knowledge of God they have. In our ungodliness, we attack the majesty of God. Through our unrighteousness, we continually violate God's created order. This is the default condition of humanity separated from God. This is the condition we are saved from.

Righteous standing before God is the condition our faith saves us to. The righteousness of God is not earned; it is revealed in the gospel. What is revealed in the gospel is God's answer to sin, and the answer is Jesus Christ. Jesus took human form to show us the way home and to open the way home for us. He died on the cross to settle our sin-debt with God and open the way for those who have faith in Him.

I am not ashamed of the gospel. The gospel of Jesus Christ completely and explosively changed and revived me spiritually and retooled my entire life. Jesus Christ blew up my previous existence—completely. Jesus saved me. It would be shameful for me to be ashamed of the gospel. "It is the power of God for salvation to everyone who believes."

What about you? Are you ashamed of the gospel? Have you experienced the Good News, or have you only heard it? Where do you stand with God? *Do* you stand with God?

SUPPRESSING THE TRUTH (ROMANS 1:21-32)

Since the beginning of humanity, the enemy tells us this: *God is holding out on you. You will never be happy living with the limitations God puts on you. Step away from God, and go your own way. Take what God does not want you to have and enjoy the power of freedom from God. Then you can create your own gods, or just be as gods yourselves.*

However, in the first commandment God tells us this: "You shall have no other gods before me." And in the second commandment God tells us this: "You shall not make for yourself an idol. . . . You shall not worship them or serve them."

How many times have you seen a family at a restaurant, and every one of them is staring at a cell phone that is drawing their attention away from the meal and each other? That is idolatrous behavior. I did a little research and found that people check their Facebook twelve to twenty times a day, for an average of three to five minutes each time. Do you think they checked in with Jesus that much? Probably not. This is social media serving—or being served—as an idol.

If you are saved, what do you fill your thoughts with? What in your life takes your attention away from God? What things in your life can be offered up to God as you do them? What things can't be offered to God, no matter how you do them? How many times do you check your phone every day? Do you check in with Jesus in prayer that many times? Your smartphone might be helping you stay spiritually dumb. Your phone might be serving as an idol. Do you think about some new possession you are wanting or trying to get more than you think about Jesus and what He did for you? Any of your world's possessions can become idols.

Do you have to have a screen on all the time? How much secular "news" do you absorb each day? Does Jesus get at least that much of your time? And, how would you feel if all of that—the internet, cable TV, social media—just went away or went dark? How would that affect you? How big are those idols in your life? How would you feel if Jesus just went away or went dark? Would you even know the difference? Where is your attention on a day-to-day basis? What idols have control of your thoughts?

Any worldly thought or mental wave of worldly thought that prevents you from focusing on Jesus and resting in His finished work at Calvary is an idol. If you cannot turn that thought off, the amount of time that you then devote to that thought is idol worship. God wants your heart, mind, and soul to be saturated with His word, immersed in His Spirit, and occupied with His presence all the time. Christianity is the path of total surrender to God through Jesus Christ.

God wants us to be the men and women He designed us to be and not the men and women we too often let ourselves become. He wants us to exchange the lies of the world for the truth of God and worship and serve Jesus Christ rather than creature culture and idols to our enemy.

JUDGMENT TO CONDEMNATION (ROMANS 2:1-11)

Verse 11 states, "[T]here is no partiality with God." Said another way, "God is a God of no faces." God is no respecter of persons or personalities. There is no way to game or work God. Everyone is under the full penalty of the Law and stands condemned. God is impartial—there are no exceptions. All unbelievers will stand before God one day, and they will be judged to condemnation. Their condemnation will be proven to be warranted and just by all that they have done in their life—things they will have long forgotten and have not given a passing thought for decades. There will be no place for excuses. Cries of "but I was this" or "I thought that" will mean nothing.

The main thrust of Paul's presentation here is humanity's powerlessness under sin. Under our own power, none of us can work our way out of sin or work our way into God's grace. Once saved, a person in union with Christ becomes capable of producing works that are acceptable to God at the final judgment. But it is not the good works that earn eternal life; it is the spiritual condition of the person doing the works. For all-knowing, all-seeing God, the outward works reflect the inner condition. The promise of eternal life rendered "to each person according to his deeds" is therefore valid.

Followers of Jesus Christ should understand the idea of judgment to condemnation. It is the same for us. There is no partiality with God. There is no way to game or work God, or impress God with good works. No one can meet God's standard on their own. The power of sin prevents anyone from doing good to the degree necessary to earn or sustain salvation.

Our works in and of themselves do not afford us any special spiritual merit or earn us any elevated status in relation to God. Our Spirit-driven, sanctifying works will simply stand as testimony to God's "not guilty" verdict rendered to those who have saving faith in the person and work of Jesus Christ. God's work at salvation is the spiritual cause that allows "those who by perseverance in doing good [to] seek for glory and honor and immortality."

GOD'S JUDGMENT AND THE LAW (ROMANS 2:12-16)

When the person who has God's Law or the person who does not is judged by God, their conscience will bear witness to how their thoughts wrestled with what is placed in every heart by God. God judges the heart; all will be revealed. To enter God's courtroom as your own defendant is a losing proposition every time.

Nobody has ever lived a life of doing evil one hundred percent of the time. Even the smallest act of good reveals an innate awareness of right and wrong—and highlights that every choice to do evil was deliberate. Even without knowing God's law, lost people show that some moral aspects of the Law of Moses are written on their hearts by way of natural revelation. Their conscience also bears judgmental witness against their conflicting thoughts that wrestle with whether to accuse or even find a way to excuse themselves. This is the dance lost people will be dancing as they are exposed before God when He judges them to condemnation. But this internal issue of conscience and thought wrestling with sin plays out in time as well.

Go back to verse 4 in Romans 2. The Holman Christian Standard Bible (HCSB) translates it this way: "[D]o you despise the riches of God's kindness, restraint, and patience . . . ?" We are given this idea of people lost in the internal conflict of wrestling with their conscience as they excuse and accuse themselves, coming to a point where they despise some of God's attributes. They despise God.

Who are these people? They are the self-righteous, lost in their own will and way, who can never get out of their own way and let God lead. Self-righteous people are the ones most prone to thinking lightly of, or despising God. Once they have built up enough momentum in thinking lightly about something, they will start disregarding it. Disregard it, and they will trivialize it. Trivialize it, and they will learn to ridicule it. Eventually, especially in the case of God's Law, they will hate and despise it.

Once you start treating God and the subject of God in a cavalier or casual way, certain things are bound to happen in your life. When you hear someone testifying how good God has been to them, you will dismiss it or refuse to acknowledge it as real. You may even find yourself making fun of them.

Treat God lightly and you will start to mock people whose lives demonstrate God's hand at work. You will disregard their experience, trivialize their witness, and maybe even start to ridicule and make fun of them. And, you will find plenty of twisted, lost people who are only too happy to join in on the mocking and the ridicule. Eventually, this type of behavior morphs into hate, and you will despise God. Look around our country right now. This dynamic is everywhere.

When someone exploits God's patience, goodness, and mercy by thinking that they are getting away with living by their own sinful, unrighteous, self-righteous standard, the accusing and excusing feedback in their own heads and hearts with eventually poison their thinking and their living, and they will begin to think lightly about God and how He chooses to do things. This always leads to despising God because according to the first chapter of Romans, the reality of God is in their face all the time.

Even a saved person can mess up this way. When we see God extend mercy, patience, and goodness to others who are obviously not living a righteous, holy, or upright life by any biblical standard (or who are not living a sufficiently righteous, holy, or upright life by our standards), we get self-righteous in our heads and hearts and say to God, *What the heck is going on here?* We take God lightly when we question why He shows mercy, patience, and goodness to a sinner who, in our judgment, does not deserve it. When we treat God in a light and cavalier manner, we trivialize His hand at work in our lives and the lives of others. Trivialize God, and the pathway is open to ridicule God, God's word, and God's people.

This is precisely how lost people learn to sneer at God and His majesty. They do not want to hear about it nor see it occurring in their own life or anyone else's life. They diminish it, dismiss it, push it aside. Eventually, they want to destroy it. And it does not matter who or what gets in their path. They just want the accusing and excusing of their conscience as God's revelation rips at it to go away.

Here is an exercise for you to prove out this dynamic. Try and pay attention to how many external things around you—cultural conventions, shows, commercials, web articles, people's behaviors—treat God and Jesus lightly.

Pay attention and take note. Then consider that each example you see is a seed that leads to despising God. This is what happens when the God portrayed in Romans 1 is treated lightly by those folks who should know better described in Romans 2. This is what happens when anyone treats God lightly.

And then, according to verse 16, "on the day when, according to my gospel, God will judge the secrets of men through Christ Jesus," the accusing and excusing games we play on ourselves in our thoughts will be exposed. God will judge the secrets, the innermost places, the dark places, the secret sins. You cannot fool—or fool with—God.

CIRCUMCISION OF THE HEART (ROMANS 2:17-29)

In our fallen condition, we tend to default to the lowest available spiritual bar. We prefer mechanical behaviors to Spirit-motivated actions. We prefer ritual pointed at God to actual relationship with God. We want a religion that tells us the minimum we must do instead of a Bible that teaches us who we must become.

When a person does not have the Spirit of God indwelling them, the outward marks of church life mean nothing to God, and Christianity becomes nothing more than the death march of worldly religion. When a person has a Bible, and even knows some of it, the mere possession of the Book or possession of some amount of Bible knowledge accomplishes nothing unless there is a real relationship with Jesus Christ. In the Gospel of Matthew, Jesus says this is the person who is going to stand before Him at the final judgment and say, "Lord, Lord, it's me. Look at everything I've done in Your name." And Jesus is going to reply, "Go away from Me. I never knew You."

You can know everything there is to know about Christianity and the Bible and still turn your back on Jesus Christ and walk away. Knowledge in and of itself delivers no security. Ritual church attendance in and of itself also accomplishes nothing. What you know intellectually is not the issue; what you do about it spiritually is. Romans 1 and 2 make it clear that if all of your knowledge about God just remains in your head, it only becomes the basis for greater condemnation.

The main thrust of this part of Romans is to strip away all of the false securities that lost people—and people lost in religion—hide in. Without faith in Jesus Christ, you are spiritually lost. Unless you are born again, you will not see the kingdom of God. There has to be the work of the Spirit in your heart, or you have nothing of eternal worth. Circumcision of the heart, by the Spirit, is what made a Jew a real Jew in the Old Testament time period and what makes a Christian a real Christian in the New Testament time period to today.

NO ONE IS RIGHTEOUS (ROMANS 3:1-20)

The Law of Moses offers no hope for defense. There is no justification by works, by good deeds, by good deeds done in the name of God, or by good deeds done with some sort of enabling grace. Works do not save you; works do not keep you saved. Ritual religious behavior will not get you saved.

The Law was given to define sin. It was given to make us specifically aware of sin. By interacting with the Law and experiencing our inability to keep it, the friction of sin is amplified. This dynamic should drive us into ever more dependance on the grace of God.

So what advantage do you have as a Christian? Well, like Paul said, you have God's word. If you read the Bible, you have everything you need to come to an understanding of where you stand with God and what it means to surrender your life to Jesus Christ. By interacting with the Bible and experiencing where you stand with God, the friction of sin will amplify. This dynamic should drive you into ever more dependance on the grace of God.

But even if you experience this friction and call yourself Christian, all of your Bible studies, your church services, and your denominational affectations add up to nothing if your heart has not been circumcised by the Holy Spirit. Spiritually real, authentic understanding of the Bible can only be accessed through the teaching of the Holy Spirit. And the condition for the presence of the Holy Spirit in your life is a life totally surrendered to Jesus Christ. Total surrender to Jesus Christ, the power and presence of the Holy Spirit, and the knowledge of God are the things that mark a true Christian.

The religious Jews back then did not get it. Lots of religious Christians today do not get it. You need saving faith. Not head faith, not intellectual faith—saving faith. If you have been saved by faith through the grace of God, as mysterious as the dynamic is, you will know it. If you are not sure that you have received the gift of salvation, then maybe you have not, and you should think and reflect on that.

So what advantage has the Christian? The Christian has the work of Jesus Christ on the cross and the power and personal presence of the Holy Spirit. Believe and abide in Christ. It's all about the relationship.

THE HEART OF THE GOSPEL (ROMANS 3:21-26)

Jesus Christ is the public demonstration—the pointer to the righteousness of God. The work on the cross demonstrates how God can maintain His righteousness, His holy standard, and still let sinners be with Him in heaven. "Justifier" is used here in a legal sense. It is the language of law. God is just. His holy justice demands satisfaction.

By the standard of God's Law, we all stand condemned. And God's Law still stands. Jesus did not come to abolish it; He came to fulfill it. The penalty for sin is not removed—it is paid for by Christ. God is the Justifier—the One who provides the means of justification, of forgiveness. Justification is not based on anything we bring to the table.

God's holy justice, holy love, and holy mercy meet at the cross and satisfy God's holy wrath. God has paid the sin-debt for us by the redemption of the blood of Christ shed for our sins. This makes God, in His righteousness, "just and the justifier of the one who has faith in Jesus Christ."

God has a very specific way to deal with the sin-poisoned world, its sin-poisoned inhabitants, and the wrath He has toward sin: propitiation. If we want to fully comprehend God's holy love for us, then propitiation is the key. Our sin is horrible and wretched to God. Sin hurts people and devastates lives. Sin is destroying our planet, and from a biblical worldview it seems that most of the people on it will die in sin.

Sovereign God hears, sees, and knows every sinful thought, word, or action that you have—and every sinful thought, word, and action of everyone in the entire world since the beginning of human history to right now and for the rest of time. What would you do if you could hear, see, and know all of that sin? It would destroy you. Holy God's wrath and indignation and righteous fury over humanity allowing sin into His creation is beyond our ability to state.

So how does God deal with it? One person of the Triune God became a man and was slaughtered to propitiate God's righteous, holy anger and indignation. How does that sound? Biblical Christianity is tough. God the Son became man, and God the Father hurled all of His righteous, holy anger and indignation at His Son. God the Father slaughtered God the Son in a redemptive act of unimaginable eternal proportions so we could be cleansed of the sin poison that we let into His creation.

Because of this, we can be justified as a gift by the grace of God. Even though we can intellectually understand this by way of Paul's legal courtroom model, God does not fix our sin legally through some work of the Law. Propitiation is the mechanism that accomplishes justification.

173

It is a person-God thing—a God to person thing. Jesus did not give us propitiation. He *is* propitiation.

---

propitiation: *noun*

the incomprehensible cost of the cross that manifests the possibility of . . .

justification: *noun*

the impossibly gracious act of God declaring us "not guilty," resulting in . . .

redemption: *noun*

the underserved gift that can only be received by faith

If you die lost, you will stand alone before God the Judge in His courtroom and act as your own defense attorney. Jesus Christ will then be the Prosecutor, and your only defense will be your life's work. In other words, you will have no defense.

When you surrender your life to Christ through faith you, in effect, stand before God in His courtroom with Jesus at your side as your Defense Attorney. In that moment, your only defense before God and the Law is the person and work of Jesus Christ. Because the atoning sacrifice of Jesus Christ has covered your sins, you are then declared "not guilty" by God. This is the justification aspect of salvation.

WE ESTABLISH THE LAW (ROMANS 3:27-31)

The Law was not given to save anyone from sin; it was given to expose sin to humanity. The Law does its job. It establishes a standard that no one can keep. Where the Law is read and contemplated, sin against the Law of God increases. The Law of God exposes and amplifies sin so as to convict sinners in their consciences and drive them to repentance.

When a sinner is justified and redeemed—when they have saving faith—they receive the supernatural, regenerating presence of the Holy Spirit. The Spirit changes their heart from a default condition of rebelling *against* God and His word to a default condition of desiring obedience *to* God and His word.

Here's an old riff: *Before I was saved, sin was my occupation. Now that I'm saved, sin is my aggravation.* Faithful, obedient Christians, now living on the aggravation side of sin, are expected to uphold the moral norms of the Law. Jesus said, "If you love Me, you will keep My commandments" (John 14:15) This is salvation language. No one who is lost loves Jesus by God's standard.

If you love Jesus, if you are surrendered to Jesus and you have received the gift of the Spirit, you will strive to keep His commandments. This is the law of faith completing the Law of Moses. The Old Testament Law points forward to Jesus Christ. The Law is not complete without Jesus to fulfill it. Jesus did not abolish the Law—He fulfilled it. The Law is still doing its job.

The gospel is the completion of the Law of Moses. To use the language of this passage, the gospel of Jesus Christ establishes the Law. The Old Testament Law smashes your ego, your self-absorption, your self-righteousness, so that you can hear the gospel calling you home—calling you back to God.

- If you are not saved, you must give your life to God by way of faith to be saved.
- If you are saved, you had to turn from the world to Christ by faith to be saved.
- If you call yourself a Christian, but the profession of faith in your mind does not include a supernaturally turned heart, then you are not saved.
- If you know that you are a Christian, if your faith is a faith that saves by God's standard, then a life surrendered to Jesus Christ is supposed to be your default stance for the rest of your life.

JUSTIFICATION BY FAITH (ROMANS 4:1-8)

The example of Abraham shows that God does not take our version of good works into account when He forgives and saves us. What is equally important, or maybe more important from a human standpoint, is that the example of David shows that God does not take the quality or quantity of our bad works into account when He forgives and saves us. Our sins have been covered by the blood of Christ. It is God *not* taking our "lawless deeds" into account that establishes forgiveness. Abraham and David are both examples of this. Abraham is before the Law. He got a blessing from God that he did not deserve. David is after the Law. He got a blessing from God by not getting what he deserved.

No one is righteous by God's holy standard. This is a hard truth of biblical Christianity. None of our standards for good behaviors, righteous undertakings, or anything else we can file under the idea of good works, matter to Holy God in terms of justification.

There is a world of difference between having a solely intellectual faith in Jesus Christ mixed in with a bunch of other competing stuff, and having a supernaturally driven faith in Jesus Christ alone. The expression of a faith that saves must exist beyond mere intellection, otherwise demons have saving faith. The conviction the Spirit brings yields a brokenness to the point that you realize you bring nothing to the cross but your sin. The convicting power and presence of the Holy Spirit smashes the human ego and reduces the sinner to nothingness before Holy God.

Everything we have encountered in Romans so far, what is driven home in this passage—the absolute sinfulness of humanity, our depravity, our inability to do anything about our relationship to Holy God on our terms—this is the stuff that makes people angry when they hear the gospel. This is the stuff that makes people hate the message and the messenger and want to destroy both.

Who is saved? The one whose faith is credited to him as righteousness—the one who has saving faith in Jesus Christ. Faith alone is the measure, but it is supernaturally transactional not just ritually mechanical. It's all in or not in with Jesus.

SIGN AND SEAL (ROMANS 4:9-12)

Because he believed, Abraham was qualified by God to be the spiritual father of "all who follow in the footsteps of the faith." Later, when he was circumcised, Abraham was specifically qualified by God to be the father of the Jewish nation and all Jewish believers. God gave Israel a covenant sign that marked them before the world as members of His covenant community and representatives of His covenant promise, but the sign had no individual effect if the person did not believe.

That sign of circumcision was also a seal that God would keep His promise. The only reason we can be saved is because God made a promise and set His seal on it. That seal was a bloodline seal guaranteeing all of the births and deaths that would take place from Abraham all the way up to Christ. That seal was a guarantee across time on the coming incarnation. The mark of circumcision was God's seal—God swearing to humanity: *I will send Jesus Christ to you.*

Go all the way back to verse 17 of chapter 1. Through the promise of God, through the gospel of Jesus Christ, the righteousness of God is revealed from faith to faith. The only way we can receive the imputed righteousness of God is through faith in the person and work of Jesus Christ. Like Abraham, you must "follow in the footsteps of the faith." Abraham is the biblical model for salvation by faith apart from any religious works or rituals.

The Jews had misunderstood the dynamic of faith. They developed a works-based system and believed that they could earn salvation by doing a variety of personal-moral and ceremonial-religious acts. Instead of justification by faith, the Jews had made circumcision the centerpiece of salvation eventually coming to believe that the mechanical act of circumcision saved them. If you were circumcised, and if you were part of national Israel, you were saved. It ceased to be a ritual sign of separation from the world and became a sacramental magic spell.

Here are just a few excerpts from extra-biblical Jewish writings:

> *So absolute is circumcision as a mark of God's favor that if an Israelite has practiced idolatry, his circumcision must first be removed before he can go down to Gehenna.*[1]

> *God swore to Abraham that no one who was circumcised should be sent to hell.*[2]

> *Abraham sits before the gate of hell and does not allow any circumcised Israelite to enter there.*[3]

Wherever Paul taught the gospel, this is the kind of stuff he was fighting against as he was clarifying the Scriptures. Acts 15:1 says, "But some men came down from Judea and were teaching the brothers, 'Unless you are circumcised according to the custom of Moses, you cannot be saved.'" They had forgotten the prophets. All through the prophetic books, they were warned that God judges the heart and that mechanical professions and ritual activities were not the heart of the matter. All through the prophetic

---

1. *Book of Jubilees*, trans. R. H. Charles (Oxford: Clarendon Press, 1913).
2. This quote is commonly attributed (in concept) to Midrash Tehillim (Psalms), Midrash Tanchuma, or Midrash Rabbah, but it's a paraphrase of traditional rabbinic teaching rather than a direct quote from a standard English edition.
3. Paraphrase or a commonly repeated rabbinic legend, also found in Midrashic or Talmudic texts.

books, God sends a prophet to warn them to get their hearts right with God by way of authentic faith, and they missed the message again and again.

If you miss justification by grace through faith, you miss everything. Why? Because religious works do not work for getting saved. They not only do not work, but they get in the way. Only faith saves. Said another way, the quality of faith that Paul keeps pointing at by way of language—and that can only be truly known when experienced by an individual believer justified by and rejoined to God—is the only faith that saves. Works do not work toward justification. Chapter 6 deals with sanctification and the place for works in the life of a justified believer. But that information is of no use if you have not been justified—that is, saved by the grace of God through faith.

GUARANTEED (ROMANS 4:13-16)

The Law does not rescue anyone from condemnation—it amplifies sin, produces more wrath, and confirms judgment to condemnation. God's wrath existed before the Mosaic Law and exists outside of the Mosaic Law. No one gets a pass on sin. By clearly defining what God requires of humanity, the Law amplifies sin and makes us even more accountable to God. Exposure to the Law amplifies the frictional condition of who we are versus who we are supposed to be.

Church buildings and denominations do not save us. Hearing and experiencing the word of God knocks us into a condition where we become savable. Ongoing exposure to the word of God, if it is preached faithfully, amplifies the frictional condition of who we are versus who we are supposed to be. It all comes down to the response of faith, or the rejection of faith. The word has the power to soften your heart toward God. The word has the power to harden your heart against God.

In verse 15, Paul drives the point in a reverse sort of way: "[B]ut where there is no law, there also is no violation." He puts forward a principle: if there is no command to obey any given specific law, there cannot be a deliberate violation of that specific law. The first two chapters have already established that everyone sins and is accountable to God. Since that is a baseline truth, then Paul is teaching here that a Jew who knew the Law, and by design of the Law inevitably violated it, was even more accountable to God than those without the Law. Turning Paul's point around, where there is God's Law, there is always a direct violation.

Paul is poking at the belief of most of the Jews back then who thought that mere possession of the Law and hearing the Law read guaranteed them salvation. He is poking at anyone today who thinks they are safe from the wrath of God because they go to church regularly or have a good Sunday school attendance record.

Faith is all that is left when God's Law makes it clear to you that you cannot do anything to save yourself. By the grace of God you become saved and not of yourself. There is no room for self-righteous boasting at the foot of the cross. Christ and Christ alone can save you.

Paul will go full steam into assurance of salvation later in the letter, but it is here also. If you are saved, can you lose your salvation? No. Your righteousness is imputed to you, credited to you by the work of Christ. You do not do anything to earn it; you just come to the realization of how helplessly lost you are, throw yourself at the foot of the cross, and beg God for mercy in repentance in the expression of your faith. Jesus takes over from there. The promise is guaranteed.

If saved—there's the catch: *if.* This is one of the things Paul has been steadily beating into our noggins: *if* saved, always saved. God will not break His promise. And *if* you are saved, if you are justified, God did not get it wrong. If you are saved, you are then commanded to engage certain Christian works. But your salvation does not depend on how well you do them. If faith is dependent on the quality of your works—on keeping the Law—"faith is made void and the promise is nullified."

Salvation is getting in agreement with what God already did. After salvation, Christian works can begin, and sanctification can begin to take place. But works are only Christian works by God's standard, and you will only be sanctified if the works are done by the Spirit of God working through you. And that can only happen if you are already justified. If you have a relationship with God, you will change. How much? I don't know. From the time-bound view, it seems to be different for each believer.

Work out your salvation. Test yourself and your relationship to the Law. Every time you do something nice or good, every time you cut someone some slack, every time you pray for someone or for yourself, are you doing it because you think it will get you into heaven? Or, do you think that you are atoning for some past sin with your current good deeds? If you are holding Christianity that way, you are acting like you are still under the Law. If you are not justified, then you are still under the Law, and no amount of churchy or religious-themed behavior is going to help you one bit.

You must come to terms with justification. You cannot save yourself—only Jesus saves. Jesus did the saving work. There is nothing you can add to the work of Jesus. Justification is God's act of declaring you "not guilty" based on *His* all-knowing evaluation of you, not your limited evaluation of Him. Justification, regeneration, and sanctification all exist in relation to each other, but the moment of justification is all of God.

THE NATURE OF FAITH (ROMANS 4:16-25)

"Abraham believed God, and it was credited to him as righteousness" (4:3b). Abraham simply believed and then abided in God. He seems to have known that everything else in life was extra to the fundamental of faith. This stance also enabled him to perform all of the "extra" things God had for him to do in time. These verses do not imply that Abraham's faith was perfect. Abraham was a sinner. But despite the evidence of his senses, his understandings in the world, and how he wrestled with those things, Abraham never "wavered in unbelief"—he never lost his faith.

Abraham did not waste himself creating a crisis of faith between some of the apparent physical evidence in time and the timeless promises of God. He continued trusting in God, and his faith grew as he waited instead of waning as he worried. Abraham had saving faith; "Therefore it was also credited to him as righteousness" (4:22).

The story of Abraham is not a one-off about some biblical super-believer. The story of Abraham is the example for all people and for all time. Abraham was challenged to believe in God's ability to bring life from a dead womb and to believe in a down-the-road prophecy that he would not even live to see fulfilled.

We are challenged by the word of God to "believe in [God] who raised Jesus our Lord from the dead." This verse emphasizes God as the One who raised Jesus. This is to emphasize the relationship between Abraham's faith and our Christian faith. Christians and Abraham share the same faith-based justification. And while Abraham did not know Jesus Christ as the specific content of the promise, the object of our faith is the same.

Paul is showing us that the Old Testament is directly connected with the New Testament and that it speaks directly to Christians. In this passage, "[Jesus Christ] was delivered over because of our transgressions, and was raised because of our justification." In Isaiah 53, "[Jesus Christ] was numbered with the transgressors . . . bore the sin of many, and interceded for the transgressors."

Like Abraham, we have faith in a supernatural God who exists beyond this time-bound universe. That means that we should have faith that relinquishes control over our lives to God. We should have faith that trusts in God's revealed word.

This forms the basis of a faith that grows stronger as we exercise it in time. And unlike Abraham, our faith does not just have a promise—we have a person in Jesus Christ.

Our faith is credited to us as righteousness when we fully trust in the promise of Jesus Christ by surrendering everything we are to the person of Jesus Christ by way of faith. The promise made to Abraham is fully manifested in the person and work of Jesus Christ. We are to believe and abide in Jesus Christ—everything else in this life is extra.

Do you want to make these passages sing in your heart? As you go about your week, try being like Abraham—simply believe and abide. Just do that. When you start getting tangled up in your goals and desires—when the world starts throwing complications at you—return to just believing. Go into the Bible and sort yourself out. Allow the Scriptures to work in your heart as you let the Holy Spirit do the same. As the Spirit works in you, the Scriptures will take root—and as the Scriptures work in you, the Spirit will transform your heart.

Our work of faith is to believe and then abide in Jesus Christ. See what happens when you spend more time immersed in your faith—being constant in prayer and immersing in the word as often as you can. Then, if you get bound up by the world's sin—or your own—just crawl up in your Father's lap and abide with Him. Sit with Him and rest—for five minutes or five hours, or anything in between. Rest in your faith; rest in God's promise. If you can simply believe and simply abide, you will, like Abraham, have a simple faith, and, just like Abraham, it will change how you move through time.

PEACE AND HOPE (ROMANS 5:1-11)

Anyone who is stumbling and/or struggling with their day-to-day faith should contemplate what they have in Christ: justification and reconciliation, resulting in peace with God. It's something "we have now received." We have received justification; we have been reconciled to God. It's done.

What about when we screw up? What about when we stumble and blow our witness before the world? Well then, we own up. We fall down, we beg forgiveness, we get back up and get on with following Jesus. Living the Christian life is never supposed to be about what we can do by our own power. It is always supposed to be all about what Jesus will do *through* us. In and of itself, our righteousness should never be the measure. We don't just exult in God—we cannot only exult in God—we exult in God through our Lord Jesus Christ.

Is Jesus Christ Lord of your life? Your answer to this question means everything. If we have real, saving faith, then we are justified and at peace with God. We are no longer God's enemy, and He is no longer our enemy. But too often we still behave as if we are God's enemy, and we worry and fret and pray in strange ways to counterbalance the friction that we are causing in the relationship.

Paul tells us that if we are justified, we do not have to go through all of that; we can be at peace with the God who is now at peace with us. Now that we are at peace with God, we can have access to His grace and blessings any day, any time, any place, to deal with anything we need to deal with. We can stand in God's grace.

Before we were at peace with God, any suffering or pressure that felt like hurt, pain, discomfort, or discontent seemed to be happening to us with no purpose nor direction. For those of us at peace with God, we realize that suffering has direction and purpose, and that tribulations exist to spiritually shape and refine us. The deeper we move into the reality of our salvation, the more of God's love we can feel in tribulation.

Through it all, there is a connection we can sense and experience. The Bible promises that if we are at peace with God, we can have peace *in* God as we move through our days. The love of God has been poured out within our hearts through the Holy Spirit who was given to us. That's a real thing and a promise of God.

Hope fortifies and strengthens in this dynamic in a way that it never would without trials and tribulations. We persevere, and in so doing we prove out our Christian character in time, and our hope in Christ strengthens. This process of patient perseverance yields a spiritual *knowing* deep inside our hearts.

We surrender in faith to the Christian reality that even though we do not know why something is happening, the God we are at peace with does know, and He tells us to be at peace. Jesus has us.

THE TRANSGRESSION—THE GIFT (ROMANS 5:12-21)

We are born into a sin-poisoned universe through a sin-poisoned bloodline. Spiritual death and eventual physical death spreads to everyone because everyone sins and death reigns. The result of this dynamic is condemnation for everyone under sin.

A lot of people do not like the forward-rolling consequences of the sin in the Garden, but the Bible insists on it. We are dealing with the result of what Adam did, even though we were not there when he did it. But this is far outweighed by the promise that we can receive the benefits of what Jesus did, even though we had no part in that either.

Because we receive the timeless imputed righteousness of Christ, we escape the timeless consequences of the sin in the Garden. We are justified before God; we are declared "not guilty." Because we receive the indwelling of the Holy Spirit, our imparted sin nature can be transformed. In Christ, we are able to engage a new Spirit-driven nature and live in a way that tends toward righteousness.

Because we now have the indwelling and guidance of the Spirit, we can offset a great deal of intentional, time-bound sinning by centering our lives around private and corporate prayer, worship, and immersion in the Bible. Because of the Holy Spirit, our Christian works can now work in ways they could not before.

The more I learn, the more I am convinced that God simplifies the complex things that Satan tries to complicate—God does simple; Satan does complicated. Jesus didn't come to fix every wrong detail in the world. That's what the Jews were expecting from the Messiah. Jesus came to fix what Adam broke: our connection with God.

The Christian answer is not in the details. Details can point to perfection, but the perfection of Christ is not about the details. You have to understand the essence of sin before you can help anyone with the details. And the only way you can really help anyone with the details is to help them understand the essence. Everything that is wrong with the world today is the result of Adam's failure.

Jesus fixed what Adam broke—our ability to connect with God. In the big picture, this is what needed fixing. All the rest of it—all of the crazy, sinful details of human drama—are going to get rolled up in the end and no longer amount to anything worth remembering.

THE NEWNESS OF LIFE (ROMANS 6:1-7)

When you are justified, the blood of Christ covers all of your sins—past, present, and (here is the crazy part) all of your future sins too. If God declared you "not guilty," God cannot get it wrong. God then promises that you cannot lose your justification no matter what you do after you are saved. So the implication of this security is that no matter how much you sin after you have been justified, God will not remove your justification.

This part of justification really troubled some people in the early church. It still troubles lots of people today. Back then, Paul was accused of antinomianism—being against the Law. The concern was that Christians, seeing themselves as free from the Law and free from any afterlife punishment no matter what they did, would corrupt society by doing anything and everything they wanted. The belief was that Christians would become the ultimate anarchists and that their supposed freedom in Christ would destroy civilization itself.

Does "if saved—always saved" result in lots of regenerate Christians willfully, mindfully indulging their favorite sinful activities because they know they can get away with it? Paul writes, "May it never be." That expression in the original language carries the meaning, "No, it cannot be."

What we see in the world are all sorts of lost people taking up the name "Christian" without taking up their cross and laying down their lives. No denomination is immune to this phenomena. Some denominations are demonstrably more biblically sound than others, but the issue plays out everywhere. When you are saved by God, you are changed; you become a Christian. You are supernaturally regenerated, and you become a new person. There will be a difference in who you are and how you are in the world.

When you claim to be "Christian" and you have not been justified by God, you are not supernaturally regenerated. You are not changed; You are not a Christian by God's standard. A person in that condition is no different than a Jew at the time of Paul believing he was made righteous by being a good Jew. If you made a profession of faith with your mind and you were not under conviction in your heart, God knew, and you have nothing (except maybe a church membership).

When you see someone claiming to be Christian who displays no sign of repentance for sin, who does not come under conviction while repeatedly engaging in overt and biblically obvious sinful actions, you are not looking at someone who has lost their salvation. You are more likely looking at someone who never had it to begin with. And only God (and possibly that person) knows the truth of their condition.

Supernaturally transformed Christians know "that our old self was crucified with Him." We know it deep inside. There is no real Christianity without this knowing. The reason God crucifies our old self—our flesh—with Jesus is so that our body of sin can be made powerless "so that we would no longer be slaves to sin." These verses are not commands to obey—they are realities to be experienced and observed. There is no hint of Christian perfectionism here; we will still wrestle with sin, we will still stumble. But we are "no longer . . . slaves to sin." When you are justified, when you are saved, the penalty of sin is removed, "for he who has died is freed [acquitted] from sin."

After we physically die, when we are raised from the dead, the presence of sin will be removed—it will be gone. That is where we are headed; that is the hope of our faith. But that is not where we are yet. Between conversion and resurrection, the power sin had over us is broken, but the presence of sin remains.

Regeneration does not make us morally or ethically perfect, but it does change our nature and our relationship to sin and sinful actions. If saved, it should now be in our nature for sin to grieve us. Whether we stumble ourselves, or just see and sense sin in the world, sin should bother us in the extreme. Sin and sinful actions, as laid out in the Bible, should now go against our very nature.

If you are saved, and you are maturing as a believer, every action that the Bible calls out as sinful should offend and grieve you. Even if you are wrestling with some parts of the Bible, you should be wrestling under conviction over a truth that is difficult for you. You should not be wrestling with trying to take control back from God by rejecting biblical truth.

As Christians, we do not have two forces at work in us—our sin nature wrestling with our Christ nature. That would reduce being in Christ to just one side of two equal and opposite forces at work in us. The usual accompanying thought process to that is this: whichever nature gets the most attention will dominate. That is the kind of thinking that tends to reject the reality and presence of the demonic, making evil nothing more than a condition of the human mind.

Holding sin and salvation that way yields a very humanistic view of sin that puts the believer in control. It is bad theology. If we are saved, we do not—according to the Bible, we cannot—have two equal and opposite natures inside of us vying for control because "our old self was crucified with Him, in order that our body of sin [our sin nature] might be done away with [made powerless]."

The old self is dead. God gives us a new nature in Christ to begin our new walk in newness of life. We go from being enemies of God and slaves to sin to being servants of Christ and haters of sin. That is our new natural. The power of sin to completely control us is broken, and we are no longer automatically given over to separation from God. The presence of sin is still all around us, and it still affects us, but greater is He who is in us than he who is in the world.

We now recognize evil for what and who it is, and it is not us. We have a very real enemy, and now that the blinders are off, we can see him. He is not in us anymore; we are in Christ. Real Christianity does not and cannot produce rebellion against God's Law. What Paul describes here is a condition not a commandment.

DEAD TO SIN—ALIVE IN CHRIST (ROMANS 6:8-14)

Ultimately, if you are saved, "sin shall not be master over you." You are no longer under the penalty of the Law, and you are no longer a slave to the amplification of sin that the presence of the Law produces. Christians are under grace. Grace is not some abstract theological concept; grace is a real power that changes people.

We are not under sin any longer. Satan is no longer our master. We are under grace, and Jesus Christ is our Master. Sin will no longer dominate us. We are now supposed to sanctify—move toward holiness. We will still sin, but we are not supposed to be in the business of testing just how much willful, mindful sinning we can survive.

When we fully realize what Jesus did for us at the cross with regard to sin, and we have added it all up and deeply considered these things, then we need to apply what we now know and live by our new nature. We are told that whatever has been done for us beyond time, sanctification requires active immersion in surrendered living here in time.

When we were lost, we were separated *from* God by sin. When we are saved, we are separated *for* God. That is the beginning of personal holiness. A Christian is supposed to turn away from the world by no longer embracing things that the Bible defines as sinful. We are separated for God once we are saved, and we are supposed to live in a way that reflects that.

Rules and structures are a part of the Christian life, but they are not the core. If we pursue holiness through rules and regulations and the policing of culture, then we are no better than the Pharisees. Holiness is not just about keeping biblical rules, even though that is part of it. Holiness is not just about what you are feeling and sensing, although emotional and sensory awarenesses are valid and important parts of it. We cannot attain Christian holiness by pursuing it with rule-keeping, ritual spiritual discipline, or ecstatic worship. None of these things are stand-alone formulas for holiness. But because we share in the death and life of Christ, the power of sin to unavoidably rule over us has been broken. We are no longer defaulted to separation from God and the embracing of sinful actions. The presence of sin is still all around us, and it still affects us, but greater is He who is in us than he who is in the world.

The old self is dead at justification. At regeneration, God gives us a new nature in Christ to begin our new walk in newness of life. We go from being enemies of God and slaves to sin, to being servants of Christ and enemies of sin. That stance becomes our new natural. When we are regenerated, we are put on the path toward holiness called sanctification.

If we are regenerated, and we have considered and deeply realize and appreciate what Jesus did for us, then we can willfully respond to the presence of the Spirit and walk right past all manner of sinful temptation. Whatever sin a regenerate person is dealing with at any point in their life, that sin is, in reality, completely powerless in light of the cross. That is a biblical promise.

When you are about to give in to lust, idolatry, anger, hatred, or gossiping, stop yourself and pray out loud or in your mind. Separate yourself in prayer and ask Jesus to help you. The more you do this, the easier and more natural it gets. This type of *stop and drop* praying is so easy and such a plain solution that many Christians forget to do it—or they just will not do it.

If you practice the discipline of taking a step back from sin when its presence is about to overwhelm your senses, and just pray for help whenever and wherever temptation happens, you will be amazed how fast and how much your inclination to sin will decrease. "For sin shall not be master over you, for you are not under law but under grace."

ENSLAVED TO GOD (ROMANS 6:15-23)

We have all earned and deserve physical and eternal death, "but the free gift of God is eternal life in Christ Jesus our Lord." The free gift is the opposite of what we deserve. And even though eternal life is freely gifted to us, it had to be paid for by someone.

The free gift of God is eternal life, paid for by Jesus Christ, and is available to us if "Christ Jesus [is] our Lord." So then, is grace the freedom to do whatever you want? No; may it never be! It cannot be. The release from the power of sin and condemnation under the Law is not to be perverted into an excuse for sinning. Being under grace carries with it obligations of obedience that can only be carried out by the power of grace.

In the sanctifying dynamic of grace, whatever your personal sins are, they are going to grab at you and try to grind you into the world's dust. The enemy cannot take your justification, so he wants to wreck what he can of your new life and destroy your witness and testimony before the world. Do not let him do it. Be obedient and righteous in Christ. Anchor your life in prayer, in the Bible, and in worship. Be, think, and do what God says.

Grace is the power of God to bring you in sync with God's will moving in your life. Before salvation, God's way of being, thinking, and doing was not available to you. You could not have done it, no matter how hard you tried.

Too many Christians who give every indication of actual salvation lose the memory of just how rotten they were before salvation—how much garbage was in their lives and the effect their sin was having on everyone and everything around them. Maybe, about once per year, they should sit down and briefly reflect on how bad it really was and what kind of eternal trouble they were really in.

Do not dwell on it for too long or get lost in it; just prayerfully reflect for a little while. Then put those thoughts away again for another year. Make it a semi-ritualized, private, personal, you-and-God-alone remembrance of who you were before God sorted you out. Think of it as a brief time of being prayerfully ashamed on purpose, and then come right back to *now*. Now, God's grace gives you the power to do what you should. Now, do what you should. There are rules and responsibilities to being a Christian.

JOINED TO GOD (ROMANS 7:1-6)

The purpose of the Law has always been to clarify sin and let us know where we stand with God. The problem of God's Law has always been that humanity cannot keep it. God's Law is of holy origin; it is divine and good, but it does not save. The primary job of the Law is to make us savable by driving us into a deep awareness of sin, a deep awareness of our helplessness, and the realization of our need for a Savior.

The testimony of Israel in the Old Testament is one of sustained inability to obey God's Law "in oldness of the letter." Abraham believed God, and his faith was credited to him as righteousness. No one goes to heaven by keeping God's Law "in oldness of the letter."

We can now exist in a state of obedience to God's Law that was not available to us before we were converted. By the grace of God, we can now "serve in newness of the Spirit." Christians are able to serve in a way that pleases God because we are now able to love God in a way that pleases God. By the transforming power of the Holy Spirit, we have been given the ability to reverentially love God. Paul is showing us who we are as Christians. To be a Christian is to be in Christ. To be in Christ is to strive for obedience as we "serve in newness of the Spirit."

Sanctification is not based on attaining some level of mystical or emotional experience. You may have mystical experiences, you might not. You might enjoy times of prayer or worship that have a profound emotional impact on you, you might not. These things can and do happen and can be useful. Sanctification is not dependent on these things.

Sanctification does not happen because you ritually memorize a lot of Bible verses or spend lots of time reading commentaries. You may have been gifted with a great memory for detail or a talent for academics—or you may not have. Sanctification is not dependent on these things.

To be sanctified is to live a life of ever-increasing surrender to the will of God. The purpose of surrendered living is so that "we might bear fruit for God" while we are on our way home. The model for surrendered Christian living is Christ Himself as recorded in the Gospels. The method for surrendered Christian living is obedience to God's revealed word. And the only way we can do any of this is if we have been saved (converted), supernaturally transformed by the grace of God into new creations.

A saved person does not obey to earn salvation. A saved person does not obey out of fear of losing salvation. A saved person strives for obedience because they have been given a new nature in Christ, and they want to obey—they are driven by the Spirit to obey.

One way to work out your salvation is to check yourself in light of these verses. Instead of tearing yourself to pieces with doubt every time you stumble in sin, ask yourself, *Despite my weaknesses and failings, what is in my heart? Do I want to obey God?*

Practical application: If you are saved, be obedient.

IS THE LAW SINFUL? (ROMANS 7:7-12)

The problem with rules is that they are external to our condition—they are on the outside looking in. Or maybe better, we are on the inside of ourselves looking out at an external Law. The Law cannot change our hearts; the Law can only show us what ought to be.

The Law amplifies sin for both the saved and the lost. When we are exposed to God's Law, our human condition will inevitably default to looking for covetous loopholes. Our enemy takes advantage of this dynamic and can outplay us at every turn when we try to go it alone. We are not dealing with moral concepts in these passages; we are dealing with the underlying mechanism of sin itself—how sin affects us at an essence level regardless of how each of us manifests sin into sinful action.

Sin used the commandment in the Garden to deceive the first human pair, resulting in spiritual death. Sin used the Law to deceive Israel into thinking they could attain spiritual life by keeping the Law, resulting in spiritual death. Sin uses the Law's power to amplify sinful behaviors to deceive humanity with regard to the true nature of sin. Sin beguiles and cheats us by playing to our fallen natures. Sin twists the Law's amplification of sin and lies to us about what we are seeing, resulting in the Law being weaponized against us.

The enemy tells us, *Go ahead. Dive in. Surely you will not die.* Left to fend for ourselves, the inevitable result is the embracing of sin and spiritual death. It is a pretty bleak picture when viewed by a lost person from inside of time. But in the big picture, the ultimate intention of all of this on both sides of the cross is the potential for the dynamic interplay of sin and the Law to break us before God and drive us to repentance. The Law has the potential to expose sin for what it is and show us where we stand with God.

Is the Law sin? No. Is the Law frictional in a sin-poisoned world? Yes—in the extreme. The Law serves as God intended it to serve. The Law has never been the problem. The problem has always been the way the enemy distorts the Law and deceives us. Adam could not sustain his relationship with God in the Garden by keeping one commandment. Israel could not earn salvation by keeping God's Law—a Law they claimed to revere. The experience of Israel is recorded for all time to remind us that no Christian should ever seek salvation through works or ritual Law keeping. Institutional religious rules and rituals do not get it done—never have, never will.

WHO WILL SAVE ME? (ROMANS 7:13-25)

Is Paul, from his new Christian perspective, describing his condition as unregenerate Saul wrestling with the Law while under the power of sin? Or, is Paul, from his new Christian perspective, describing his condition as a regenerate Christian wrestling with the ongoing presence of sin? Arguments for both positions have been in play since the early church. What we need to know is that both theological positions are proved out in multiple other parts of Scripture. This is not a case of which position yields true theology. The arguments are just about which position is being taught in these specific verses.

The majority of early church fathers believed that these verses describe an unregenerate person. For lost people, the Law exists to amplify sin and either drive a person further away from or drive them toward God—which is true. This was Augustine's early view as well. At one point in his life, Augustine got into some heavy theological debates with a guy named Pelagius over the freedom of the will, and in the course of those arguments, for a variety of reasons, he changed his position on these verses to the regenerate view.

Fast-forward to the Reformation. Almost all of the reformers went with Augustine's regenerate position. These passages were, for the most part, taught as describing a part of a normal regenerate experience. After conversion, Christians will still wrestle with the presence of sin—which is true.

At the end of the seventeenth century, a group of Christians called Pietists reacted against what they called the "dead orthodoxy" they believed they were seeing in Reformation churches. They asserted that because of the intensity of the sin problem as presented in this passage, it could not be describing a regenerate Christian. For the Pietists, this level of struggle left too much room to justify too much quantity and too much depth of sinning.

The Pietists believed the regenerate interpretation was out of bounds to Paul's other teachings on what the presence of sin can and cannot do in a saved person. They went back to the teaching of the early fathers, which was that Paul is describing himself as representative of Jews under the Law. The Pietist position resurfaced with a lot of scholarly support in the early 1900s and became pretty much orthodox among the academic crowd, while at the same time the pulpits continued to preach the regenerate Christian "epic wrestle with sin" model.

Right now, the regenerate position is being preached and taught by a great many faithful theologians—guys who I have a lot of respect for. And right now, the unregenerate position is being preached and taught by a great many faithful theologians—guys who I have a lot of respect for. Remember, the question here is not, *Which of these two positions is true?* The question theologians have been dancing back and forth on for centuries is, *Which position is this passage teaching us about?*

Here is a summary what's been going on. Intense and detailed linguistic and contextual study of these verses in the original language yields some really solid evidence that *Paul is writing about his experience as a saved person wrestling with the ongoing presence of sin.* Also, intense and detailed linguistic and contextual study of these verses in the original language yields some really solid evidence that *Paul is writing about his experience as a lost person wrestling with the Law and sin.*

Based on that, and a great many other things, at my current level of ignorance and understanding, here's what I believe has really been going on: Many faithful theologians—guys who should know better—either wrestle with or outright deny the paradox that God has placed us in and that the Bible clearly teaches. Instead, they continue trying to "solve" the Bible through some version of the pure reason model.

For the most part, the Western church has labored diligently to find an intellectual work-around for the mystical paradoxical nature of large swaths of Scripture. Timeless, divine sovereignty surrounding and encompassing the time-bound universe and its movements in time is untenable foolishness to a theological mind grounded in Aristotle and Aquinas. The ongoing dynamic of trying to solve God's paradox with the Greek philosophical method has left us with all sorts of unnecessary separations and sinful frictions.

In light of this, and because of the abuses of understanding caused by a lot of folks throughout church history who call themselves "mystics," the biblical presentation of that which actually is mystical—and even the supernatural underpinning of the Bible—gets dumbed down or just flat-out disavowed in what are otherwise mostly solid seminary environments.

The historical back and forth over whether these verses represent Paul reflecting back on unregenerate Saul or looking at his struggling with sin as a Christian is a good example of what I just wrote. Paul's mystical musings yield two interpretive positions: both do honor to the language and the context, and both have tons of solid scholarly and theological support. Yet the ghosts of Aristotle and Aquinas insist that we pick one or the other.

The entire sweep of church history has shown us that both positional assertions inherent in this passage result in sound doctrine and can yield faithful practice. I am somewhat well-read in the works of the more prominent Christian mystics throughout history, and there is a tendency for Christian mystics to speak from their own journey and their own arrival point at the same time. I believe that is what Paul is doing here. Paul, very well-versed in Scripture beyond most all of his contemporaries, knocked into conviction by the risen Christ, converted and regenerated by the Spirit, and then discipled by Jesus Christ in what can only be defined as a mystical teacher-student relationship, is doing some seriously mystical writing. This is not a case of, *Which is it?* This is a case of Paul telling it like it is from his view in Christ.

On the one hand, Saul was ritually and academically serving the law of God as a Pharisee, but on the other hand, he was lost to the power and penalty of sin. In like manner, on the one hand, Paul was saved, freed from the penalty and the power of sin, but on the other hand, he found himself too often succumbing to the presence of sin in the world.

In both cases, there is the conflict between mental assent to the law of God and ongoing practical failure to keep the Law. It is an intense portrait of the universal sin problem viewed from both sides of salvation, with the law of God front and center for focus and clarity.

As a Pharisee, Saul wrestled endlessly with the *how* and the *what* of God until Saul finally realizes that it is all about Jesus—the *Who* of salvation—and Saul becomes Paul the Christian. What does this tell us? The *how* and *what* of theology can only get us to a certain depth, and that's it.

This points to why rules, rituals, programs, and procedures within a church culture never get it done. Usually the institutions that chase after God from that starting point end up wrestling with varying levels of spiritual despair. And when despair intensifies, churchy folks cry out for more rules, rituals, programs, and procedures. Or they go looking for a church with a more alluring set of rules, rituals, programs, and procedures . . . or just a better band and a coffee shop.

Rinse and repeat; the sin battle rages on. There is no way around what the Law was intended to do. It is a dead end when carnal Christian flesh screams out for more *how* and *what* when it has always been about *Who*—when the Holy Spirit and the Bible are always whispering, *Him.*

This is the heart of the letter to the Romans. The answer is not found in the mechanics of the principles, or the achievements of human understanding, or in any other way. Salvation is personal and relational. It has to be. The answer to sin is only found in a deep, experiential, intimate, and personal relationship with Jesus Christ, initiated by God Himself at justification, and sustained only by the power of the Holy Spirit through regeneration.

Christianity ultimately is not about the mechanics of how we get set free, or the metaphysics behind what sets us free. Christianity is all about *Who* will set us free. Who will set us free from this body of death? And the only answer is Jesus Christ our Lord. Without a real relationship with Jesus Christ, there is no saving faith, no real spiritual joy, no peace that passes all human understanding, no grace to sustain.

Without Jesus, we have nothing. With Jesus, we have everything. Who will set us free from this body of death? Jesus Christ our Lord. Why? Because we believe. Believe and abide in Christ; everything else is extra.

As a saved person, God's rod and staff may comfort me, but that rod of discipline still hurts when I sin. There's just no other way. I couldn't be saved by works of the Law, and I can't maintain my salvation by works of the Law. Left to myself, I am a wretched man. Paul's mystical reflection on lost Saul and saved Paul is humbling. It should be. It is a fitting soliloquy for ushering us into the magnificence that is chapter 8.

FREEDOM IN CHRIST (ROMANS 8:1-4)

The only role we really play in the big picture is the surrendered servant. The requirement of total surrender, as the reality of saving faith, is so direct and straightforward, and flies so strongly in the face of our sin-poisoned natures, that most of humanity will not accept the idea, let alone do it. But those of us who have accepted Jesus Christ will no longer have our lives determined and directed by rebellion against God "according to the flesh"; we will give inward and outward evidence of our salvation by living in obedience "according to the Spirit."

When the enemy gets after you and starts showing you those sinful pictures from your past, go to Romans 8:1 and reflect on who you are in Jesus Christ. Remember that "there is now no condemnation for those who are in Christ Jesus." It does not say that there is *less* condemnation, or *modified* condemnation, or some afterlife holding tank to pay back remaining condemnation. Jesus did it all—one and done, for all time.

Remember that by faith you received a gift. You did not earn it, you did not deserve it. You still do not deserve it. Remember that any claim to spiritual righteousness you have comes from Christ and Christ alone. Jesus Christ was condemned in place of you. Because of that, and only because of that, "there is now no condemnation for those who are in Christ Jesus."

If you are in Christ, when the enemy nags you about your sinful past, remind him that you stand in the righteousness of Christ. Rest in that knowledge. When the enemy tries to drag you back "according to the flesh," remember who you are in Christ, and "walk . . . according to the Spirit." Let the Spirit bring you peace.

Chapter 8 is all about our assurance as believers, and it begins by reminding us that our assurance is all about Jesus.

THE INDWELLING SPIRIT (ROMANS 8:5-11)

The Bible is full of propositional statements that can be digested and examined by the human intellect. And the human intellect, with itself as the standard, can render varying degrees of intellectual acceptance or rejection of these ideas. But salvation is not just about taking an intellectual stance based on the body of truth statements made in the Bible. A supernatural conversion must take place for a lost person to become a real Christian.

If you are saved, you received salvation as a gift by faith because deep inside yourself, in a place beyond words, in the power and presence of the Holy Spirit, you repented of your sins in the midst of whatever level of intellectual clarity you were or were not experiencing at that time. You turned back to loving God with all of your heart, all of your soul, all of your strength, and all of your mind, even though your mind was a mess and still is by God's standard. What is important is that by God's mystical standard, your faith was genuine. In that supernatural, mystical, transactional moment, you got the gift of salvation. That is how a lost person becomes a Christian, regardless of their theological acumen (or lack thereof).

You did not earn it; you did not deserve it. What the Law could not do for you in your lost condition, God did. The requirement of the Law was fulfilled in you. You are no longer defaulted to blindly walking under the power of sin. You are now able to walk according to the Spirit of God.

Salvation is more than just a legal decree stating that we are no longer guilty before God. Salvation is more than just justification and the thought that when we die, we go to be with God. Salvation is also about the assurance we have as believers and how and why we can experience that right now. When God justified us, declared us "not guilty," He also regenerated us, freeing us from the power of sin. God spiritually transformed us at conversion by the power and indwelling presence of the Spirit.

Because of regeneration, the transformational aspect of our salvation has already begun. We are saved right now. We are not glorified right now, but we are moving in that direction. We are in the midst of the process we call *sanctification*. A real Christian moves through the world differently than a lost person because a real Christian is different than a lost person.

There are a handful of ways to interpret the word *flesh*, depending on where you are at in the Bible, which language it is translated from, and the immediate context surrounding its usage. In these verses, *flesh* references the sinful condition of humanity apart from Jesus Christ and the Holy Spirit. It references fallen human nature in a state that is incapable of conforming to God's holiness.

In Romans, the word *flesh* gives the sense of humanity surrounded and encompassed by both the innate power and tangible presence of sin. In these verses, "flesh" does not mean "human body." Lots of people throughout history took "flesh" to mean "human body" in these passages and then developed the notion that their physical bodies were inherently evil in opposition to their soul and spirit. This led to the invention of all manner of twisted and weird spiritual disciplines that are not the least bit spiritual in their form, function, or result.

In the Western church, the idea that the physical human body is inherently evil and an obstacle to spiritual growth originally came from the Greek philosopher Plato, and the idea is still worming its way through Christendom. Lots of Christians today are making this mistake.

The human body is subjected to the fleshly world, but it is still God's creation and was originally created for good. And it can still be used for God's good when it is used in the service of God. The Bible teaches that each regenerated human body is a temple of the Holy Spirit. Christ Himself incarnated and lived a sinless life in a real human body, despite being subjected to the presence of the fleshly world.

For a lost person, walking in the flesh means being in slavery to the power of sin and being unavoidably given over to the temptations manifested by the presence of sin. For a saved person, being in the flesh means going beyond temptation and willfully giving in to some manifestation of the presence of sin. That's why Jesus taught us to pray, *Do not allow us to go into temptation, but keep us safe from evil.* When we sin now, the devil does not make us do it; he just lures us back into the fleshly world with all manner of temptations.

If you are saved, the Holy Spirit of God is now dwelling in you and will never leave you. This is the result of conversion. The Spirit of God dwells in you. The only way to not be in the flesh is to be in the Spirit. And the only way to be in the Spirit is "if indeed the Spirit of God dwells in you." There's that "if" word again. If the Spirit of God dwells in you, it is because you were saved.

You cannot be justified, have your sins forgiven, become a Christian, and then have to do some extra something to receive the Holy Spirit. Justification and regeneration are distinct but inseparable. Salvation is all of God.

If you are saved, it is because the Holy Spirit did the convicting work on your heart by the grace of God when you surrendered control to Jesus by faith. God does all of the work. The Holy Spirit does not convict people to the point of conversion and then stand back while they figure out some works-based ritual activity to earn His indwelling presence.

Note that the Spirit does not come and go. If you are a Christian, the indwelling of the Spirit is permanent and constant. You are never alone. Consider that reality. And then consider this: How many times per week, or even per day, do you drag the Holy Spirit into an activity that He wants no part of? Whenever you engage any sinful frequency, the Holy Spirit is right there as witness. That is a sobering thought.

By the power of the Holy Spirit, your human spirit has been quickened toward God—made alive to God through the person and work of Jesus Christ. That is something you should know and experience at least to some degree. However you experience your new life in Christ, you should know what I am talking about at a level so deep inside of you that it passes all intellectual understanding. The power of the Spirit raised Jesus from the dead. If you die in Christ, the same Spirit will raise you from the dead, giving "life to your mortal body." There is the future hope of faith that is unfolding in you right now.

This does not mean that we will not live contrary to the Spirit at times. Other places in Scripture make it clear that is going to happen. Our own walks make it painfully clear to us that sin is still a present and pernicious influence. But for those of us in Christ, we have been changed, transformed, converted, and regenerated by the power of the Holy Spirit. God did it. And once it is done, it is done. That is our security.

As Christians we have security because we know beyond knowing that we are taking part in a salvation that has already begun and that God is going to complete in us. And now, our human spirits testify inside of us at such a profound depth that we know beyond knowing who we are in Christ and where we are going when we die. That is our assurance.

There is an inner witness that the Holy Spirit communicates to our (small *s*) spirits that affirms and seals God's word in us. There is an authoritative and all-encompassing presence that comes with regeneration that only a follower of Christ can know. This tremendous inner outpouring of holy peace and holy love is impossible to convey to another person by intellectual description, yet it is something that countless believers experience in a place beyond words as central to their new life in Christ.

The experience of the indwelling presence of the Spirit does not replace or override the objective truths presented in the Bible. The objective, subjective, and mystical aspects of Christianity are a series of interrelated "ands" and are in no way presented as *either-or* in the Bible. Each of these things does not exist in a believer without the other. Everyone who is really saved has at least some degree of a deep, inner sense—a peace in God—that passes all human ability to control or completely understand.

1. We have the objective assurance of the written word.
2. We have the subjective assurance of who we know ourselves to be in Christ.
3. We have the mystical assurance of the undeniable, indwelling presence of the Spirit teaching us about all of this in context of the other parts.

Most of the problems a believer experiences moving through sanctification are the product of the human mind either unintentionally or intentionally unbalancing these three aspects.

CHILDREN OF GOD (ROMANS 8:12-17)

If you live in this life indebted to the devil as your father, then when you die you go to be with your father, the devil. You go where he is to be with him and suffer his fate. You go to the place of permanent separation from God.

A Christian still lives in the presence of sin, and the enemy uses that presence to pull at the body. But the assurance of salvation is not to be taken as an excuse for spiritual idleness or ongoing adventures in idolatry. You are to put to death the deeds. It does not say that you are to put to death the *presence* of sin in the world around you; the sin-poisoned universe is the way of things right now. It does not say that you are to put to death all temptation; our enemy is on the loose right now, and that is his turf.

In the big picture of timelessness, the devil has already lost the war, but he is still fighting crazy battles in time as he rails against and tries to subvert what he has been told is coming. If you are saved, then the devil has lost the war for your soul even here in time—but he still fights to diminish your witness and testimony any way he can.

Sanctification is not a test of wills—yours against the enemy. That is a fool's game. You may win a few going that way—and you are going to lose more than a few—but you are guaranteed to miss out on the peace and power of total surrender in the Spirit. The Spirit is right there waiting to help, but you have got to let the Helper help by getting out of your own way.

If you are a Christian, the war for your soul is over. Now you have an obligation to fight the ongoing battle of continuously "putting to death the deeds of the body." And with the Spirit leading, and you immersed in obedience, you will be able to fight.

The result of this immersion will have a practical base. There are biblical rules in play, and there are commands in play, but this type of fighting is a matter of heart, of conforming to the holy love of Christ. Sanctification is an ongoing test of obedience of the heart. Who are you answering to every day . . . every moment?

Back in chapter 1, Paul introduced himself as a bond-slave of Christ. There is a world of difference in Paul's mind between a slave and a bond-slave. A slave to sin can only fear God as a distant and cold judge. The only kind of fear in that condition is the fear of punishment. Now, as a completely surrendered bond-slave of Christ, Paul understands the relational nature of reverentially fearing God.

Jesus said to His followers, when you pray, use the word "Father" to address God. Paul picks up on that here. Followers of Jesus are on family terms with God now. A bond-slave of Jesus obeys God in a family relationship built on trust, respect, and loving reverence in the sense of a little child respectfully and obediently obeying their parents.

Christian spirits are no longer fearful slaves to the enemy; we are adopted as sons and daughters into the family of God as reverentially fearful bond-servants to Jesus Christ. We are learning about the relational nature of holy love, a love that transcends any experience or notion of love we can muster on our own. Loving reverence for God and reverential fear of God are inseparable.

We have been welcomed back into God's family, but only on God's terms. By the bond-servant limitations God puts on us in time, we can experience the real love for God that gives birth to the reality of God-honoring reverential fear. It is the biblical limits that our loving Father puts on us in time that yield the intensity of sanctified living in the Spirit. The deeper we surrender into these sanctifying limitations, the more the intensity of this awareness striking at every level of our being becomes an overwhelming mixture of form, fact, and feeling "by which we cry out, 'Abba! Father!'"

In the biblical sense of reverential fear, all that is available to a lost person is the terror and the dread of being confronted by the living God. When we were lost, we had much to be afraid of. All we could do in response to the dynamic of sin was immerse ourselves in covetousness and idolatry. But now, we have the spirit of adoption. We know the Truth, and the Truth has set us free.

> The cross of Christ is God saying, *This is how I loved the world.*
>
> The gift of salvation is God saying, *This is how I love you.*

We now know the love of God and the indwelling of the Spirit, and we know that the appropriate response to the Spirit's outpouring of holy love is to be respectful, humbled, surrendered, obedient, awestruck, worshipful— all of that summed up as reverential fear.

The Spirit converts us, the Spirit gives us a new heart, and the Spirit lives in us. This is how we know that our salvation is assured; this is the inner awareness that drives our security. How do we communicate this to an unbeliever? All of this stuff is foolishness to the lost mind. We can give them the objective truth of the Bible. We can tell them about our subjective relationship to all of that. We can tell them our stories. But we cannot give them our Inner experience of life in Christ. Our justification and regeneration and everything that goes along with it is the gift of God.

As children of God, we have already been adopted; we are already saved. As heirs, we are growing into our inheritance; we are growing toward glorification. We are obligated by God and driven by the Spirit to walk with Jesus. No one can make a case for a legitimate claim to salvation while living in continuous, intentional, ongoing rebellion against God's revealed word. There must be surrender to the touch of the Spirit.

There is no room for self-righteous moralism or works-based legalism here. The process of sanctification is completely dependent on the power and presence of the Spirit. No one can go it alone. That is a fool's game—or, said another way, a game of religious foolishness.

The other extreme is to become obsessed with non-accountable immersion. But life in the Spirit is not about achieving a place of mindless surrender, leading to some sort of dissolution of the self. We are not subsumed into the Spirit to the point that we have no individual will. We are commanded to work with the Spirit—to be an active part of the process. These verses insist that there must be an ongoing, accountable, human response taking place in time.

And so it is. We cry out to our Father as His adopted children in Christ, and we thank God that "[t]he Spirit Himself testifies with our spirit that we are children of God." We can count it as nothing that we suffer with Christ in this life because we know with the deepest kind of knowing that we will be glorified with Him.

Here is how God loves us: "[W]e are children of God . . . and fellow heirs with Christ," and we will be glorified with Christ. We are going home.

IN HOPE WE HAVE BEEN SAVED (ROMANS 8:18-25)

As Christians, we are heirs to all of the biblical promises regarding eternal life. But we also inherit all of the time-bound consequences of following Christ in a lost world. Everyone who is really saved has come to grips on some level with the awesome and terrifying power of sin. Our relationship to the power of sin has been supernaturally changed, and the sin blinders are off—at least intellectually.

Now we have to walk out our new lives in Christ in a world that is dying in sin. We are now spiritually out of alignment with the lost world and out of bondage to the enemy, and our enemy knows it and is coming for us. During the time between salvation and glory, we will have to endure periods of suffering with Christ. This is the way of things. This will be the way home.

The history of real Christianity is the history of the enemy using the lost world to lash out at Christ's faithful and the history of the faithful persevering against all human odds by way of the certain hope for the future that drives our present faith. In these verses we learn about how we should hold all of this in our minds during the waiting period between salvation and glorification.

We cannot see the Holy Spirit indwelling us, but we can sense His presence. The Spirit of God is inside of us, nourishing us, growing us, shaping us, changing us. Because of the presence of the Spirit, our hope is alive. Without the Holy Spirit, there is no real faith and no holy love in us— only a broken spirit and an intellect running on sensory data and whatever degree of intellection we possess. Even with the indwelling of the Holy Spirit, we will experience degrees of frustration with the incompleteness of our faith playing out in the world.

If you are having problems with your faith, you might want to look to how you are holding hope. Saving faith in Christ is inseparable from the hope of salvation. Knowing what you have been saved from includes knowing what you are being saved to. Hope gives faith a target beyond what can be seen. Stay focused on eternal things, and the hope that faith engenders will drive your perseverance, and you will be able to faithfully and eagerly wait out your time on earth.

THE SPIRIT'S INTERCESSION (ROMANS 8:26-27)

The Holy Spirit is our teacher in time. The Spirit illuminates God's revealed truth so that we can go beyond mere intellection and authentically live out the truths in the Bible. We cannot live out an authentic Christian life without the power and presence of the Holy Spirit. It cannot be done.

If God had justified us and not regenerated us, we would be the exact same people after salvation as before. The only difference would be our "not-guilty" verdict before the Law. (Let's be clear, that is no small thing. Without justification, we would all stand condemned.)

Left to ourselves, we are spiritually weak. When we try to run on the human power of self, we fall right back into the world. We've all seen and experienced enough less than optimal churchy behaviors to know the truth of this. We need help. If justification did not include regeneration, we would be saved in eternity and left to our own devices here in time, "for we do not know how to pray as we should."

The Spirit helps us in all sorts of ways, but Paul addresses the help here in terms of prayer. The gift of prayer is so simple and straightforward that too many Christians are convinced they cannot do it, or it does not work, or they are not doing it right, or there must be some mystical method they are missing. But prayer is simply talking with God. We lift up worship *to* God as humble, respectful servants; we talk *with* God in prayer as adopted children.

The reason we too often struggle with prayer is clearly spelled out for us: "we do not know how to pray as we should." Many of us tend to pray like little two- and three-year-old children struggling to find words to communicate with their parents. Sometimes the idea is right there, and the words do not get it across. Sometimes we just repeat words we have heard in an effort to sound the way we think we should sound. Sometimes the words just pour out and do not have any real connection to what is going on inside of us. In terms of what we are to pray for, how can we get that right? It is easy enough to think in general terms: pray for each other, pray for justice, pray for the conversion of lost souls—things like that. But the more detailed we get, the more prayer starts to become about our perceived wants and what we think needs to happen in time, and less about what timeless, sovereign God ordains and knows that must happen in time.

Too often we take the simple and straightforward activity of prayer and complicate it with our perceptions of what should and should not be happening in the world. None of us know the mind of God. None of us are God. Prayer that focuses exclusively on the results in time that we want is not surrendered prayer. Prayer is not about carefully punching the right buttons on a spiritual vending machine called "God" to get what we want. Authentic prayer helps us to draw closer to God as we learn to move in His will and way, despite all the craziness unfolding in the world.

Real prayer is not about structurally accurate lists of requests, soaring poetry, or mechanically correct formulas. Real prayer is about authentic communication with God. And God knows that we are not very good at that. We are learning to walk in alignment with God's will, but there is no perfection in sanctification. God doesn't ask us to pray by some lofty, perfected standard; He just asks us to pray.

God did not establish prayer to be tricky or for it to be difficult. Prayer is not the mechanical thing that we do; it is an expression of the relationship that we have. Prayer is talking with God—not *at* God, *with* God—as we learn to spend more time in an attitude of listening instead of attitudes of worrying or insisting.

As Christians, the Holy Spirit now intercedes on our behalf by aligning our prayers with the will of God. The Spirit's intercession makes the prayer of a believer powerful and effective, despite our inability to pray as we should and regardless of our perception as to the way the prayer is answered.

Chapter 8 is about the assurance of our salvation both beyond time and in time. We are not supposed to worry, be afraid, or be anxious. Our hope keeps us focused on what God has done, what God is doing, and what God is going to do (which are all really the same thing from God's perspective). God has got this. He does not need our help. He does not need our prayers, but He wants us *living in* prayer. Do your best to pray authentically and from your heart. The Holy Spirit will handle the rest.

> **Paraphrase:** *In the same way that faith-driven hope sustains us, the Spirit joins with us to help our weakness, for we are unable to clearly discern God's will in the things we pray for, and our wills are not perfectly in alignment with the will of God, but the Spirit Himself intervenes on our behalf in an unspoken groaning way that perfectly matches the will of God; and God, who knows the innermost hearts of humans, perfectly knows the mind of the Spirit because the Spirit prays on behalf of believers in perfect alignment with God's will.*

Just pray. God already knows your innermost thoughts. Just pray.

THE SOVEREIGNTY PARADOX (ROMANS 8:28-30)

We have been told that we are secure in Christ. We are heirs to the promise of God. We will inherit the kingdom. But the Bible makes it clear that in the time between salvation and glorification, we will have times of suffering with Christ. It's going to happen.

At the very least, the friction between being a temple of the Holy Spirit while living in the presence of sin is going to make for times of serious spiritual discomfort. And, even with the Spirit indwelling us, we do not know how to pray as we should. There is a lot we do not know, a lot we cannot know right now.

In verses 28-30, Paul is telling us about something we can know spiritually even though it is difficult to process intellectually. The foundation of our security is the sovereignty of God. God is not subject to the boundaries of time and space. However things look to us here in time, God knows the end from the beginning, and He has got this.

There is a whole lot of stuff going on that is extremely and extraordinarily bad. And we can know and understand that things are going to end badly for a whole lot of people regardless of what they can or cannot see right now. Part of our assurance is that all of these things are causally related and perfectly understood by God. "God causes all things to work together for good"—and then the limiter —"to those who love God." Regardless of how bad things can get in time, God is using all of it toward what will ultimately be good ends for His people. Everything that we can see in time, and a lot of things we cannot see, are working "together for good to those who love God."

That is a pretty weighty assertion given the amount and intensity of evil playing out in the world. But, as Christians, we are learning to take a step back from our time-bound notions and view all of history through our biblical Jesus glasses. From the time-bound biblical viewpoint, the worst, most evil event in human history is humanity humiliating, torturing, and murdering the incarnate Son of God. At the same time, with a view from beyond time, the best thing that has ever happened for humanity in time is Jesus Christ dying on the cross for us. God caused all of that to "work together for good to those who love God."

So all things in creation are not currently good, but from a longer view of history, things are moving as they must according to the will and way of God for the good of His kingdom. Whatever is currently happening in us or around us, as soon as the event moves from the present moment to the past, sovereignty gets a little easier to deal with. You can look at whatever has happened in and around your life and reflect on 1 Thessalonians 5:18: "[T]his is God's will for you in Jesus Christ." Even if it was something tough, or mind-boggling, or something you're ashamed of, once the event moves into your past, take the lesson and "in everything give thanks, for this is God's will for you in Jesus Christ."

If God saved you, then you are among "those who are called according to His purpose." God does not serve; God saves—and then we serve the God who saved us. If words like *chance, luck,* and *coincidence* are pointers to actual occurrences in time, then God is not sovereign, and we have no reason to trust His promises. If we are called according to God's purpose, but His purpose is subject to random natural forces like chance, luck, or coincidence playing out in time, then we have no assurance and no security. Our faith is rooted in a deep knowing that however things look from a time-bound perspective, God is all-knowing and all-powerful.

Two words in these verses point us into the mind of God: "foreknew" and "predestined." To foreknow an event is to know about it before it happens. It is an incredibly weighty idea when contemplating God, but the definition is that simple and demands to be taken that simply. The Bible insists that God has complete knowledge of all things past, present, and future. God knows the end from the beginning.

To predestine an event is to decide upon the outcome of an event before it happens. Again, the definition is simple enough. Taken together, the assertion is plain. God has perfect knowledge of everything past, present, and future. Therefore, if someone gets saved, it is no surprise to God.

When you approach these verses, and any like them, remember that they teach us about how God is relating to us from beyond time, not how we relate to God from our time-bound perspective.

Humanity exists in time in context of timeless sovereignty. The Bible books move freely back and forth between lessons rooted in time and instruction about the nature of sovereign God. In some places, the two viewpoints are clearly delineated; in some places they switch back and forth across paragraphs and verses; in other places they mix and mingle, pointing at both viewpoints simultaneously. Human willfulness in context of the sovereignty of God is the contextual basis for the entire Bible. We have two parallel realities, one only existing in context of the other, both of which are presented as real and true, running side by side throughout the Bible.

This presentation of the human will making meaningful decisions in time while everything in time is completely subject to the absolute sovereignty of God creates an unsolvable paradox. Time-bound logic breaks down here. If one presentation is true by human logic, the other must be false—or less true—and vice-versa. And yet, the biblical writers place these two viewpoints side by side and make no attempt to reconcile them or apologize for the paradox the presentation creates.

In verse 30, it is God who predestined, called, justified, and glorified. They are all in the same tense. If God predestines, calls, and justifies, then glorification is a done deal. Why is this timeless presentation important for time-bound believers? As individual believers, we are assured that God is working for our ultimate good regardless of how things look to us in time. God will glorify us beyond time. God is in control. This time-bound view into timeless sovereignty, when held in mystical tension, yields security and the inner spiritual knowing of assurance.

God's paradox is foolishness to human logic and will always break attempts to systematize away the essence of the presentation. But what is logically foolish becomes spiritually reasonable in a place beyond human logic with the illumination provided by the Holy Spirit. Part of the power of the hope of our faith is that we can rest in what we do not know.

God did not give us this paradox to confuse us or to give theologians something to argue about until the end of time. He gave us this presentation to grow us spiritually. We are to take in everything the Bible says about humanity in time—moral agency, accountability for what we do and think, the real decisions we make in time. We are to take in everything the Bible says about the nature of God in timelessness—that God is all-knowing and all-powerful, that God foreknows and predestines beyond any understanding we can come to by time-bound intellection. Then, we are to hold all of this in the tension of ongoing contemplation and trust in the Lord while not leaning on our own understanding. The Bible does not say that we are not to have understandings; we just are not supposed to elevate them over our faith or limit God or the Bible by our time-bound standards of what can and cannot be.

None of this diminishes the importance or reality of the human response of faith. Like the biblical writers, we are to live in the midst of the paradox and let the tension stretch us and grow us spiritually. Ongoing immersion in the paradox of sovereignty drives us into deeper knowing of what it means to be and live surrendered to God. Timeless sovereignty held in tension with time-bound humanity places our limited and skewed time-anchored perception in proper context within God's timeless and actual reality.

We are walking through a world lost in sin, and the Bible promises that if we are in Christ, then one way or another we will suffer with Christ as we move toward the hope of glory. The lost world is nuts. To follow Jesus in time, we need assurance from God. That may be why these verses go hard over to the timeless side of the biblical paradox and give us a glimpse into the mystery of sovereignty. That is where our security is based. From God's viewpoint, nothing is uncertain, unknowable, or unknown. No matter how things appear to those of us in time, God is causing all of the stuff going on in humanity and human history to work together for good to those who are in Christ.

When you engage the Bible, you need to know what you are reading and which position is being emphasized or when the positions are, to varying degrees, intertwining. And then you are to subordinate your detailed intellectual understandings to your faith and cultivate your knowing with ongoing prayer, worship, and further immersion in the word.

When dealing with the human will in context of sovereignty, surrendering the certainty of systematic mental gymnastics and meditating on the illogical intermix of that which is timeless and that which is time-bound points us into the mystery of Christianity and encourages deeper immersion in the Bible. There is no solution to the paradox of time-bound human moral agency existing amidst the timeless sovereignty of Holy God—there is not supposed to be. Take the ongoing, unsolvable, mysterious lesson and let the spiritual tension it creates change you—do not try to change or solve it.

IF SAVED, ALWAYS SAVED (ROMANS 8:31-39)

"What then shall we say to these things?" Well, because we are followers of Christ, existing in time while stretched in the spiritual paradox of time meeting timelessness, we can simply say God is for us. And then we can ask ourselves, each other, and the world, *If God is for us, who is against us?* Who can ultimately stand against God and His family in an eternal way? No one.

Here in time, there have been plenty of people against us. Real Christians, walking with the Spirit, have dealt with all manner of persecution since the time of the apostles. But take heart as you survey time. God loved the world in this way: He did not spare His own Son. Here is the holy standard of God's love. If God did the much greater thing of sacrificing His own Son, then how much more can He be trusted to get us home despite what the worlds throws at us?

God's holy love is the relational standard that we are drawn into at salvation. This is the standard that drives our hope forward. Not our time-bound understandings of love, but our exposure to the holy love of God.

Who is against us? It does not matter—bring it! God is for us, and we have a hope that defies whatever the world throws at us. Who is accusing us? Who is bringing a charge against our faith? It does not matter. God has justified us, and His revealed word transcends all other words. Who cares if some court of the human mind condemns us.

We stand in the shadow of the righteousness of Jesus Christ. The question isn't, *Will I sin after salvation?* or, *Will my sinful actions as a saved person cause me to lose my salvation?* The question is, *Can Jesus sin?* God's verdict of "not guilty" is anchored to the person and work of Jesus Christ. Jesus is our security, and Jesus does not sin. The righteousness we have is imputed to us through Jesus Christ. Jesus is interceding on our behalf right now and always. We can get sloppy with our walks; Jesus Christ never gets sloppy with our salvation.

"Who will separate us from the love of Christ? Will tribulation, or distress, or persecution, or famine, or nakedness, or peril, or sword?" This is prophecy and lesson. When Paul wrote this, all of these things were about to happen to lots of real Christians. All of these still happen to real Christians all around the world. Some amount or degree of this comes to all of us in one way, shape, or form. There are tens of thousands of people lining up at churches where they are told that they are doing great if God is giving them lots of money and stuff. They also tell them that if they are dealing with "tribulation, or distress, or persecution, or famine, or nakedness, or peril, or sword," then there is something wrong with them spiritually. But in previous verses in this letter alone, we were told that if we are in Christ, we will suffer with Christ.

The first assertion is this: the love of Christ does not separate us from sufferings in time. The second assertion is, sufferings in time have no power to separate us from the love of Christ. There is no promise of Christian perfection or perfect Christian circumstances in this life, just warnings of imminent persecution and suffering and teachings on how to deal with it. For the sake of the gospel of Jesus Christ, many Christians have been and continue to be persecuted up to and including being put to death. But if we are in Christ, then whatever face persecution takes, "in all these things we overwhelmingly conquer through Him who loved us."

Nothing that can happen to a Christian in this life, including the end of this life, "will be able to separate us from the love of God, which is in Christ Jesus our Lord." That is the promise of God. This also applies to angels and principalities ("principalities" is a Paul word for *demons*). Neither angels nor demons have any power over God, nor can they wrest your salvation away from God. If God justified you, you are saved. Your salvation is secured by God in Christ, not by you.

Neither things present nor things to come can undo what God has done. Do not worry about the forces arrayed against us in the world. Worrying that way will cause you to project fear into the future. And then you will be worrying in the present about things to come. Do not worry about what the powers that be are doing. Political leaders come and go, nations come and go. That stuff can get real ugly, but none of it can separate us from God.

What about real worldly power? The evil one is more powerful and capable than all of the most evil leaders in history combined. And here he is referenced generally as a principality and power, relegated to a list of things that simply cannot cause you to lose your justification. Neither height nor depth can separate you. It does not matter where you go. There is nowhere on earth where God is absent. Wherever you find yourself, and whatever condition the world around you is in, Jesus Christ will not allow you to be separated from the love of God.

Then Paul ties it all up with, "nor any other created thing." Everything in the universe is a created thing. Paul is writing about security and assurance here, and he wants to make sure we get the picture. In the big picture of timeless sovereignty, God is in control. "Any other created thing" also includes you. You are a created thing. If God justified you, if you are really saved, even you cannot separate yourself "from the love of God, which is in Christ Jesus our Lord." *Once saved, always saved* is such a clumsy and semantically treacherous representation. *If saved, always saved* is more accurate and God-honoring.

Satan will accuse us. Enemies of God will accuse us. Our own thoughts will accuse and excuse us because of the presence of sin. These are the ones who condemn. But we have been freed from the condemnation of God if Christ is in us. Since God is both just and the justifier of the one who has faith in Jesus Christ, none of these other accusations can override or overrule God's "not-guilty" verdict.

Who has the power to undo what God has done? No *one* and no *thing* can come along and alter what God has declared to be. God is not bound by humanity in time or by the limits of time-bound thought processes and systems of thought. We have a trustworthy Bible because of the sovereignty of God. We are still here in the presence of sin. God doesn't promise separation from the presence of sin as we walk this out. He promises that sin will no longer separate us from Him because "in all these things we overwhelmingly conquer through Him who loved us."

Believe and abide in Christ. That is where you will find security and assurance.

BECAUSE OF HIM WHO CALLS (ROMANS 9:1-18)

Salvation now belongs to Christians whether from Jewish or Gentile background. Many Jews in the early church would not accept this. To accept the message of Jesus was to accept that individual Jews started out condemned right alongside the Gentiles. It seemed to them that if Jews are under the same penalty as Gentiles, then God is unfaithful to His promises. But they had lost sight of the faith of Abraham and gotten lost in the notion that just being a Jew was in and of itself enough to secure salvation. The Jews that would not accept the gospel accused Paul of being a blasphemer against God, anti-Semitic, and an enemy of Israel. The Roman Christians, and many others, were studying the Old Testament Scriptures and trying to figure out how much of Jewish heritage should be part of their Christian faith.

God never promised to save every Jew. God was never obligated to Israel in that way. In the same sense, God never promised to save everyone who calls themselves Christian. It is the same God on both sides of the cross, the sovereign God over all humanity who is not and has never been bound by institutional religious organizations.

There are no business meetings with God. There are no votes that can bind or limit God. Nothing you encounter in your institutional denomination of choice changes the will of God the least single bit. Lots of Jews back then found out about this the hard way. Lots of Jews are still finding out about this the hard way. Lots of unjustified, unregenerate, unconverted people, who have based their claim to salvation on denominational traditions and rituals, have died and found out the hard way that God is not bound by human traditions. God is free to harden this person and have mercy on that person regardless of how things look to us. We are just not in control.

To be hardened is to be spiritually insensitive. Spiritual hardening renders a person unresponsive to God and to the Scriptures. The case of Pharaoh uses this idea to plainly display the paradox. Exodus 9:34 says that Pharaoh sinned and hardened his heart. Exodus 9:35 says God hardened Pharaoh's heart. Which verse is true?

In our puny little brains, God exercising His divine foreknowledge and predestining things is incompatible with our sense of willful moral agency. When the two positions are set side by side, our logic circuits lock up. God's reality creates a paradox in time that breaks the boundaries of time-bound logic.

The first tendency when this happens is to look for an either/or solution. One position must be false for the other to be true. And yet, the Scriptures present both viewpoints and assert the truth of both conditions. The place where human moral agency meets divine sovereignty cannot be penetrated with time-bound systems of logic.

The Bible presents us with the mystical nature of our existence and simply demands that we surrender to the gospel message. Then, with the indwelling of the Holy Spirit, what once seemed impossibly illogical becomes more and more spiritually reasonable. The place where human moral agency is enveloped in God's sovereignty is the place where spiritually mature Christians should be living.

Try to reflect and weigh your life playing out in time in the context these verses present. Weigh your life playing out in time against the biblical standard of holiness, and reflect on how you appear to Holy God. It is *supposed* to be humbling; it is *supposed* to unsettle your time-bound-ness. Let it.

THE POTTER AND THE CLAY (ROMANS 9:19-24)

In the John 15, Jesus said to His apostles, "You did not choose Me, but I have chosen you." That is just one example from other Bible books of this dynamic, mysterious intermix that Paul has been teaching us about.

You will find both viewpoints—the view from time and the view from sovereignty—running through all of the books of the Bible. Some biblical passages focus on one view or the other, some start with one and move to the other, some work them back and forth, some mix and mingle them at the same time. This is the overarching biblical context.

The central teaching in the letter to the Romans is the justification of a lost person by grace through faith in the person and work of the Lord Jesus Christ. Romans 8:29 gives us a stark picture of sovereignty. However things seem to us, God foreknew us, predestinated us, called us, and justified us. God foreknew it all; God did it all. Salvation is all of God.

There is no getting around the mysterious paradoxical underpinnings at the heart of biblical theology. And yet generations of Christian theologians, embracing varying degrees of the Greek philosophical pure reason model, have done everything they can to find logical ways to lock out one side or the other of the paradox to rid themselves of the biblical tension.

Before I encountered the world of Western systematic theology, I was taught that the heart of biblical theology was simple. We are supposed to contemplate the sovereignty of God in salvation. We are supposed to contemplate the human aspect of salvation in time. We are supposed to immerse in everything that the Bible teaches about our responsibilities in time and deal with it. We are supposed to immerse in everything the Bible teaches about sovereign God and accept the truth of it. Then, we are to hold all of our time-bound understandings in context of sovereignty, and let the two positions pull at us spiritually as we grow in grace and spiritual understanding of this dynamic.

Yes, the paradox of sovereignty raises difficult questions from our time-bound perspective. It is supposed to. But when the human questioner becomes an accuser of God, Paul shuts the whole thing down. If you approach God that way, the creature is judging the Creator by the limited understandings of the creature. The created being is then elevating the human mind over the mind of God.

Paul says to the clay, *Hey, we are not going there. Go back to Romans 1. You are worshipping anything and everything in time, including yourself, in order to reject this truth I am giving you.* The argument is not answered by Paul; it is rejected. We are not to elevate pure-reason-style philosophical word games as the path to what the Bible calls wisdom. We are not to blame God because we cannot or will not surrender in the walled-off, tiny little courts of our minds. This type of thinking is where my biblical journey began.

After many years in seminary and acquiring four theological degrees, this is where I have returned.

Human intellection has tremendous potential to create things in time. Nowhere does the Bible command us that we should not use the reasoning faculties God has given us—God's specially revealed truth is delivered in human language in the Bible. The Bible has a lot to say about how we should use our reasoning faculties for the glory of God. But human intellection can only take us so far. We are not saved by the grace of God through intellection and perfected reasoning. We are saved by the grace of God through the surrender of faith. People of the Book are people of faith. Paul is amplifying the case made throughout the Bible: *Human, here is where you stand in relation to God. Deal with it.*

In some places, the Bible puts forward clear teachings about human responsibility and moral agency. In some places, the Bible puts forward clear teachings about the divine sovereignty of God. The Bible never offers— here or anywhere else—a logical solution to the tension this presentation creates. The Bible asserts the truth of both positions, makes no attempt to reconcile them, and expects us to do the same.

God is the Creator. He has the power and authority to create what He creates for His own purposes. A baseline assertion here is that God has the authority to deal with sinful creatures according to His will. God has the right to use people as He sees fit to complete His plan of salvation.

Throughout the Bible, some people are spiritually hardened to fulfill some purpose of God. Throughout the Bible, some people are renewed by repentance. If we view the end from the beginning—which is way over our heads—God can make from the same rebellious lump of sinful humanity a justified and regenerated Christian totally surrendered to Jesus Christ, and at the same time a hopelessly lost person who refuses to surrender control to God.

The bottom line here is that ultimately, no one escapes the glory of sovereign God. We are all of the same lump. We all belong to God. The Bible points to total surrender to God or total rejection of God, as measured by God, as the only two possible human positions. All of the rest is mental noise that we make.

What if God . . . ? You can put everything we have learned after that. *What if God is sovereign? What if God is holy? What if all of God's attributes are holy—holy love, holy mercy, holy justice, holy anger, holy wrath (holy sense of humor)?* Each of these is an important point to contemplate.

What if God, who is willing and able to demonstrate His wrath and power at any time, has indeed let certain people live out their unrepentant destinies in time, while knowing beyond anything we can comprehend that they were "vessels of wrath prepared for destruction"? And what if He allowed all of that sinful history to unfold just to amplify the contrast between sin and His glory so that those of us who are "vessels of mercy, which He prepared beforehand for glory" would be able to deeply know "the riches of His glory" that we have received in salvation?

Paul's point: *What if He did?* What if it is as plain and straightforward as this language makes it? The mature Christian takes the teaching and grows with it. What if God is sovereign? What if God knows the end from the beginning? Deal with it, and be obedient here in time. God is not bound by our perception of His purpose, period. We have no control over God. Paul is pointing at total surrender to God through Christ. There is a tremendous letting go of control that has to take place to accept the word of God.

Here is where we stand in relation to God, the all-powerful sovereign God who has offered us a way home on His terms and on His terms only. These teachings are not given to confuse us; they are given to humble us and open us, to shatter our sense of self-righteousness and self-elevation. These teachings are given to stimulate reverential fear of God. Properly fearing God is the beginning of spiritual wisdom.

On the one side of reverential fear is the terror and dread of the anger and wrath of Holy God. It is a terrible thing for a lost person to fall into the hands of the living God. But for those of us who are saved by God, we can remember a time when the gospel of Jesus Christ caused us to be respectful of God—humbled, surrendered. That is all part of reverentially fearing God too.

And now, as we walk closer to Christ in obedience, these same teachings make us awestruck and worshipful. It's all part of being deeply, reverentially, appropriately fearful of God in the peace and joy we now know as His adopted children.

Our faith connects us to a place beyond the limits of time, a place beyond the time-bound polarizations of good and evil, a place of hope. We do not have to worry. God has got this; God has got us.

216

For I am convinced that neither death, nor life, nor angels, nor principalities, nor things present, nor things to come, nor powers, nor height, nor depth, nor any other created thing, will be able to separate us from the love of God, which is in Christ Jesus our Lord. (Romans 8:38-39)

This is right where we are supposed to be right now, stretched between time and timelessness, alive in Christ, growing in the grace and knowledge of our Lord and Savior, and resting in the sovereignty of God.

I LAY A STONE IN ZION (ROMANS 9:25-33)

Think about how angry some lost people get when you tell them about Jesus Christ and sin and salvation. Christ confronts the sinner, the sinner is offended by Christ and keeps stumbling around in the dark. When I reflect on how angry I used to get about the God I did not know, and about His Book that I had never read, I deeply understand what it means for Jesus to be "a stone of stumbling."

When I was lost, Jesus was a "rock of offense" to me. He was an offensive presence in my mind. Mention the name Jesus Christ to me back then, and you were in for a fight. I do not have that particular problem anymore. I am getting clearer and clearer regarding where I stand with God. I am a spiritually dull, sinfully weak man in absolute need of a Savior.

Left to myself, I will go into temptation over and over as the enemy has his way with me. The only real righteousness I can lay claim to is given to me by Jesus. It is not mine; it is His. I am just another wicked, sinful man saved by the grace of God. By the power of the Holy Spirit I surrendered; I let go. I took God at His word and let go of everything except Jesus. I put my faith in Jesus, and I am not disappointed. I belong to Jesus, and I am not ashamed of who I am; I am ashamed of who I was. Now I am in Christ and Christ is in me, and that is nothing to be ashamed of.

I still wrestle with sin, but now I know who I really am and where I am going. I know at a deeper level than I know anything else that following and serving Christ will not disappoint me. Jesus will not put me to shame; He is going to bring me home.

There is nothing new in time that ultimately matters. Cultures invest in different details, technologies expand and collapse, philosophical systems come and go, and here we are, two thousand years later, confronted with the same Christ and the same evil forces attempting to keep us in the darkness.

All that ultimately matters is where you stand with Jesus. He is either a "a stone of stumbling and a rock of offense," or He is the foundation of your faith.

THE WORD IS NEAR YOU (ROMANS 10:1-10)

Jesus Christ became a man. The perfect life that none of us can live has already been lived. The work is done. There is nothing we can do to get more truth than what has been revealed to us. There is no more truth needed than what has been revealed to us. There is nothing we can do to earn our salvation. The work is done. The written word is complete and sufficient; the living Word is complete and sufficient. Jesus said it on the cross: It is finished.

> *If you confess with your mouth Jesus as Lord, and believe in your heart that God raised Him from the dead, you will be saved. (Romans 10:9)*

To "confess with your mouth" is to give outward evidence of the inward condition of saving faith. To confess "Jesus as Lord" is to recognize Jesus Christ, the God-Man who died for your sin, as your Lord with total power and authority over your life. To "believe in your heart that God raised [Jesus] from the dead" is to have an understanding that goes beyond intellection of the meaning and significance of the resurrection as it relates to sin and salvation. To "believe in your heart" is to experience a supernaturally induced place beyond mere intellectual agreement. Intellectual assent, left to itself, is just another human work. Heart belief is a Spirit-fueled, deep inward trust and all-in surrender of the totality of one's being to Jesus Christ as your Lord and Savior. Anyone who meets these requirements "will be saved."

Heart faith is between you and God—God judges the heart. And only you and God know whether or not your profession of faith is true and acceptable to God, "for with the heart a person believes, resulting in righteousness, and with the mouth he confesses, resulting in salvation." Here is belief, righteousness, salvation—the theme of the letter to the Romans.

Paul is not presenting verbal confession as a second requirement for salvation after heart belief. Confession is the outward mental expression and evidence of the inner response of heart belief. It is two aspects of the Spirit-led experience of conversion. If you do these time-bound things, and timeless God (has judged, is judging, judges) your profession of faith to be true as He (initiates, oversees, responds) to the process, then God justifies you by your faith in Jesus Christ, and you are saved.

The focus is not on zealous spiritual seeking with faith as an abstract. The focus is on the object of our faith. We are not saved by a mystical, unknowable something; we are saved by faith in a Someone—Jesus the Messiah.

You must believe in the innermost depths of your being that Jesus Christ died to pay the sin-debt that you cannot pay, and that He rose from the dead to authenticate and seal the deal. And you must confess the reality of Jesus Christ as your Lord and Savior out into the world. You do these things in agreement with the Holy Spirit, and the result is salvation. You will be saved.

Real saving faith arises out of a heart stimulated by the gospel through the power and presence of the Holy Spirit. A Christian is someone who professes to live—and actually does live—in faithful submission to Jesus Christ, the Son of God.

ACCOUNTABILITY (ROMANS 10:11-21)

Most of the ancient Jews did the same thing lots of us do. They picked out the Scripture verses that they liked and built their entire theology around them. Taking verses out of context did the same thing to them that it does to us; they formed an incomplete and flawed understanding of God's plan for humanity. That led to an elevation of ritual and religious tradition over the Scriptures.

By selectively filtering the Scriptures, and by getting lost in their traditions, there are two truths in the Old Testament that the Jews had lost sight of. The first is that the only way a sinful human can be saved is by faith through the grace of God. Salvation by grace through faith is the foundation of the Torah, and the Jews had lost track of it. By the time of Saul, the idea of Messiah had been reduced to that of a time-bound military leader, a great earthly king who would lead armies of Jews to physically conquer the world. The Jews lost sight of the need for personal redemption and saw only the need for national vindication. They put their faith in their own works, idolized the Law, and became self-righteous.

The second reason the Jews rejected the Messiah was an outgrowth of the first. The Jews would not believe that they were in the same spiritual condition as the Gentiles. If the only way to God is by grace through faith, then anyone who has faith can be saved by grace—anyone. This was a complete dismantling of the works- and ritual-based Jewish religious tradition. Instead of humbling themselves before God and fulfilling their role as God's representatives to the lost world, the Jews had, for a long time, set themselves above the rest of humanity as the only people who could have a relationship with God. They could not and would not accept the teaching that we are all in this sin mess together and that without saving faith they were ultimately no better off than the rest of the lost world.

In Acts 22:21, as part of his testimony, Paul told the Jews about his mission to the Gentiles. "And [God] said to me, 'Go! For I will send you far away to the Gentiles.'" Here is the next verse: "They listened to him up to this statement, and then they raised their voices and said, 'Away with such a fellow from the earth, for he should not be allowed to live!'" The thought that Gentiles could be saved by grace without becoming Jews upset them more than the thought that they needed to be saved by grace. However they were receiving the gospel up to that point, when they heard about the inclusion of the Gentiles, they got so angry they wanted to murder Paul. They did not understand that the inclusion of the Gentiles was not fabricated by Paul during his ministry.

In Luke chapter 4, Jesus is preaching in the synagogue of His hometown, Nazareth. When He declared, "Today this Scripture has been fulfilled in your hearing" (Luke 4:21), the initial response was positive: "All were speaking well of Him, and wondering at the gracious words which were falling from His lips" (Luke 4:22). However, when Jesus reminded them of how God's blessings had been extended to Gentiles—specifically in Luke 4:25-27, referencing the widow of Zarephath and Naaman the Syrian— everything changed. "All the people in the synagogue were filled with rage as they heard these things; and they got up and drove Him out of the city, and led Him to the brow of the hill on which their city had been built, in order to throw Him down the cliff. But passing through their midst, He went His way" (Luke 4:28-30).

However receptive they had been to the gospel at first, they clearly did not understand that the inclusion of the Gentiles was not a new teaching that Jesus was revealing to humanity for the first time. When they heard about the inclusion of the Gentiles and the exclusion of the Jews, they got so enraged they hauled Jesus out of the synagogue and attempted to murder

Him. What was Jesus's response? "Passing through their midst, He went His way" (Luke 4:30). He left them.

In Romans 10:19 Paul's antagonist asks, "But I say, surely Israel did not know, did they?" Surely this is a new idea; surely the Jews could not have known. Surely they did not know about salvation by faith. Surely they did not know that God's mercy extended to the Gentiles. Paul replies with Old Testament proofs: "First Moses says, 'I will make you jealous by that which is not a nation, by a nation without understanding will I anger you.'"

Because of Jewish faithlessness and rejection of the Messiah, God has made them jealous by those who were not the chosen nation of God (that's all of us). By a nation that is spiritually stupid and spiritually foolish (that's all of us), God has angered the Jews. The Jews should have known, but they forgot who they were and what they were supposed to be about. Self-righteousness wrecked their understanding of faith, and pride sealed their rejection of the Messiah. Do not forget where we stand in this picture. We are the spiritually stupid and spiritually ignorant people that God has called to His purposes.

Paul continues from the Old Testament in verse 20: "And Isaiah is very bold and says, 'I was found by those who did not seek Me, I became manifest to those who did not ask for Me.'" Corporate Israel should have "found" Jesus Christ through correct understanding of the Scriptures. But Israel did not, so God sent the gospel to the Gentiles, "a [spiritually] foolish nation." And you can still see the prophetic result playing out today. Try preaching Jesus to orthodox rabbis and you will see jealous and angry Jews in fulfillment of Isaiah 65:1.

In verse 21 we here from Isaiah again: "[A]s for Israel He says, 'All the day long I have stretched out My hands to a disobedient and obstinate people.'" The Isaiah quote is from verse 2 in chapter 65, and it stretches across time. "All the day long I have stretched out My hands." God's timeless extension of grace remains constant across time. God keeps His word.

The prophecies clearly state that the majority of Jews were predestined to rebel—prophecies are prophetic. The prophecies clearly state that the Jews were willfully choosing to rebel—the prophecies have been authenticated by the human actions in time.

"All the day long I have stretched out My hands . . . to a disobedient and obstinate people."

Here is the rest of the Isaiah verse:

> ". . . *who walk in the way which is not good, following their own thoughts.*"
> (Isaiah 65:2b)

The Old Testament story of time-bound Israel is, for the most part, about "a disobedient and obstinate people" who, despite having the Scriptures, continually chose to indulge their own thoughts and words instead of following the word of God. And so, the gospel left Old Testament Israel and has moved from the Near East to the West and to the Far East—two thousand years of massive moments of the Holy Spirit and enormous amounts of conversions all over the world—and nowhere in church history to date do you see anything but a small remnant of Jews coming to Christ. Lots to ponder there.

There is no other way. All other spiritual paths are counterfeits. Jesus Christ is the standard, the saving faith of true repentance is the measure, and God, as judge of the heart, is the decider. There is no favoritism here. There is no cultural or national elitism.

So, who is elect, who is predetermined, who is predestined? We do not get to know. That information exists on the timeless, divine, sovereign side of the paradox; it is above our pay-grade as Cristians. In that sense, it is none of our business. We engage the gospel right here, right now. And on the time-bound side of the paradox, "Whoever will call on the name of the Lord will be saved."

Paul makes three time-bound assertions:

1. People can't call *on* Jesus Christ if they don't believe *in* Jesus Christ.
2. People can't believe *in* Jesus Christ if they don't have true knowledge *about* Jesus Christ.
3. People can't have true knowledge *about* Jesus Christ without biblical preaching in all of the forms it can take.

WHAT THEN? (ROMANS 11:1-10)

Is God through with Israel? No. Corporate Israel is spiritually asleep and under judgment while here and there a remnant of Jews become Christians. That is not happy news, especially for corporate Israel at the moment. But that is God's story, and we are to remain sober in our minds and stick to it.

When the Romans destroyed the Jerusalem temple in 70 AD, everything was either destroyed or carried away. Loud trumpets, huge cymbals, great bells, and the like—all specifically designed to make loud and joyful noises to God—were lost. After the destruction, musical instruments were banned from synagogue services. One of the reasons was that musical instruments suggested celebration and joy. Celebration and joy were officially mandated out of Jewish worship service.

In a traditional Jewish worship service, only the cantor sings, and the music is always mournful, lamenting, and in a minor key. It can be hauntingly beautiful in its own way, but it is sadness music—victim music. That has been the way of things in synagogue Judaism for almost two thousand years. They created a new tradition of sadness and institutionalized it to commemorate the sadness at the tail end of the old tradition.

There are now some synagogues that are bringing musical instruments back into their services in an effort to make things less depressing and off-putting for younger Jews. But the overall presentation is the same. If you ask why they do not make joyful music to the Lord, they tell you the story of the Temple. If you press them past that, you get more theology of sadness, some sort of dismissive answer, or just "I don't know."

The Jews as a corporate entity blew it so bad that God put them to sleep spiritually, and they are still in that "spirit of stupor" that Paul writes about. The Jews are lost. They are bound up in their allegiance to tradition. They study the Talmud and get lost in the extra-biblical meanderings of Jewish commentary. They have settled on a system of good works compensating for sin. Keep the Old Testament laws and customs, observe the festival days, and try to do more good than evil.

But behind the robes, the prayer shawls, the mournful lamenting, and the ritual readings, the Jews are imprisoned in a static and spiritually dead tradition that is an empty shell of what it used to be. Rabbis are now mystical curators of a God-less religious museum. And Jews are spending lifetimes wandering through those dead halls.

Jesus Christ took us to God, and, except for a remnant, the Jews went away from God. God cannot be controlled by religious scholarship or religious traditions. God's plan and pattern from the start has always been relational and revelatory. Jesus is only accessed through the direct revelation of salvation by grace through faith.

God is in control; you and I are not. The more we learn from the Bible, and the more we let that learning change how we think about things, the more that should be our default stance when confronted with all of the fears the enemy throws our way. God is in control, and His plan will unfold on His terms.

We tend to wring our hands and lament and worry about the future. One of the reasons we are given things like chapter 11 of Romans is to jar us out of that sort of thing. We are a people with hope for the future. We have a hope that makes sense out of the downward spiraling, time-bound mess called human history. Instead of worrying ourselves sick about this and that, instead of all of the little games we play to exert some degree of control over the people, places, and things around us, we should be rejoicing in our complete and total inability to control God or His plan for humanity.

Take God at His word. "God gave [Israel] a spirit of stupor," and He tells us why in His Book. The Jewish religious tradition is spiritually dead and a spiritual dead end. Real Judaism points to faith in the Messiah. And without grace, most Jews could not see the Messiah when He was standing right in front of them. And now, by the will of God, most of them still cannot see clearly. Take God at His word. God gave us the Messiah, and He tells us why in His Book. And without the grace of God, we cannot see Jesus clearly either.

What extra-biblical traditions are you trapped in? What part of your denominational structure is in the way of the revelation of Jesus Christ? Do you live in an "I don't know" place regarding sin and salvation? Do you know what to do regarding sin and salvation? Think on these things. Reflect on these verses, and apply them to your religious life. Then give thanks to God for the gift of unmerited grace. Without grace, even God's chosen people have nothing. If you have been justified by the grace of God, you have everything.

GRAFTED IN AMONG THEM (ROMANS 11:11-27)

God is not through with Israel. Part of the purpose of two thousand years of Gentiles getting saved is to make the Jews jealous for God. Paul's use of this time-bound motif of human jealousy reminds us that human action and response is important to God.

Gentiles study the Torah; Gentiles read the prophets; Gentiles celebrate the Messiah. And the Jew says, "Hey, that's my Torah. Those are my prophets. We are still waiting for the Messiah." The Christian reply is, "No. The Messiah came, your ancestors rejected Him, and you are still rejecting Him." And when Jews hear that, there is room in time for them to be jealous of us and want the Messiah. Those who respond to that conviction, they are the remnant. It is a slightly different version of the exact same thing that any lost person deals with when they hear the gospel of Jesus Christ. Corporate Israel is under judgment until the second coming, and there is room at the cross for the individual repentant Jew.

From one point of view in time, any given Jew, like anyone else, can be saved if their unbelief becomes belief, because salvation is all of God and God is all-powerful. From another point of view in time, one day, after Israel ceases to continue in their disbelief, God will graft them in again. From the sovereign side of the paradox, one day, God will wake Israel up, graft them in again, and they will cease to continue in their disbelief. Take those two points of view side by side and do not try to solve them against each other.

Paul's calling is to preach to Gentiles, but he knows that a remnant of Jews will be saved along the way, and he himself is part of that remnant. He does not speculate about how many Jews will be saved; he does not know that. He does not say, "Ah well, that's somebody else's job." His personal mission is to the Gentile nations, but his Christian heart bleeds for everyone, especially his "fellow countrymen." Paul does what he can with what he has been given. That is all any of us can do. We are here now. Paul did his part in salvation history, and we are to do our part in this phase of salvation history.

Do not elevate yourself above anyone else. You are running on faith, and the only reason you are here running on faith is because of God's extension of grace. Do not get lost in cultural Christianity. Do not make the traditional Jewish mistake. Even though Israel had the prophets, the writings, the Temple, and the Law, God did not spare those who did not have saving faith. Priests, popes, preachers, patriarchs, sacraments, rituals, traditions—none of those save. God did not spare the faithless of Israel. If you do not have saving faith in Jesus Christ, "He will not spare you either." The judgment of Israel stands as God's witness and warning to the Gentile nations. Do not be arrogant. Do not be spiritually foolish. Reverentially fear God. Work out your salvation with reverential fear and respectful trembling.

You cannot "continue in [God's] kindness" if you aren't "in God's kindness." You can't be in God's kindness if you are not in Christ and Christ is not in you. If you are saved, if Christ is in you, you *will* "continue in [God's] kindness." Otherwise, if you are not saved, and you are just ritually doing church while putting your faith in some denomination or institution instead of in the person and work of Jesus Christ, "you also will be cut off."

When people drop away from Christianity, they do not lose their salvation. In most cases, they just prove that they never had it to begin with. They do not "continue in [God's] kindness" because they never took advantage of God's saving kindness to begin with. They spoke words with their mouth that they did not believe in their unchanged hearts.

If you are saved, you are always saved because it's God who does the justifying. And your walk will prove that out as you "continue in [God's] kindness" (to use Paul's language). If you are not justified by God, no amount of self-righteous religious behavior, no amount of works, no amount of doing religious things at a building called "church" will save you.

A partial hardening has happened to corporate Israel. There is no salvation in Judaism. They are not on some separate but equal salvation track alongside Christianity. A remnant of Jews is being saved while God gathers those He calls from the Gentile nations. Things have to play out this way because God's word is true, and there is a future for Israel because God gave His word.

Accepting God at His word is central to the surrender of faith. None of this is subject to human will or whim. We are not in control. It has never been about us except in the limited context of time-bound history. It has always been about Jesus Christ. It will always be about Jesus Christ. Take God at His word. Get right with Jesus Christ, "otherwise you also will be cut off."

TO GOD BE THE GLORY FOREVER (ROMANS 11:28-36)

Things can look pretty messy from the time-bound view. So many crazy people, so many places and events. The unfolding drama of human existence can appear to be a chaotic, random, haphazard mess if you view it through secular histories. But if you view time through the Bible, what appears to be the complicated history of humanity gets reduced to the merely complex. The Bible then takes those time-bound complexities and places them on the foundation of the sovereignty of God.

The complex interactions of humans throughout time-bound history then fall into the same, predictable patterns playing out over and over again in context of God's eternal, unchanging purpose. What Satan tries to complicate—which is everything—God's plan for humanity simplifies. We call this plan the doctrine of God's eternal decree, and it runs consistently though the Bible from the beginning in Genesis until the end in Revelation. The Bible presents this singularly focused plan as the will of the timeless, divine, triune God playing out across time.

The books of the Bible collectively adhere to one storyline—that is, the creation of the universe, the presence of sin in the universe, the appearance of humanity in perfect alignment with God, humanity's fall from that alignment, and God's plan for bringing people back to alignment. The sixty-six books share one common theme—that is, God's holy wrath and holy anger over sin in context of His holy love for all of humanity. The sixty-six books share one common message: salvation and the return to complete and total alignment is available to anyone who turns away from sin and the ways of the world and turns back to loving God with all their heart, mind, soul, and strength. To turn away from sin and turn back to God on the basis of faith in the person and work of Jesus Christ is to repent.

This unfolding plan of salvation is the vehicle God has chosen to reveal His character and nature to humanity. And the focal point of this revelation is the God-Man, the Word made flesh, Jesus Christ. That is the big thing. But God's plan, by its nature, encompasses every little thing as well. Nothing in time is excluded from God's eternal decree. There is nothing, not even the smallest thing, that occurs in time that is outside of God's timeless plan. That is inherent in the idea of sovereignty.

So when you contemplate the implications of God's eternal decree, you will always be driven to one of two possible understandings: either God is absolutely sovereign over every time-bound event in the universe, or He is not. The very definition of sovereignty leaves no room for some kind of partial or qualified sovereignty.

This is the point of the biblical paradox. You have to go one way or the other with it. It is all-in or not-in. There is no middle ground. God's plan demands total surrender by way of a presentation that is foolishness to the Greek who seeks time-bound wisdom and to the Jew who seeks time-bound religion. Anything short of total surrender always results in wrangling with God in varying degrees of not surrendering.

The decree of God's sovereign plan does not allow for the time-bound notions of chance, luck, coincidence, or accident. Those are errant viewpoints generated by human minds stuck firmly in time. Everything that has happened, happens, and will happen in time ultimately serves to drive home the sovereignty side of the paradox and demonstrate the glory of God. As a world historian, this has been a difficult idea for me to reconcile in my time-bound studies of the major movements of human history. My mentor has been consistent since day one: "Keep praying, keep learning, surrender more." Biblical Christianity is not for the faint of heart.

For followers of Christ, everything that has happened, is happening, and will happen in our lives ultimately serves to drive us into a deeper awareness of where we stand in time in context of the glory of sovereign God. If you are not saved, you are God's enemy and God is your enemy. The Jews do not get a pass on the gospel. At this point in salvation history, a Jew without Jesus is in the exact same spiritual condition as a Gentile without Jesus: they are enemies of God.

Christians are not Israel. Christians are never called *Israel* in the New Testament. Israel is still Israel. We are called the church. God has called corporate Israel to salvation, and one day Israel will answer the call. The plan is straightforward—simple. God does simple. The saving promises made to corporate Israel will happen because God keeps His word.

Paul has made his case. These things are playing out this way "for your sake"—that is, you and me, the Gentiles. What appeared to Israel to be an impossible complication has been shown to be a straightforward expression of the gospel. Israel crucified their Messiah. God now offers the Messiah to us. What they meant for evil in time, God meant for good in His sovereignty. Israel got spiritually put to sleep for their disobedience with the result that we can be spiritually awakened in ours. That is a sobering point of contemplation.

The biblical presentation demands a response as it executes judgment. Each individual human response, or refusal to respond, results in either judgment to salvation or judgment to condemnation. There is no middle ground expressed or allowed for here. To respond with any of the varying degrees of time-bound rejection that everyone from atheists to lost churchy people indulge in results in judgment to condemnation.

Amen. That is how mature believers respond to God's plan. Amen—so be it. I surrender.

Can I intellectually explain time in context of timelessness? Yes. Does that mean that I have some degree of control inherent in my understandings? No. The models my mentor taught me are just models, pointers handed down from one generation to the next since ancient times. The intellectual plateaus we arrive at are nothing more than pointers into the mystery of God's holiness.

The focal point of a Christian life should not be the accumulation and organization of biblical facts and data in an attempt to arrive at a perfect time-bound systematized theology. Any form of time-bound Christian perfectionism is an affront to the holiness of God. A balanced Christian life is one given over to praying (all types), worship (with or without music), and immersion in the Bible. Biblical immersion should include both extended times of study and extended times of contemplative reflection. While these three disciplines can and should be engaged separately, for the mature believer they will regularly intertwine.

When I was at my second seminary and wrestling with varying systematic presentations, my mentor emailed me this: *The largest book in the Bible is a songbook, the book of Psalms. The largest book in the Bible is God's worship book. And it's all about worshipping Holy God.*

TOTAL DEVOTION TO GOD (ROMANS 12:1-2)

Paul is the ambassador of Christ and His authoritative representative—God is speaking through Paul's writings. Paul does not command us on his own personal authority; he authoritatively "urges" us to respond. We are to respond appropriately to the experience of God's mercy and to the authority of the gospel. We are to respond "by the mercies of God." Everything Romans has taught us so far is summed up singularly as the plural "mercies of God."

The section of Romans on practical life application begins with the truth of where we stand as Christians. God has done everything with regard to salvation; we have done nothing. Now that we have Christ, we have everything. We are not here right now to get anything else; we are learning how to live in a state of continually giving back to God. We want to be in such a condition of ongoing spiritual renewal that the Holy Spirit will put us on like a suit of clothes and use us in ways beyond our human limitations.

> **Paraphrase:** *Therefore, in light of all you have learned about the righteousness of God, on my authority as God's ambassador I urge you, in view of the mercy of God in action, to present the entirety of yourselves as continuous, ongoing sacrifices set apart as holy and acceptable to God, which is your reasonable, authentic, true worship. And do not immerse in or go along with this age where the world is dominated by sin and Satan, but apply yourself to progressing in spiritual change at the deepest level by the ongoing, Spirit-driven reprogramming of your moral consciousness and practical reasoning, so that you may discover so as to carry out what the will of God is, that which is good, acceptable to God and perfect.*

A MEASURE OF FAITH (ROMANS 12:3-8)

We are learning how to live in a state of continuously giving back to God. Because of our regeneration, we are able to discern and understand what is acceptable to God. The foundation of sound judgment in time is remembering where we stand in context of sovereign God. Whatever measure of faith we have, it is God who allotted it to us. We now have the Spirit-led ability to effectively apply ourselves to obedience. The Spirit is leading us in the process of sanctification, and we are to follow.

Our understanding of faith is only a measure of God's understanding. Acknowledging and embracing this humbling reality is the foundation for sober and sound self-assessment. When you are weighing your personal strengths and weaknesses, do not think more highly of yourself than you ought to think.

Saving faith is the common standard for all Christians. The standard of saving faith applies equally to everyone. The moment of salvation is personal, but Christian existence from the moment of salvation on is corporate. In this timeless sense—the most important sense—we are all equal in the body of Christ. While it is obvious that a wide range of personal abilities are distributed throughout the body, no one in the body of Christ is more important to God than anyone else.

I like the visible-invisible model. The physical appearance of Christianity in time is what we call the visible (institutional) church. That is the totality of the organizational structures that reasonably represent biblical truth. Even though the gospel is present in faithful institutions, these human-designed structures create the illusion of isolated groups of Christians at odds with each other in their diversity. But the real body of Christ is the invisible (actual) church made up of all of the justified, regenerate believers past, present, and future. Regardless of the institutional details, all supernaturally converted followers of Jesus Christ are "one body in Christ."

If you are saved, then we are all in this together. Do not act like you can separate yourself. I can no more walk away from the spiritually connected body of Christ than my foot could walk away from my physical body. The body functions best when all of the parts are healthy and doing their part. We are all responsible for active participation in the invisible body of Christ through some sort of visible action. This is the meaning of the priesthood of all believers. How did this biblical truth get so completely twisted in the institutionalized churches?

What happened can be summed up in the misguided observations of a guy named Eusebius. A long time ago, he put forward the idea that there are two Christian lives in time: the perfect life and the permitted life. Priests, bishops, monks, and nuns were leading the perfect life. Everyone else was living the permitted life.

By virtue of their position, church people were somehow defaulted to being holier than everyone else. They were thought to have a special connection with God that no one else could have. Everyone else was completely dependent on their priests and bishops to mediate their relationship with God. What the permitted life people did for an occupation was necessary, but they could never live the so-called perfect life of the professional ministry caste.

The Protestant reformers did away with most of the extra-biblical, sacramental, magic show stuff that had poisoned the church up to that point, but the basic idea behind the perfect life / permitted life model hung on and morphed into what many of us still do today. There is still a tendency for Christians to act like there is an essence division between "regular" Christians and those who are called into full-time vocational ministry. In this sense, the ghost of Eusebius is alive and well.

None of us have the right as Christians to sit back and watch the lost world go by. That is not the way of following Christ. The early institutional churches sold that nonsense to the world and then went about enforcing the model. It was wrong then; it is still wrong today. We serve in a wide variety of ways, but every Christian is supposed to serve. There is no biblical allowance for an uninvolved regenerate lay person. There is just the priesthood of all faithful believers justified and regenerated by God.

Humbly, prayerfully sort out what you can and cannot do for Jesus. When you have discerned the gifts you have, use them for the good of the body of Christ. We offer ourselves to God, and we offer ourselves to each other. One is the outgrowth of the other. God saved us to serve.

OTHERS-CENTERED LOVE (ROMANS 12:9-16)

We are supposed to love one another. But what kind of love are we supposed to love with? It is easy to love someone who is giving us something we want, or who makes us feel the way we want to feel, but if I am loving you because of what I am getting from you, I am expressing a worldly and self-serving love. There does not need to be any godliness present to love in this way. Jesus said that this kind of love is no big deal. Even lost people do it.

The love that the Bible teaches, the love that Jesus commands of His followers, is an outgrowth of who we are in Christ; it is an other-centered love. As Christians, we do not love because of what we get from others, we love because of what we have been given in Christ. Christian love exists because of who Jesus Christ is, and we can only manifest it because of who we are in Jesus Christ. Because of the work of the Holy Spirit in us, we can learn to love with no thought of what we are going to get in return. This is the selfless, self-sacrificial love modeled by Jesus in the Bible. We love not because of what we can get from each other, or what we want from each other; we love because of who we are in Christ.

There are a whole lot of people running around in churches insisting that their self-absorbed version of love is what the Bible is talking about, and they demand that the body of Christ love them the way that they want to be loved. When this sort of love dominates in a church, self-centeredness takes over, the biblical model collapses, discipling collapses, spiritual growth collapses. And any ministry efforts—if there are any ministry efforts—will be driven by worldly desires and not by Christ-centered hearts.

God will not bless a life powered by self-centered love. We are supposed to love one another the way that Christ loves us. To do this we must know what love in the body of Christ is supposed to look like. Christian love is an outgrowth of God's holy love. Genuine Christian love is a love without hypocrisy. A hypocrite is a phony, an actor hiding what they really believe behind a false face and empty words. Faking love is always bad. Smiling at someone and saying, "I love you!" while saying in your heart, *I don't like that person!* isn't just fake love—it is evil behavior. There is no Christian love in politically correct, inauthentic churchy behavior.

Paul tells us to abhor what is evil and hold fast to what is good. The evil in this verse is the hypocrisy of fake love. Paul tells us to abhor it, be disgusted by it, hate it. We are supposed to hate the behavior when we do it, not hate ourselves. We are supposed to hate the behavior when other people do it, not hate the person.

Real Christian love is a passionate love. Our spirits should crave alignment with the Holy Spirit. Our day-to-day stance should be this: *I will not let myself not serve the Lord. I am going to learn to love you with a holy love. I am going to learn to love you with an others-centered love.* But then I have to take it to the next level. *I am going to reach out to you and help you do better, and I am going to let you reach out to me and help me do better. Then you and I will keep each other going in our walks, and we will both be better equipped to make other disciples.*

Nobody serves the Lord in isolation. If you have the Holy Spirit in you, then you are a member of the body of Christ. If you are a member of the body of Christ, you are never alone. Alone is an illusion that the enemy creates to make you feel isolated from the body of Christ. But if you are saved, you are never alone, and you are never supposed to act like you can go it alone.

Christian love perseveres, it sustains, it lasts. Our faith is sustained by the Holy Spirit working in us and driven forward by our hope in the promise of eternal life. The interplay of hope and faith gives us the strength to be patient with each other when times get tough. Even when the circumstances fall far short of happiness, we do not surrender our joy. Always remember, there is a plan. There is a purpose to all of this. And followers of Christ are on the right side of that plan, come what may.

Christian love must have a practical aspect. When a brother or sister needs help, if you can help, help them. Large Christian churches will send tens of thousands of dollars to missions and denominational structures, and nobody checks to see if the person sitting next to them has enough to eat, or has enough money to properly clothe their children, or has a life situation they cannot handle.

Paul writes that not only are we to be hospitable toward each other, we are supposed to do what we can to help each other in tangible, practical ways.

It is not enough just to pray; sometimes you have got to put some physical or financial skin in the game.

At the same time, when we help a weaker Christian brother or sister, we have to be mindful of what kind of help they really need. Today, just as in the early church, there are lots of folks who prey on Christian sensibilities and always seem to have their hands out for the wrong reasons. In 2 Thessalonians 3, Paul makes it clear to all people claiming Christianity: If you won't work, you don't eat. We are not to encourage idleness in the body, and we are not to reward people who make no effort or who refuse to live within their means. Contributing to the needs of the saints also means knowing what kind of help not to give.

Remember the baseline: It is impossible to do any of this without Jesus. Jesus is the Way, the Truth, and the Life. Our minds, our bodies, our thoughts, our actions, our choices, are supposed to be focused on Jesus every day, all of the time. None of what Paul talks about in this passage can be accomplished on our own. And if we try to do it by our own efforts, by the force of our wills, that is the flesh, that is mechanical works.

These verses are not just instructions about how we are to live our lives in community. These verses describe a thoroughly transformed follower of Christ moving through the world under the power of God. Do not think of them as commands; think of them as promises to the faithful.

- Verse 9: If you love without hypocrisy, you won't be a fake Christian. If you are disgusted by evil, you'll stay away from all the evil stuff. You will be drawn to, and hang on to, the good things.
- Verse 10: If you devote yourself to manifesting authentic Christian love, you will treat others with true affection and be sincerely respectful of others.
- Verse 11: If you keep your (small s) spirit focused, and move in alignment with the (big S) Holy Spirit, you will find yourself excited about whatever you're doing in your life and ministry.
- Verse 12: If you are devoted to a prayerful life, you will be full of hope, even in the tough times, and you will persevere no matter what this life throws at you.
- Verse 13: If you are practicing Christian hospitality as a way of life, you will find yourself naturally drawn to taking care of the people God puts around you.
- Verse 14: If you practice loving through the lens of holy love, you will compassionately understand people who do not understand the

gospel message and bless them, hoping that they will one day have a relationship with Jesus before it's too late for them.

- Verse 15: If you love through the lens of Christ's holy love, you will be able to behave naturally and authentically in whatever situation you find yourself.
- Verse 16: If you genuinely understand where you stand in relation to Holy God, you won't be "wise in your own estimation," and you will manifest an authentic, natural humility.

If you have a living, breathing relationship with Jesus that you cultivate through regular immersion in prayer, worship, and the Bible, your life will naturally display Christian authenticity, and these things will shape you and happen. Selfless Christian love will not be something you work at doing, it will become a natural outgrowth of who you authentically are in Christ.

Serve the Lord by surrendering to the touch of the Holy Spirit every day and living in the reality of the corporate body of Christ. How do we do that? Stay focused on Jesus. Pray a lot. Leave time in your life for worship. Contemplate passages like this, and let the word of God sink into your bones. And then let Jesus love the world through you. Only Jesus can love the world the way God wants it loved. The amazing and exciting part of Christianity is that Jesus will do it through us if we obediently follow His will and way.

OVERCOME (ROMANS 12:17-21)

What about people outside of the body of Christ who do not like us or even hate us? If we respond to evil with evil, we lose our Christian witness; we lose our credibility as witnesses for the truth of the gospel. We are not to respond to evil by emulating evil. If we fight the fire of evil with evil fire, evil wins. When that dynamic happens, we allow ourselves to be motivated by evil thoughts, and the enemy then drags us down into evil behaviors. The embracing of evil is never right. We do right by the biblical standard, even when we are treated wrongly.

We know why they are embracing evil stuff. If they are lost, they are in Adam. Whether they know it or not, they are serving the wrong master, and they are prone to calling evil *good*. Since we know this, we can take a step back and respond to their evil with understanding. We know what they are up against because we have all been there; we all know what it is to be lost. We bless them with a heartfelt desire and prayer for their salvation—other-centered love. That does not mean respect them or trust them, just pray for them and mean it.

Before we act, we are to reflect on what is right and proper by God's standard and strive to be above reproach in the sight of everyone. Lost people are watching and will respond to our Christian witness—or lack of Christian witness. When they see some of us who claim to be Christian behaving as bad or worse than lost people, why would they want to hear us tell them about Jesus? At best, we appear to be hypocrites. At worst, we will come across as frauds and phonies.

We are to manifest what is right as a witness to all people by never meeting evil with evil. Retaliation is not the Christian way. We are not to live or behave that way. If you are in a situation where someone is stinging you with evil, and the only thing at risk is your pride, turn the other cheek. Do not fight evil with evil. Realize the evil for what it is, and do not become party to it by joining with it.

Lost people are under the power of the enemy whether they know that or accept it, but they are not the real enemy. We are fighting a spiritual war against spiritual enemies, and we are supposed to be reaching as many lost people as we are able. It is not always possible to be at peace with other people when they start manifesting serious evil, but we should default whenever possible to maintaining our Christian witness.

It is not for us to react to the lost world with wrath. That is God's prerogative. God is holy. All of God's attributes are holy. Wrathful vengeance is a power only God can wield without sinning. Never respond to the evil of others with evil thoughts or actions of your own. When humans are given over to wrath, it is never holy. Wrath is not an attribute that can ever be used by a human for the glory of God. Holy wrath is only of God, and only God has the right to express it.

Do not give yourself over to vengeful, wrathful thoughts. "[L]eave room for the wrath of God" by staying out of that dynamic. This does not mean that we are not allowed to get angry at the evil we see and experience. Christians are not called to be passive in response to evil. In Ephesians we are told, "Be angry and yet do not sin" (Ephesians 4:26a). Sin manifesting around you should anger and offend you at the deepest level. Go ahead and burn with a righteous anger born out of biblical wisdom and Spirit-filled discernment, but do not sin. Do not let your anger turn into vengeful wrath. "[D]o not let the sun go down on your anger, and do not give the devil an opportunity"

(Ephesians 4:26b-27). Rightly judge the sinful actions of others, but do not judge the sinner to condemnation either in thought or action.

To give yourself over to wrathful vengeance is to become a self-appointed judge, jury, and executioner of human souls. Remember where you stand—and where you used to stand—with God. Never hold an attitude of seeking revenge regardless of the circumstances. Evildoers, who are lost in Adam, are going to have it bad enough if they die in that condition.

The verse has nothing to do with self-defense, or defending your family, or church discipline, or courtroom proceedings under the law of the land. The verse is about not responding with wrathful, vengeful anger to evil that has been done to you or done toward you. No good can come of it. The evil response lowers the responder to the level of the person who initiated the evil. Responding to evil with evil, fighting fire with fire, is the way of the lost world, not the Christian way.

There are times for a Christian to pick up the sword and fight, but whoever lives by the sword by giving themselves over to wrathful anger will spiritually die by the sword. And whatever righteous expression they thought they were going to communicate with their self-righteous, wrathful anger will die with them.

"But if your enemy is hungry, feed him, and if he is thirsty, give him a drink; for in so doing you will heap burning coals on his head." This was not some radical new Christian teaching. The first two phrases are from Proverbs 25. The last phrase is Old Testament metaphor representing God's presence and judgment. Instead of responding with anger when persecution or tribulation comes your way, remember where the lost person stands with God. If they die lost, they are going to directly experience the wrath of Holy God as He judges them to condemnation. How does your puny expression of anger or limited ability to exact revenge compare to that? Just remember where you stand with God and how badly that person needs what you have.

"Do not be overcome by evil, but overcome evil with good." If you are authentically living in the peace of Christ, you will not "be overcome by evil" when tribulation comes. You will have Christian courage, a courage that does not need anger for fuel, and you will be able to "overcome evil with good." Show the character of Christ to the lost world. This not only leaves appropriate room for the wrath of God, it creates space for the convicting work of the Holy Spirit. This is practical Christian ministry as an outgrowth of authentic Christian ministry.

When verse 20 was written, fire was really important; fire was central to the survival of a household. Fires were tended so that even when the flames died, there would still be burning coals. In that time, if the fire went completely cold in your house at the wrong time, you were in serious trouble. If someone's coals went out, neighbor women would put coals into clay pots that they would carry on their heads and bring them to the house to rekindle the fire. The neighbors were providing them with the means of staying alive. If they did not share the fire, the other folks could die. This type of kindness is practical Christianity.

We bring the fire, but the fire is not us; Christianity is the fire we bring. This is at the heart of exercising Christian hospitality. This is why service to others is a high good. We metaphorically invite the lost into our homes where the fire of the Holy Spirit is burning bright and providing us with warmth and security. Christian fire is life-giving, and without it, they will perish. If we do not bring the fire, there is no way to win them to the kingdom of God.

Burning coals can warm you and your household, and they can also burn your house to the ground. If lost people mishandle the fire we bring, it will burn them up, and that is not our problem. We are just supposed to properly handle the fire and bring it to those in need. The lost world is supposed to sense the fire through us. This is the Christian life; this is it. We bring Holy Spirit fire with us wherever we go. God wants us to live out our salvation into the lost world. As we are going, we make disciples. We live to serve.

ESTABLISHED BY GOD (ROMANS 13:1-7)

The word translated here as "subjection" represents a willing act of obedience, a recognition of some type or degree of authority. It is the same word used in the passages that say to be in submission to your elders in the body, for wives to be in submission to your husbands, for children to honor your parents with obedience. In each case, these relationships are divine institutions ordained by God to keep order at all levels of human relationship.

In each case, there are times when the human end fails. Children become rebellious and disrespectful, husbands behave so badly that the one-flesh dynamic is damaged or broken, and church elders mess up so badly that they no longer qualify as leaders. Government leaders can and do implement rules and regulations that would compel us to do things that the Bible forbids. When that happens, we are not to be blindly, robotically obedient to secular authorities; we default to our Christian conscience and remain obedient to the Scriptures. But, barring rules or rulers who demand anti-Christian behaviors or actions, we are to willingly place ourselves under the governing authorities.

If the rule of law you live under does not violate God's Law, and the rulers are enforcing it reasonably, then the only reason to be afraid is if you know you are a law breaker. Be a good citizen; render unto Caesar what is Caesar's. And if you do not, and if you are punished for your crime, you brought it upon yourself.

The authority of government is supposed to be "a minister of God to you for good." Authority in the church body is supposed to be "a minister of God to you for good." Authority in the home is supposed to be "a minister of God to you for good." In almost all instances, if "you want to have no fear of authority," do your best to live out the Ten Commandments. And if the rule of law is being honored by the authorities, "it [will be] a minister of God to you for good." If you are being a good Christian, then you are honoring your family relationships—you do not murder or commit adultery, you are not stealing or lying, and you are doing your best not to covet anything other than God.

No passage in the Bible should be read out of context of its own book, and no book of the Bible should be read out of context of all of the rest of the books. Remember that as Christians we are still rooted in the Old Testament, and in the Old Testament there are two images of government:

1. Godly government is imaged as a tree. When authority is deeply rooted in godly principles, the result will be strong limbs yielding good fruit and protective covering. This is how things should be. Good authorities stabilize a society and prevent anarchy and the tyranny of the masses. Good authorities establish reasonable and necessary limitations as part of God's plan for humanity.

2. A government that moves away from God is imaged as a beast. A beast can be very powerful, but it has no conscience or morality; it

exists to serve its base impulses. A government that loses all sense of God is likened to an uncontrollable and dangerous beast.

Government in these verses is called "a minister of God," so there is an underlying assumption of good government in these verses. If the authorities are functioning reasonably well within the limits of the law, and you are functioning reasonably well within the limits of the law, then you have nothing to fear from secular authorities. But if you willfully, mindfully break the law of the land, there is always that sense of fearful dread—the fear of being caught and of the resulting punishment. And if that respectful sense of fear is not present when you bend or break laws, then you are either not paying attention, which is bad, or your conscience is badly broken, which is worse.

Good government is "a minister of God." Good governments are authorized by God to enact laws, enforce laws, and punish law breakers. Without good laws and a willingness to enforce those laws, any society will break down into anarchy. If a government is functioning properly and "you do what is evil, be afraid; for it does not bear the sword for nothing."

Capital punishment is installed in the Law of Moses. Certain aspects of the Law are now put away, but the Ten Commandments, among other things, are still in force. The sixth commandment tells us, "Do not murder." It does not say, "do not kill"—that is a faulty translation of the Hebrew text. No one at any level of society is ever authorized by the Bible to commit murder. But capital punishment is allowed under certain circumstances. Capital punishment for murder is established in Genesis 9:6: "Whoever sheds man's blood" (that's murder), "by man his blood shall be shed" (that's capital punishment). God is serious about all sinful behaviors, so in time, the punishment should fit the crime. And He is deadly serious about the sinful action of willful, mindful murder.

Side note: Several Hebrew scholars have told me that certain contextual, structural, and grammatical cues make this the only crime in ancient Israel where capital punishment had to be administered without any opportunity for repentance and lesser punishment. Other crimes were worthy of capital punishment, but the proper reading in all other cases is, "Surely they should be put to death, shouldn't they?" The only crime where capital punishment was demanded by God was premeditated murder.

When the rule of law is enforced in a society, reasonable people rightly submit to the law. An understanding of the consequences of breaking the law, and a desire not to face those consequences, is a normal part of that submission. When the rule of law is enforced in a society, criminals cannot freely roam the streets preying on the weak and the helpless. Even if they do not want to submit, the potential for swift and certain punishment can keep criminals in varying degrees of compliance.

Respectful fear of the law is a secondary reason for Christians to submit. First and foremost, we reverentially fear God, and our consciences are tuned to the convicting presence of the Holy Spirit. We live within the law of the land because God tells us to. We respectfully obey secular law because we reverentially fear God.

The Old Testament system of tithing thirty-some percent to theocratic Israel was put away at the cross. All Christian giving is what the Old Testament calls freewill giving. That is what the woman at the Temple that Jesus pointed out was doing. She had already paid her tax-tithes—they were required by Law of all Israelites. She then took the last money she had and put it in the freewill offering box. Paying your taxes to the government is our New Testament tax-tithe. Like the Old Testament system of tithes, it is not voluntary, it is mandatory—a matter of law.

To keep society functioning, we have full-time judges, police officers, lawmakers, and the like who are supposed to be "devoting themselves to this very thing"—the maintenance and support of a well-functioning and law-abiding society. To keep society safe, we have a full-time military who are supposed to be "devoting themselves to this very thing"—the protection of a well-functioning and law-abiding society.

And so, as members of this society, "Render to all what is due them: tax to whom tax is due; custom to whom custom; fear to whom fear; honor to whom honor." This is the practical application of verses 1-6. This covers direct taxes as well as indirect taxes like tolls and fees. In either case, pay your taxes. Protect yourself with a good accountant if you need to, but do not cheat. Cheating violates the eighth, ninth, and tenth commandments (which were neither abolished nor put away by Jesus).

Unless we are told to do something that directly violates the Bible, we are to be obedient as citizens. Civilizations and governments come and go, but the kingdom of Jesus Christ endures forever. And because we know this, Christians can rest in the sovereignty of God even if the civilization we find ourselves in becomes a beast.

One more thing: Do not engage in the art of selectively breaking minor laws because you know you will not get caught, or you are pretty sure you will not get caught, or you just do not like the law or see any sense in it. One of the simplest examples of this is the speed limit. I have never seen a speed sign that says, SUGGESTED AVERAGE SPEED. They all say, SPEED LIMIT. Every time you willfully, mindfully speed, you are willfully, mindfully breaking the (small *l*) law of the land. Who is being hurt by this? You are. You are creating sinful dissonance within yourself. An attitude of stretching laws as far as you can, or just flagrantly breaking them because you think you can get away with it, will build that way of thinking and living into your mind, warp your conscience, and damage your (small *s*) spirit. It is always a spiritual matter. All of Christian life is a spiritual matter. The (small *l*) law violation will always violate one or more of the Ten Commandments.

FULFILL THE LAW (ROMANS 13:8-14)

Owe nothing to your neighbor. Honor them by living right. Do good business, give good witness. Pay what you owe, and be true to your word. If you are a Christian, and you are out there cheating in business, not keeping your word, doing your best to look out for yourself and your interests at the expense of others, you have no authentic Christian witness.

The enemy will be all over you and use you to drive people away from the gospel. Someone may have heard the gospel, but then they witness bad behavior by someone who claims to be Christian, they sense the dissonance between God's word working on them and how God's word is not manifesting through that Christian, and the enemy gives them an easy out on conviction.

We are not to pander to lost people. We do not water down the gospel or just go along to get along. The love we owe is not the love of the lost world for the world. The love we owe is the holy love Christ has shown to us. This is ongoing. The extension of holy love is a Christian obligation. We are to treat our fellow humans with equity and fairness with God's Law as our guide. Yes, the Law was given to amplify sin. No, we cannot keep the Law good enough to earn salvation. But the Law itself is still holy and good. As Christians, we love Jesus, which means that He has accepted us into His holy love. And since we love Him, we want to keep His commandments.

Saved people have been brought back into a relationship where we can love the Lord our God with the entirety of our being. We do not just intellectually assent to the first and foremost commandment; by the grace of God we exist as expressions of the foundational principle of God's Law. Everything in our Christian lives stands on this foundational idea. We love God because He first loved us, and then we reflect that love of God out into the world around us.

A Christian authentically extending the love of Christ is fulfilling the second foundational point of the Law while giving evidence of fulfilling the first foundational point. The highest human expression of holy love is the ongoing fulfillment of these two commandments in the sanctifying walk of a Christian.

Every day, the final salvation of Christ's return is nearer to us than when we first were saved. And nobody, from Paul's time to now, knows how much nearer. Regardless, if you are alive at the second coming, and you are lost, you will be judged to condemnation. If you die before the second coming, and you die lost, you will be judged to condemnation. The difference for us as Christians is that we know we are watched. We know there is accountability for our lives in time.

People who indulge in sinful "deeds of darkness" do not believe anyone can see them. They believe that if they are not seen, and they do not get caught, then they are not accountable for who they are and what they do. Christians know better. We have a relationship with the living God, and we are accountable.

We put on the armor of light. We put on the protection of the righteousness of God. The armor of light is both defensive and offensive. We are to defend ourselves against the deeds of darkness while actively extending the gospel into the world. That does not mean that bad things cannot or will not happen to us in time. It means that whatever happens to us in time, God has got us beyond time.

That is the hope of our faith. We live in the light of Christ, and we are going home to the light of Christ. Let us live like Jesus is standing right next to us every day in everything we do—because He is. We are to be accountable to the supernatural reality of the faith we share.

We are not to live "in carousing and drunkenness, not in sexual promiscuity and sensuality, not in strife and jealousy." There is the underlying history of every Godless civilization there has ever been. While the governments and leaders are doing the things that historians tend to write about in detail, there is always a culture given over to varying degrees of carousing, substance abuse, sexual perversion of all types, and strife and jealousy between people. And while that dynamic is always playing out in the majority of humanity, all throughout history God has sent those who "lay aside the [sinful] deeds of darkness . . . put on the armor of light . . . [and] behave properly as in the day." And now, that is us. We are to behave in a manner appropriate to our calling. We have been released from the darkness and brought into the light. We are not to retreat to the darkness and engage in sinful and un-Christian conduct.

Because of who we are in Christ, we "put on the Lord Jesus Christ, and make no provision for the flesh in regard to its lusts." Our part is to be careful with our witness. The presence of sin is still everywhere, and all of us have the potential and capacity to go into temptation in an instant. So "make no provision for the flesh" by mindfully "putt[ing] on the Lord Jesus Christ" every day. "Love the Lord your God with all your heart, and with all your soul, and with all your mind," and then you will be able to "love your neighbor as yourself."

The ancient Jews were supposed to know this. But long before the incarnation of Christ, the Jews had split into several camps over how they should relate to the Romans and the Greeks—to the lost world. The Zealots wanted war. Their answer to dealing with the Romans and Greeks was to destroy them on the battlefield. The Herodians decided that the best answer was to go along to get along—be in the world and of the world. No sense in upsetting the secular world. The Sadducees divorced themselves from the difficult issues we confront when sovereignty meets time. They stuck their theological heads in the sand with regard to sovereignty and embraced a sort of Jewish humanism. The Pharisees dialed in on the Law to the exclusion of people. The lost world was irrelevant. All that mattered was studying, interpreting, and enforcing God's Law and getting lost in Jewish history. The Essene answer was to go out into the wilderness, focus on God, and ignore the lost world. Each one of those positions has repeated itself over and over in the New Testament church.

But the Bible says to the Zealot, *Do not make lost people the enemy in your heart, even if they make you their enemy.* The Bible says to the Herodian, *Do not go along to get along. You are set apart for God; live and act like it regardless of the secular consequences.* The Bible says to the Sadducee, *Do not shy away from the supernatural, spiritual reality the Bible presents, even if it makes you or someone around you uncomfortable.* The Bible says to the Pharisee, *This is a living faith. It is about the people of God, not just the things of God.* The Bible says to the Essene, and to all the rest of them, *Followers of God are to go and make disciples of all nations. As we are going, wherever we find ourselves, we make disciples.*

We are to be salt and light in the world. By our spiritual example, we are to make the lost hungry for God, and then we bring them the light of Christ.

THE STRONG AND THE WEAK (ROMANS 14:1-23)

We are not dealing with doctrinal issues in these verses. We solve those issues by going to the relevant Scriptures. We are also not dealing with things like intentional moral sin and church discipline here. We are addressing behaviors and beliefs that are not specifically revealed from Scripture— things where we have some degree of license in the life details.

In Paul's time, the churches he dealt with were a mix of all kinds of cultures and ethnicities. You had people coming together from lots of different nations and trying to live together as one body in Christ. The lesson is delivered in context of food. On one side of things, you had the Gentile converts. Food as a religious idol, and food offered to idols, had loomed large in their pre-Christian lives. And even though they were being taught about the falsehood of all that, many of them still wrestled with eating foods that may have been involved somewhere along the way with some pagan idol or pagan ritual.

On the other side, you had the Jews. They had never bought into the varying Greek and Roman systems. Food was food and was not affected or changed by ritual offerings to false gods. On the Jewish side, many of them were still wrestling with how to handle the Old Testament dietary laws as Christians, which was causing another kind of social mess. The result was culturally charged sub-groups pairing off against each other and destroying unity over what turns out to be non-essential details.

The first thing Paul does is establish a contrast between the actual believers who are weak in faith and actual believers who are strong in faith. Both groups are dealing with convictions about what faith in Jesus Christ allows and prohibits in their lives. But the groups are not on equal footing. The weak in faith are spiritually immature Christians. Their knowledge and understanding has not matured. The presentation insists that the best sanctifying result is to move from weakness in practical faith to strength in practical faith. The weak Christians here are not weak because they are vegetarians. They are weak because they are afraid of magic pagan meat. They are running on superstitions and not Scripture. For the strong Christian, do not go to the pagan service and participate in the ritual meal. But if you go to the market and there is some leftover meat on sale, have a steak and enjoy it.

There were also weak in faith Jewish Christians in Rome who still felt obligated to live by Old Testament dietary laws. The majority Gentile Christian population had never lived under Old Testament dietary rules and regulations and were mentally free from that stuff.

What does this lesson mean for us? Application crosses into things like dancing, having an alcoholic drink with dinner, how much and what kind of make-up is appropriate, how you think you—and usually everyone else around you—should dress in or out of the assembly. These verses deal with all of the areas of Christian life that the Bible either does not specifically address at all, specifically addresses in a way that is affected by time-bound historical context, or addresses in a more open-ended way than some of us are comfortable with.

There is a general call to unity here. That means that the type of weakness described here does not refer to core issues of salvation. The passage assumes that everyone involved is saved. The baseline is this: there will always be weaker and stronger Christians in terms of biblical understanding and spiritual wisdom. Stronger Christians are charged here to work with the errant opinions of weaker Christians without judging them to condemnation and without being too quick to judge them to separation.

Whether weak or strong, we are dealing with servants of Christ. That is the constant; that is the baseline. God has already judged to salvation (and, of course, there must be solid testimonial evidence by the biblical standard of salvation that God has indeed accepted them—a different issue). God has passed ultimate judgment. Now we are supposed to work together from our varying points of strength and weakness to honor the relationship we have with God through Jesus. The foundation is a relationship with God through Jesus. The non-revealed details of day-to-day practical Christian life are then downstream of salvation.

As far as tradition-based differences are concerned, Paul's answer is plain: You do not have to do what that other group is doing. Whether your church tradition likes it or not, most ritual issues are matters of preference, nothing more. If you want to have your congregational meeting on Sunday, have it on Sunday. If you want to have it on Thursday, have it on Thursday. If you want to meet for worship and the reading of Scripture every day, knock yourself out. Leave them alone to "be fully convinced in [their] own mind[s]."

Consider this: As Christians, how much of our lives are to be devoted to the glory of God? All. How many of our decisions are supposed to be outgrowths of our devotion to God? All. How many of our actions in time should give glory to God? All. You will have a lot less trouble with the details of your faith if you attend to the essence of your faith. Anchor your walk in the example of Jesus and be strong; the devil is in the non-revealed details.

"But you, [weaker Christian] why do you judge your brother?" Why are you getting hung up on some extra-biblical thing that you may not even correctly understand to the point that you are judging your fellow Christian to condemnation over it? "Or you again, [stronger Christian] why do you regard your brother with contempt?" So you have figured out that you can have a glass of wine with your dinner to the glory of God. Why do you use your understandings as the standard for looking down on your brothers and sisters? No believer has the right to cast doubt on the salvation of a fellow believer over non-revealed or non-salvific issues.

Each one of us will have to give an account of our lives directly to God. We are supposed to be engaging this foundational truth every day and living as reflections of it. All of our lives are to be devoted to the glory of God. All of our decisions are supposed to be outgrowths of our devotion to God. All of our actions in time should give glory to God. These are practical instructions in time, and they are simple. If you attend to the essence of your revealed faith, you will be a lot less likely to get snared in the non-revealed details of your life. Do strive to see things clearly through the biblical lens. Do not make spiritual or traditional non-essentials hills to die on.

These verses focus mainly on the responsibilities of strong believers. Other places in the Scriptures deal with what to do when weak believers go too far in their behaviors. Be careful, strong believer. Unless something really needs attention, leave people be. Do not condemn yourself publicly as a Christian jerk even if you are in the right. Building up and strengthening weak believers takes time, patience, and lots of love. This strong believer / weak believer presentation is essential church stuff.

Know that we are not talking here about biblically revealed issues regarding morality and ethics. We are not to form opinions about biblically revealed moral and ethical truths; we are to absorb biblical truth and obey. If we love Jesus, we will want to keep His commandments. The things plainly stated in Scripture are to be obeyed. Do not drag that discussion into chapter 14 of Romans.

This section of Romans is about managing your personal convictions where there is no revealed biblical rule. We are talking here about real Christians who ruin churches over personal opinion, over personal likes and dislikes—people who ruin churches over things so non-essential that the Bible either mentions them only in passing or does not even mention them at all.

Most Christians overly invested in denominational traditions take it upon themselves to fill in all of the non-revealed areas of Christian life with a bunch of extra-biblical rules, rituals, and requirements that they pursue with more zeal than the revealed word of God.

Paul goes to the heart of it: part of loving your neighbor as yourself, when you are dealing with non-revealed areas of Christian life, is to leave people be. Outside of doctrinal essentials, live and let live. In Christian non-essentials, leave people be. What they are doing is none of your business.

Keep your mind on Jesus Christ. What do you think you are going to experience when you are glorified by God? Do you think it will look like any of this time-bound churchy stuff? Not hardly. Focus on the essentials of your faith. Pray—a lot. Worship God passionately. Immerse yourself in the Bible. One foot in time, one foot in timeless sovereignty. Live from there.

STRIVE TOGETHER WITH ME (ROMANS 15:1-21)

An attitude of compassionate care does not imply pandering to those who are in direct violation of Scripture. At the same time, weak believers are still justified believers and should share in Christian fellowship. Strong believers are not to isolate themselves from the larger body of Christ in an effort to create a personally pleasing Christian environment. In the body of Christ, the whole is more important than the parts. The individual point to consider is this: your Christian walk is not supposed to be about what is best for you; it is supposed to be about what is best for the body of Christ.

Give yourself over to the grace of God. Be of the same mind—a mind focused on Jesus Christ, a mind devoted to living out the gospel and glorifying God. Then, when someone walks into your assembly, they may see a wildly differing bunch of believers, but they will sense the power and the presence of the Holy Spirit unifying your assembly "to be of the same mind with one another according to Christ Jesus," and they will experience us "with one accord . . . with one voice glorify[ing] the God and Father of our Lord Jesus Christ."

"Therefore, accept one another, just as Christ also accepted us to the glory of God." It does not say "put up with." Verse 7 does not say, "Therefore, put up with one another, just as Christ also puts up with us." Assuming saving faith on both sides, the barrier between the strong believer and the weak believer has been broken by Christ's ministry. Both are justified, and both exist for the glory of God.

Only God can "fill you with all joy and peace," and only the power of the Holy Spirit can cause you to "abound in hope." These are not abstracts. These are not just propositional truths. These are experiential realities of real Christian faith. The forward-looking hope of our faith in Jesus Christ, driven by the power and presence of the Holy Spirit indwelling us, is supposed to be the all-consuming focus of our lives every day.

The personal experience of salvation immediately ushers the new believer into the corporate reality that is the body of Christ with all of the rights and responsibilities that we have been learning about. Each of us is the offering and the priest at the same time. Each of us is entrusted with the Scriptures. Each of us is a temple of the Holy Spirit and at the same time a caretaker of that temple.

Ministry, sharing the gospel with the lost world, can seem daunting. Just remember: apart from Christ, you can do nothing. Do the things you are supposed to do, and the Holy Spirit will get you out of your own way and use you in ways that will transcend any scripted program you can come up with. In all cases, regardless of the specific details, "As you are going, make disciples of all the nations" (Matthew 28:19a).

If you lose this outward-radiating sense of what Christianity is and is supposed to be doing, you lose your identity as a Christian church. If sharing the gospel takes a back seat to mechanically doing church, more often than not the church turns in on itself and becomes self-absorbed and self-reverential. The result of this will be a church that exists to serve itself. Regardless of the details, the end result is always the same. Instead of the church body conforming to the image of Christ, Christ is conformed to the image of whoever is exerting the most control over the institutional church.

PAUL'S TRAVEL PLANS AND A PRAYER (ROMANS 15:22-33)

Priorities. There are places Paul wants to go and people he wants to see. But he has his priorities straight. Paul will not go until God "green lights" him. And he will not stay in Rome any longer than he is supposed to. That is a level of spiritual clarity and Spirit-driven relationship that I want. It does not matter what my job is; I want the clarity to know I am where I am supposed to be, and I am doing what I am supposed to be doing for the kingdom.

The Bible tells you to do things. The Bible tells you a lot about how to do those things. Nowhere does the Bible teach that you can give glory to God by attempting to do those things under your own power. Any biblical commandment is the will of God and makes no assumption that, left to ourselves, we can keep it.

Christianity is supernaturally powered, or it is not biblical Christianity. Nothing real is happening in Christian ministry unless the Holy Spirit is moving and hearts are coming under supernatural conviction. We are the conduit that God uses to connect time-bound humanity to timeless, divine sovereignty, and God tells us to use prayer to keep that connection front and center in our lives.

Anybody can join a denomination and mechanically do church. Nobody can influence God or cause the Holy Spirit to manifest and move with mechanical behaviors or rituals. Nobody can cause the salvation of a lost person based solely on skillful apologetics, or intellectually profound teaching, or emotionally charged preaching. The Holy Spirit of God moves through our ministries, or we have got nothing. What we want to see are lost people supernaturally converted into followers of Christ, not intellectually assenting lost people mechanically doing church.

"Now I urge you, brethren, [for the sake of] our Lord Jesus Christ and by the [holy] love [given by] the Spirit, to strive together [united] with me in your prayers to God." That is the baseline for how Christians get things done. Do not get hung up on non-essential matters; know the difference between essentials and non-essentials. Stay focused on what is important.

"Now the God of peace be with you all. Amen."

Part 2:

THE LETTER OF JAMES

INTRODUCTION:

THE LETTER OF JAMES

T he Letter of James is generally addressed to all Christian Jews living in various Gentile nations. These Jewish Christians were experiencing intense persecution and discrimination from the larger unconverted Jewish populations. Due to this, many of these Jewish Christians were shying away from publicly living out their faith in Christ.

James is in some ways similar in style to Proverbs in the Old Testament. There are over fifty direct commands in the five chapters. Behavioral directives follow one upon the other throughout the letter, often without clearly defined connections to each other. The letter is mainly focused on the day-to-day aspects of Christian conduct and does not directly establish any core doctrines of the Christian faith. James teaches us about practical Christian living and deals with the question, *What makes a godly person?*

COMMENTARY:

THE LETTER OF JAMES

1:1 Address and Greeting

1:1 James, a bond-servant [bond-slave] of God and of the Lord Jesus Christ, to the twelve tribes who are dispersed abroad: Greetings.

Most ancient letters opened in this way. This style indicates that James is writing a letter, not a theological treatise or a short story. If the James who wrote this letter is the half-brother of Jesus, why doesn't he mention it in his introduction? James knew that his family relationship to Jesus through Mary gave him no authority as a Christian leader. Only his spiritual relationship to Jesus mattered. So he introduces himself as "a bond-servant [bond-slave] of God." The Roman bond-servant surrendered his will to his master and served with no regard for self; only death could break the bond. The Hebrew indentured servant voluntarily became the permanent bond-slave of a master he loved and respected. By identifying Jesus as his Lord in parallel with God, James acknowledges that Jesus the Messiah is equal to God.

> "the twelve tribes"—The original Israelites were divided into twelve tribes descended from the twelve patriarchs.

The expression "dispersed abroad" literally translates as "scattered in the Diaspora." Both the Assyrians and the Babylonians had in the past conquered Israel and taken most of the tribes of Israel into exile. *Diaspora* had much earlier become a catchall term to describe all the nations outside of Palestine where Jewish people were living. James uses the language of the older Jewish dispersion to address the Jewish Christians who have been dispersed from the Jerusalem area because of persecution, as recorded in Acts 11:19. James also may be using Diaspora imagery to describe Christians as those who live in the time-bound world currently dispersed from their true heavenly home.

All of the Jewish Christian recipients of the letter would have known the identity and status of James, the head of the church at Jerusalem. The chief elder of the Jerusalem church wrote a pastoral letter to the scattered members of his flock. There would be no need for any more detail about his identity.

1:2-4 The Trials of Sanctification

1:2 Consider it all joy, my brethren, when you encounter various trials.

In verse 2, James moves from greeting directly to exhortation. By placing the issue of trials this prominently in the letter, he establishes that the spiritual difficulties they were experiencing form the main reason for writing the letter.

> "my brethren"—When used in this spiritual sense, the word "brethren" includes men and women.
>
> "Consider it all joy"—The expression suggests the intensity of the joy, not that joy is the only thing being experienced.
>
> "various"—any and all kinds of suffering that Christians can be exposed to in this fallen world
>
> "trials"—(GK) *peirasmos:* (1) an outward trial or process of testing; (2) the inner trial of temptation to sin

In this verse, to encounter "*peirasmos*" means to encounter the process of trials with the understanding that all spiritual trials have the potential for temptation to sinful immersion.

James does not tell you to be happy "when you encounter various trials"; he tells you to "consider it all joy." That does not mean that Christians are supposed to go through highly charged difficulties like grinning idiots. Personal happiness is not necessarily spiritual joy, and, for the mature believer, spiritual joy does not depend on personal happiness. James also does not suggest that the ultimate mature Christian response to trials should be nothing but joy. We just remember where things stand in relation to Holy God, where we now stand with Holy God, and then consider whatever is happening with all joy. We rest in the sovereignty of God and the security of salvation despite our circumstances.

James works from the premise that God brings trials into a believer's life for the purpose of sanctification and that the desired spiritual growth results when a believer responds properly to the trial. Trials, when properly understood, should be an occasion for authentic rejoicing.

> **TIME-BOUND:** "Consider it all joy" in no way means or implies "be happy about it."

1:3 . . . knowing that the testing of your faith produces endurance.

> "testing"—(GK) *dokimion*: the process of using heat to refine silver and gold; in this usage, the heating of faith in the crucible of suffering to refine away impurities
>
> "testing of your faith"—the refining and purifying of faith that already exists; not, a test to determine whether or not faith exists
>
> "knowing"—The joyful baseline reaction comes from the knowledge that however things appear in time, God is using the trial to make us stronger Christians.
>
> "endurance," "perseverance"—(GK) *hypomone*: to bear up while remaining under
>
> "the testing . . . produces endurance"—As Christians, we develop the mental and spiritual strength to intentionally remain faithful to God by exercising our faith in time-bound trials.

For something to be refined, it has to already exist. This "testing of your faith" is then the refining and purifying of a faith that already exists—not a test to determine whether or not faith exists. We are put through trials to develop the mental and spiritual strength we need to do our parts in the family relationship we have with God.

> **TIME-BOUND:** Through the heat and trials of suffering, we learn to intentionally remain faithful to God by exercising our faith in time.

Through the heat of trials and suffering, we learn to intentionally remain faithful to God by exercising our faith in time.

Go to the sovereign side of the paradox. Since God is sovereign, there can be no such thing as chance, luck, coincidence, or accident. Those are human-created ideas that imagine us in a closed universe system with no supernatural outside control. Those are ideas that attempt to shut out the paradoxical nature of our time-bound relationship to our timeless God.

> **TIMELESS:** Since God is sovereign, then from the sovereign viewpoint, any and every trial we encounter is an act of God.

Every trial is intentionally delivered to force a believer to a cathartic point where they must either lock down harder on trying to control their day-to-day existence or deal with what's happening while "considering it all joy" and offering it all up to God. That also means coming to and having all sorts of unpleasant understandings about where we stand in time in relation to sovereign God, and then trusting deeper in the Lord instead of leaning on those understandings.

So then, anything and everything that has happened to you in your Christian life has been allowed to happen by God in order to put you through the trials of testing that He wants you to go through whether you like it or not. Think on that and all of its implications.

As believers, we are bound to a life of testing. Jesus Christ wants His followers humble before Him and on the path of sanctification, and He is going to do what it takes to humble and sanctify His followers. In the trials of God's testing, we get to find out who we really are in time as opposed to who we think we are. Life becomes God's word and God's truth contrasted against our perception of God's word and God's truth.

Know that when things get really crazy in the world, the bottom line is that God is testing and refining your faith—not for Him, for you. Spiritually mature Christians "[c]onsider it all joy" when encountering any and all kinds of suffering, knowing that the testing of faith produces spiritual endurance.

1:4 And let endurance have its perfect result, so that you may be perfect and complete, lacking in nothing.

> "perfect"—(GK) *teleios*: mature, complete
>
> "perfect result," "complete work"—the ultimate goal of the testing of faith; all aspects of the ideal Christian character fully developed and matured

Trials only benefit the believer if they are responded to the way God intends. "Let endurance have its perfect result" by getting out of your own way and letting God lead your life. You let it happen in the course of faithful movement through trials; you let it happen in the course of works. You cannot make it happen by your works.

This perfect result has nothing to do with how we hold the idea of perfection in the English language. This verse cannot mean that we are to achieve sinless perfection in this lifetime. As just one example, we are warned in 1 John,

> *If we say that we have not sinned, we make Him a liar and His word is not in us. (1 John 1:10)*

Perfectionism is an affront to Holy God.

In the Gospel of Matthew, Jesus told His disciples, "[You] are to be perfect, as your heavenly Father is perfect" (Matthew 5:48). If you are careless with the English here and ignore the Greek, then this verse gets interpreted as, "You are to be [perfectly holy], as your heavenly Father is [perfectly holy]." That can then morph into all of that "little gods" nonsense. "Perfect" is an acceptable but incomplete translation of the Greek word in this verse. "Mature" is an equally acceptable and equally incomplete translation. But if you plug that in, then in the Gospel of Matthew Jesus is saying, "[Y]ou are to be [mature] as your heavenly Father is [mature]." That does not get it in Matthew because maturation implies a process of degree, and sovereign God does not go through a process of maturation.

The original word also carries the idea of "complete." So we have *perfect*, *mature*, and *complete*. We are left to work with the verse in light of these three shadings of the original word in context of everything the Bible teaches about sanctification. "And let endurance [in testing] have its [perfect, maturing] result, so that you may be [perfectly mature] and complete, lacking in nothing [spiritually]." This represents the ideal state of a spiritually mature believer who is satisfied to live in Christ every day, regardless of what the world offers or throws at them.

Note that this passage has nothing to do with the securing of salvation by works.

> **TIMELESS:** Can sovereign God—who judged and continues to judge my heart when I placed my faith in Christ, who declared me "not guilty" based on everything that Christ did and on nothing that I did except surrender by faith—justify me, and then by testing me find out later that He got it wrong? No.

Christians who persevere by faith under trials prove out in time what God has already established beyond time—that they have been blessed and favorably accepted by God. Those who think they can do things pleasing to God under their own power cannot. And God is showing that to them with each passing trial.

> **TIME-BOUND:** Works do not work for salvation; they work through salvation for the purpose of sanctification.

Those who know they cannot please God under their own power are learning to trust in the Lord more and more with each passing trial while considering it all joy in light of where we are going. Christians moving through the trials of time by this standard will find themselves progressively "lacking in nothing" in terms of spiritual integrity.

Whether or not this ideal, mature, and complete Christian character can be fully attained in time by God's standard, Christians are to settle for nothing less.

1:5-12 The Crown of Life

1:5 But if any of you lacks wisdom, let him ask of God, who gives to all generously and without reproach, and it will be given to him.

Wisdom is the central theme of the Old Testament book of Proverbs. For James, spiritual wisdom is a practical matter in the tradition of the Proverbs. The wisdom he is writing about only comes from the Lord: "For the Lord gives wisdom; from His mouth come knowledge and understanding" (Proverbs 2:6). And this wisdom only develops through a surrendered relationship with the Lord: "The fear of the Lord is the beginning of wisdom" (Proverbs 9:10). Spiritual wisdom is the means for discerning and living out the will of God (Proverbs 2:10-19, 3:13-14, 9:1-6).

Keep to the context of the lesson:

> **Amplification:** . . . *if any of you lacks [insight into the trials you are dealing with], let Him ask God.*

> **Amplification:** . . . *if any of you lacks [insight into what God is doing], let Him ask God.*

If you ask, God will not reproach you for asking. The wisdom you need to deal with whatever you are going through will be given to you. When you ask God for the wisdom to deal with a particular situation, God will not scold you for not having enough wisdom to deal the situation. God wants you to ask; He wants you in prayer all the time, about anything and everything.

> "generously"—(GK) *haplos:* Most English Bibles translate *haplos* as "generously" or "liberally." Those translations partially work, but they do not deliver the full meaning of *haplos. Haplos* also carries the idea of integrity, sincerity, and the simplicity of singular focus.

> **Amplification:** . . . *if any of you lacks wisdom, let him ask of God, who gives [wisdom] to all [with sincere and singularly focused integrity] and [who does not reproach].*

Verse 5 supports a central theme of sanctification in the letter of James: Christian spiritual integrity. James emphasizes God's singular intent to generously give us what He knows we need, not necessarily what we want and think we need. The wisdom we are supposed to be seeking is the wisdom of God—the wisdom to exist the way God designed us to exist.

Spiritual wisdom forms a buffer against the presence of sin and guides us on the path of sanctification. The spiritually wise are "lacking in nothing."

1:6a But he must ask in faith without any doubting.

James is writing to Jews who are now Christians. The verse is not about having faith contrasted against having no faith; the opposite of faith in this verse is doubt. When we pray for help, we "must ask in faith without any doubting."

God gives (with sincere and singularly focused integrity). That is our model. We must ask for things with singleness of intent—singular focus on God, not on self. God answers prayers on the condition of His standard of faith. When we pray for help, we do not just ask in faith—"[we] must ask in faith without any [spiritual] doubting."

Paul uses the same word in chapter 4 of Romans:

> *Without becoming weak in faith [Abraham] contemplated his own body, now as good as dead since he was about a hundred years old, and the deadness of Sarah's womb; yet, with respect to the promise of God, he did not waver [doubt] in unbelief but grew strong in faith, giving glory to God. (Romans 4:19-20)*

259

Paul knew from reading Genesis that Abraham had doubted God's promise at least once. Paul's point is the overall consistency and intensity of Abraham's faith, not that Abraham never wrestled with doubt. Likewise, in this letter, James is not teaching that prayers are only responded to when a believer has perfect faith, but that God is looking for spiritual integrity a faith that asks for things in alignment with God's will and word.

> **TIME-BOUND:** We must ask in faith without creating any distinctions, without arguing within oneself, without any inner division or wide swings of inconsistencies of attitude toward God.

Verse 6a reflects the teaching of Jesus in Matthew 21:

> *"Truly I say to you, if you have faith and do not doubt, you will not only do what was done to the fig tree, but even if you say to this mountain, 'Be taken up and cast into the sea,' it will happen. And all things you ask in prayer, believing, you will receive." (Matthew 21:21-22)*

When we ask for something in faith, we are supposed to be in the business of conforming to Christ, becoming more Christ-like. We are not supposed to lust after things of the world and pray to God for them like He is some sort of faith-powered cosmic vending machine. The prosperity gospel is perverse. It opposes and derails sanctification. We cannot grow spiritually by the standards of the world. There is no wisdom of God in that path; there is no way to ask God in faith to satisfy our worldly lusts and longings.

Both James 1:5 and Matthew 21:21-22 are used by the "health and wealth" "prosperity gospel" preachers to claim that God will give you anything you want if your faith is strong enough. But the "all things you ask in prayer" of Matthew 21:22 is conditioned by God's standard of what belief is and what constitutes spiritual doubt throughout the Bible. And the "ask of God . . . and it will be given" in this letter is clearly conditioned by verses 6, 7, and 8.

1:6b . . . for the one who doubts is like the surf of the sea, driven and tossed by the wind.

The faith "of the one who doubts [in this way]" is like the surface of the sea—never constant, always shifting and changing with the winds of the moment.

COMMENTARY: THE LETTER OF JAMES

1:7 . . . for that man ought not to expect that he will receive anything from the Lord.

A person with verse 6 faith should know better than "to expect that he will receive anything from the Lord."

1:8 . . . being a double-minded man, unstable in all his ways.

> "double-minded"—(GK) *dypsychos:* double souled; James invents a new Greek word to express an Old Testament Hebrew concept: spiritual schizophrenia.

The double-minded doubter argues within himself about God, creates inner division in his attitude toward God, and therefore does not pray with spiritual integrity or singleness of God-honoring purpose. At any given moment, the double-souled doubter is either asking for wisdom from God with one side of his heart or embracing the ways of the world with the other.

Here are some examples of mild to moderate *dypsychos* that we all deal with:

- God is in control . . . except when I decide to be in control.
- God is sovereign . . . and I walk around every week worrying about what is going to happen next.
- Instead of praying a blessing on someone, I wish them "good luck!"
- God's hand is moving purposefully in everything . . . but I refuse to see it. I observe things and say, "Wow, why did that happen?" or, "Wow, what a crazy coincidence."
- I reverentially fear God . . . except when I am more afraid of something or someone in the world.

Ratchet all of those up to their extremes, and you have a double-minded believer—a two-souled believer, a spiritual schizophrenic.

Verses 6-8 are not about the inevitable intellectual doubts that occasionally arise with regard to misunderstanding or wrestling with this biblical detail or that one. The phrase "unstable in all his ways" represents an ongoing state of schizophrenic division of the human soul that is constantly causing wild faith swings. If you are living this way while claiming to be a Christian, you are "unstable in all your [spiritual] ways."

Here is an Old Testament contrast:

They speak falsehood to one another; with flattering lips and with a double heart they speak. (Psalm 12:2)

How blessed are those who observe His testimonies, who seek Him with all their heart. (Psalm 119:2)

The person who is given over to putting one foot in with God to get what he decides he wants from God, while keeping one foot in the world to get what he decides he wants from the world, "ought not to expect that he will receive anything from the Lord, being a double-minded [spiritual schizophrenic], unstable in all his ways."

Prayer results are not achieved through personal prayer power or super-human expressions of faith; God is not a cosmic vending machine with prayer as the currency. The power of faith exists only in relationship with God. For prayer to yield results in time, it must align with the will of God.

1:9 But the brother of humble circumstances is to glory in his high position.

"the brother"—any male or female member of the family of God

"humble circumstances"—overlooked or looked down on by the world; oppressed by the world

"glory in," "take spiritual pride in," "boast about God in. . . ."

Paraphrase: *But followers of Christ who are overlooked, oppressed, or looked down on by the world are to glory in and boast about what God has done for them through Jesus Christ.*

Strong believers use whatever trials God throws at them to grow closer and closer to God.

1:10 . . . and the rich man is to glory in his humiliation, because like flowering grass he will pass away.

"rich man" (verse 10) is a modifier of "brother" (verse 9) in parallel with "humble."

"humiliation"—(GK) *tapeinosis:* lowness, low estate, be made low, (verse 10) spiritual humiliation causing one to recognize and lament their sinfulness

Amplification: *But the brother [in Christ] of humble circumstances is to glory in his high position; and the [brother in Christ who is a] rich man is to glory in [what God has done to him in his spiritual humiliation].*

James tells the poor person, *When you are tempted to feel insignificant and powerless because of how you are judged by the world's standards, instead glory in and boast about God and what He has done for you through the person and work of Jesus Christ. Ultimately, your time-bound circumstances do not matter. You will pass from this world soon enough.*

James tells the wealthy person, *When you are tempted to think too much of yourself because of your worldly wealth and status in this world, remember spiritual humility and boast instead about God and what He has done for you through the person and work of Jesus Christ. Ultimately, your time-bound circumstances do not matter. You will pass from this world soon enough.*

1:11 For the sun rises with a scorching wind and withers the grass; and its flower falls off and the beauty of its appearance is destroyed; so too the rich man in the midst of his pursuits will fade away.

As for man, his days are like grass; as a flower of the field, so he flourishes. When the wind has passed over it, it is no more, and its place acknowledges it no longer. (Psalm 103:15-16)

Do not [be awed] when a man becomes rich, when the [glory/wealth] of his house is increased; for when he dies he will carry nothing away; his [glory/wealth] will not descend after him. (Psalm 49:16-17)

All flesh is grass, and all its [loveliness/constancy] is like the flower of the field. The grass withers, the flower fades, when the breath of the Lord blows upon it; surely the people are grass. The grass withers, the flower fades, but the word of our God stands forever. (Isaiah 40:6b-8)

TIME-BOUND: A rich person dies just as surely and finally as a poor person dies, and in both cases everything of the world is left behind.

1:12 Blessed is a man who perseveres under trial; for once he has been approved, he will receive the crown of life which the Lord has promised to those who love Him.

"a man"—(GK) *aner*: stylistic equivalent to (GK) *anthropos*: a person "crown"—In the time of James, in that part of the world, the image of a crown as a laurel wreath given to winners of athletic contestants would have come to mind more readily than the headpiece worn by kings and queens.

And every man that striveth for the mastery is temperate in all things. Now they do it to obtain a corruptible crown; but we an incorruptible. (1 Corinthians 9:25 KJV)

Everyone who competes in the games exercises self-control in all things. They then do it to receive a perishable wreath, but we an imperishable. (1 Corinthians 9:25)

TIME-BOUND: "once he has been approved"—once God is done testing a believer in time

TIMELESS: "crown of life"—the reward of eternal life

TIME-BOUND / TIMELESS: "those who love [God]" = those who are saved

Once we go through all of this, and our salvation, which is already secured by God, is proved out in time before the world, "we will receive the crown of [eternal] life which the Lord has promised to those who love Him." When did God promise you the crown of life? When He justified you at your conversion based on the person and work of Jesus Christ.

Do not fear what you are about to suffer. Behold, the devil is about to cast some of you into prison, so that you will be tested, and you will have tribulation for ten days. Prove yourself faithful until death, and I will give you the crown of life. (Revelation 2:10)

Blessed is a man who perseveres under trial. (James 1:12a)

Amplification: *A [person] who perseveres under [God's] trial . . . is [proven] blessed.*

If you are saved, "consider it all joy" as God tests and refines you. Run the race God puts before you. Once God is done testing you, you are done in time, you die in time, and after your death you receive the crown of life. That is what the Lord has promised to those who have turned away from the world and turned back to God with all of their heart, soul, mind, and strength—which is the same as saying that is what "the Lord has promised to those who love Him."

James is showing us the reality of a Christian living out timeless, eternal saving faith in the time-bound world of day-to-day life. Trials are not accidents; trials are purposeful. They are tests given to break our dependence on our own power. They are tests designed to drive us into humble submission before God. Those of us with saving faith know that faith is real at the deepest level we can know anything. We then strengthen spiritually in time as we see faith being proved out before ourselves and humanity as we persevere through trials and testing God is putting us through.

Real saving faith will prove itself out in time.

1:13-18 God Doesn't Tempt

1:13 Let no one say when he is tempted, "I am being tempted by God"; for God cannot be tempted by evil, and He Himself does not tempt anyone.

Verse 13 transitions from testing to temptation. In verse 12, God promises blessing on a Christian who "perseveres under trial." Verse 13 then establishes that every trial carries with it an inner temptation to sin.

> "God cannot be tempted by evil"—(GK) *apeirastos*: "God is [unable to be tempted]."

If you are contemplating God's sovereignty, you can argue in a human way that since God is all-powerful, and since nothing can happen that He does not know about and allow to happen, then He is in fact the one causing everything that is happening in the universe. This thought process then makes God the creator and ultimate causal agent for sin. But that would be an abuse of the sovereignty paradox and an improper time-bound thought. God's sovereignty cannot be evaluated or fully understood through the lens of time or time-bound logic. Teachings on sovereignty are not given to us for that purpose.

God allows trials; God brings trials—but "He Himself does not tempt anyone." Temptation is an impulse to sin, a desire to sin. Since God has no desire to sin, He cannot be viewed as causing the desire to sin in humanity.

James is dealing with the practical aspects of Christianity playing out in time and writes from that standpoint. A trial is a test of faith. For many Christians, it is all good and fine to praise God when the sun is shining and there is money in the bank. But when God ratchets up the trials, and things seem to be spiraling out of control from the perspective of time, lots of sunshine Christians fall apart. Then, instead of calmly asking the spiritually discerning question, *Why is God testing me this way?*, misunderstanding skews the trial and the question becomes a challenge: *Why is God doing this to me?* The double-minded often ratchet it up to, *I won't worship a God who will let this happen.* In all cases, it is Proverbs 19 kicking in: "The [spiritual] foolishness of man ruins his way, and his heart rages against the Lord" (Proverbs 19:3). That type of Christian needs to come to grips with the letter of James.

Every test carries with it an inner temptation to sin stimulated by the sinful human longing for what God has forbidden, but salvation has broken the power of sin over us. A lost person can say, "The devil made me do it"; a Christian cannot. All a Christian can say is, "The devil suggested it, and I went along."

> **TIMELESS:** God is sovereign. He is beyond time, all-knowing, all-seeing, all-powerful.

> **TIME-BOUND** question: Then how can we make willful, meaningful decisions in time and be held accountable for them?

> **TIME-BOUND / TIMELESS** answer: Because God says we can.

And so we pray, "Do not permit us to go into temptation" (Matthew 6:13a).

As we go deeper into the Scriptures, as we go deeper into the mystery that the sovereignty paradox intentionally creates for us, we are ultimately being tested to "trust in the Lord" while not "leaning on [our] own understandings." The verse does not say, "do not have any understandings." All throughout the Bible we are challenged to grow in spiritual wisdom through our ever-increasing biblical understandings. Those types of understandings inform our faith, but they are not our faith. The foundation of faith is in trusting in the Lord. Everything else rides on that.

God's testing never has the purpose of inducing sin or weakening faith; He is testing us to refine our faith and prove ourselves to the world in time. The blessing of perseverance from verse 12 demands that we overcome the temptations that rise out of trials.

1:14 But each one is tempted when he is carried away and enticed by his own lust.

"lust"—lustful desire, the human longing for what God has forbidden

The temptation to sin comes from our own sinful natures joining with the presence of sin around us. The outer trial we are put through is not the inner temptation to sin. Sin takes place "when he is carried away and enticed by his own lust." God is absolutely sovereign, and James makes it clear that each of us is personally responsible for our personal excursions into sinful behaviors. The presence of sin remains around us, but salvation has broken the power of sin over us.

TIME-BOUND: Each one of us moves from trial to temptation "when [we are] carried away and enticed by [our] own [lustful desire]."

None of this is about whether a person is saved or not. Those distinctions are made in other books of the Bible—not here. James is presenting the reality of the post-conversion sanctifying process. We are being refined through testing and trials. One result of this testing should be a deep and intuitive knowing that sin is separation from God. Christians in the process of sanctification should deeply, intuitively, and by experience know that indulgence in sinful living is a kind of spiritual death.

1:15 Then when lust has conceived, it gives birth to sin; and when sin is accomplished, it brings forth death.

This verse spells out the active process and the consequence of responding to temptation.

Temptation is the superficial attractiveness of sin enticing our inherent desire toward evil. If you go into temptation instead of resisting it, the union of the external presence of sin and the inner lust of the person "gives birth to sin." At this point the temptation becomes sin in the person.

Therefore, ongoing experiences of temptation do not indicate a person who is not on the sanctifying path. Spiritual maturity is not defined by the amount of temptation we deal with but by how often we go into it. As we mature, the power of temptation should have less of a hold on us.

Sin is separation from God. Indulgence in sin is spiritual death.

> *Now therefore, O sons, listen to [wisdom], for blessed are they who keep [wisdom's] ways. Heed instruction and be wise, and do not neglect it. (Proverbs 8:32-33)*
>
> *For he who finds [wisdom] finds life and obtains favor from the Lord. But he who sins against [wisdom] injures himself; all those who hate [wisdom] love death. (Proverbs 8:35-36).*

1:16 Do not be deceived, my beloved brethren.

Verse 16 is a transitional phrase. Looking back to verses 13-15, "Do not be deceived beloved followers of Christ," God is never tempting you to do evil. Looking forward to verses 17-18, "Do not be deceived beloved followers of Christ," God is the source of "every good thing given and every perfect gift."

1:17 Every good thing given and every perfect gift is from above, coming down from the Father of lights, with whom there is no variation or shifting shadow.

God is called the "Father of lights," the "[Father of all, the giver of] lights." This is God as the creator of all heavenly bodies. The phrase "coming down from the Father of lights" represents God's ongoing care for the world. James then employs two ancient astronomical terms in this verse to make his point about God's nature. "Variation" is the orderly yet constantly changing movement of all celestial bodies. "Shifting shadow" can be read, "shadow due to change," referencing the orderly yet always changing phases of the moon—the constant variation of day and night.

Everything in God's creation is ordered according to God, yet always shifting and changing with the seasons. Unlike everything in the universe box, God is constant; God does not change. In the midst of a complex universe, the diagnostic application for our lives is simple: Satan cannot give us anything that is spiritually good for us. If something really is a "good thing" in our lives or a "perfect gift" by God's standard, it is from God—it can only come from God.

1:18 In the exercise of His will He brought us forth by the word of truth, so that we would be a kind of first fruits among His creatures.

There is an old Jewish morning prayer that recognizes God as the creator of the heavenly lights and then God as the redeemer of His people. Jewish Christians at the time of James would have been aware of the creation context inherent in "Father of lights" and "word of truth." James presents the ancient images in a new Christian context:

> "the word of truth"—the instrument of God's salvation
>
> "first fruits"—early Christians (in this context)

Salvation "by the word of truth," "in the exercise of [God's] will," establishing the existence of the first Christians in time serving as "a kind of first fruits among His creatures," is the preeminent example of "every good thing given and every perfect gift . . . from above, coming down from [God] the Father of lights, with whom there is no shifting [of intention or integrity]."

When you were saved, God brought you forth from the spiritual womb by the gospel of Jesus Christ. And for someone else at some point, your witness and testimony will be a first fruit for their conversion. And you do not get to know when or where that will be happening in your life. So, in the spirit of James, and for the sake of the lost people God places around you in your life, behave yourself.

1:19-27 Doers of the Word

1:19 This you know, my beloved brethren. But everyone must be quick to hear, slow to speak and slow to anger.

> **Amplification:** *"This you know [from the Scriptures, so take note]."*

The expression "my beloved brethren" is used three times in this letter to shift topics. James is going to move off of the "word of truth" theme for two verses and then pick it up again in verse 21. This verse restates an old wisdom literature principal. Here are five examples from Proverbs:

> *When there are many words, transgression is unavoidable, but he who restrains his lips is wise. (Proverbs 10:19)*
>
> *He who despises his neighbor lacks [heart] sense, but a man of understanding keeps silent. (Proverbs 11:12)*

The one who guards his mouth preserves his life; the one who opens wide his lips comes to ruin. (Proverbs 13:3)

He who restrains his words has knowledge, and he who has a cool spirit is a man of understanding. (Proverbs 17:27)

Even a fool, when he keeps silent, is considered wise; when he closes his lips, he is considered prudent. (Proverbs 17:27-28)

James does not tell us we should never be angry. He tells us to be "slow to anger." Sin in all of its manifestations should not only bother us, it should upset us, make us righteously angry, fill us with righteous indignation—whether it's our sinful actions or someone else's. But that is as far as we are to go with it.

Tremble [with anger], and do not sin; meditate in your heart upon your bed, and be still. (Psalm 4:4)

Do not be comfortable with sin. Do not get intellectually or emotionally numb to your sinful actions or anyone else's. Be angry, but do not let your anger escalate beyond the indignation of righteous anger.

Be angry, and yet do not sin; do not let the sun go down on your anger, and do not give the devil an opportunity. (Ephesians 4:26-27)

Amplification: *Be [slow to righteous anger], [so that you] do not [go into the] sin [of mean-spirited, malicious, or prideful anger]; do not [nurse or brood] on your anger, [so as not to] give the devil an opportunity [to exert his influence].*

In verse 19, James introduces a "tongue" motif that will move through the rest of the letter (1:26, 3:1-12, 4:1-3, 4:11-12, 5:12).

1:20 . . . for the anger of man does not achieve the righteousness of God.

Bring the "slow to anger" idea into verse 20:

Amplification: *. . . for the [unbridled] anger of man does not [produce behavior that is pleasing to God].*

Amplification: *. . . for the [unbridled] anger of man does not [bring about what God requires of his people].*

There is a time and place for righteous anger and righteous indignation, but unbridled anger is sinful and makes a person slow to hear clearly and quick to speak unwisely. As part of the process of sanctification, we learn to keep the emotion of anger under control, "for the [unbridled] anger of man does not achieve the righteousness of God."

1:21 Therefore, putting aside all filthiness and all that remains of wickedness, in humility receive the word implanted, which is able to save your souls.

"Therefore" ties "receive the word" in this verse back to "word of truth" in verse 18. There is a similar presentation in 1 Peter:

> [F]or you have been born again not of seed which is perishable but imperishable, that is, through the living and enduring word of God. For, "All flesh is like grass, and all its glory like the flower of grass. The grass withers, and the flower falls off, but the word of the Lord endures forever." And this is the word which was preached to you. Therefore, putting aside all malice and all deceit and hypocrisy and envy and all slander, like newborn babies, long for the pure milk of the word, so that by it you may grow in respect to salvation. (1 Peter 1:23–2:2)

New believers are reminded of the new spiritual life they have received through the word of God and are then challenged to put away their old sinful ways and live out biblical truth in their day-to-day lives.

> . . . the word implanted, which is able to save your souls.

In several places in the New Testament, the verb *save* and the noun *save* refer to the final deliverance from sin and death at the return of Christ.

TIME-BOUND / TIMELESS: For James, salvation at conversion and ultimate salvation at the second coming are a package deal, with sanctifying obedience in time as the connecting point.

Amplification: *The "word implanted [which has saved you at your conversion], is able to save your souls [at the second coming]."*

God has saved you. You have the word that God implanted in you, which is able to save your soul. Now, put aside all of the filthy old behaviors of your sinful past, steer clear of the abundance of remaining wickedness around you, and humbly be receptive to the work of the word in your heart.

1:22 But prove yourselves doers of the word, and not merely hearers who delude themselves.

You have spiritual access to a deeper understanding of the Bible after conversion; you do not suddenly achieve perfect understanding of God's will at conversion. The image of salvation as the implanted words of Scripture is surrounded in this letter and throughout the Bible with admonitions to study and learn the Scriptures and put them into practical use. Salvation, as the supernaturally implanted word, is how you are now able to do that, and regeneration, as the supernaturally implanted word, gives you the desire to do that.

> **TIME-BOUND:** There is no contrast or conflict here between the importance of doing the biblical word (the practical application of obedience) and hearing the biblical word (immersion leading to understanding).

> *While Jesus was saying these things, one of the women in the crowd raised her voice and said to Him, "Blessed is the womb that bore You and the breasts at which You nursed." But [Jesus] said, "On the contrary, blessed are those who hear the word of God and observe it." (Luke 11:28)*

If you do not or will not immerse in the Bible, how will you know what it commands you to do? If you claim to be a Christian because you have heard things about sin and salvation, but you do not have the inner desire to immerse in the biblical word and be obedient to it, you may be running on head faith and deluding yourself—you may have heard the biblical word but not received it. James is pointing at lost people claiming to be saved while deluding themselves. They have heard biblical things, but they have not received what James calls "the word implanted."

If your soul has been saved because by faith you received the supernatural word of God implanted in you, your faith must and will play out in time in authentic practical obedience. That is the proof to yourself and the world that you are doing the biblical word and not just deluding yourself by doing church.

> *The one who says, "I have come to know [Jesus]," and does not keep His commandments, is a liar, and the truth is not in him; but whoever keeps His word, in him the love of God has truly been perfected. By this we know that we are in [Jesus Christ]: the one who says he abides in Him ought himself to walk in the same manner as [Jesus] walked. (1 John 2:4-6)*

TIME-BOUND / TIMELESS: Justification does not exist without regeneration, and the result of regeneration will always be some amount of sanctification in time.

"Therefore everyone who hears these words of Mine and acts on them, may be compared to a wise man who built his house on the rock. And the rain fell, and the floods came, and the winds blew and slammed against that house; and yet it did not fall, for it had been founded on the rock. Everyone who hears these words of Mine and does not act on them, will be like a foolish man who built his house on the sand. The rain fell, and the floods came, and the winds blew and slammed against that house; and it fell— and great was its fall." (Matthew 7:24-27)

TIMELESS: If saved . . .

TIME-BOUND / TIMELESS: . . . always saved.

TIME-BOUND: Believe and abide in Christ.

If saved, always saved. Believe and abide in Jesus Christ.

1:23-24 For if anyone is a hearer of the word and not a doer, he is like a man who looks at his natural face in a mirror, for once he has looked at himself and gone away, he has immediately forgotten what kind of person he was.

The original word translated here as "natural" is itself translating the word *genesis*. *Genesis* translates literally into English as either "beginning" or "existence." Genesis as "beginning" is never used in the Bible to represent the original spiritual condition of humanity. The immediate context suggests the meaning in the verse to be "existence." So why translate it as "natural"? Why not just go with the literal meaning and render the sentence as, "he is like a man who looks at his [existence face] in a mirror"? I like it better that way to get to the meaning even if the wording is unusual or seems a bit clumsy. These are the types of decisions translators wrestle with as they try to get these ancient texts into our ears in ways we can understand.

"look"—(GK) *kataneo*: contemplate, consider carefully

The person "looks . . . in a mirror." This is the process of moral self-reflection. This was the most common usage of the mirror metaphor in James's time. There is also a subtle underlying theme of the limits of self-guided introspection.

> **Paraphrase:** *Once he is done looking at himself in this way, he will immediately forget what he has seen.*

> **Amplification:** *For if anyone is a hearer of the word and not a doer, he is like a man who [contemplates] his [existence] in a mirror; for once he has [carefully considered] himself and gone away [back into the world], he has immediately forgotten what kind of person he was [shown to be].*

The hearer of the biblical word who does not do the word looks at his existence, contemplates things, and goes about his life without changing and conforming to the word. This idea of spiritually forgetting who we are is incredibly important. Romans 1:28 can be rendered, "And just as they did not see fit to have God in knowledge any longer, God gave them over to a depraved mind" (Romans 1:28a).

> **TIME-BOUND:** It's part of the doomed condition of lost humanity that we forget what's important.

The person who forgets only hears or reads the Bible on a superficial level; what they read or hear has no lasting effect on their soul. Whatever they intellectually remember from exposure to the Scriptures, they "immediately forget" in their soul—they have not been changed spiritually.

The Israelites were constantly warned not to forget about what God had done for them:

> *Moses said to the people, "Remember this day in which you went out from Egypt, from the house of slavery; for by a powerful hand the Lord brought you out from this place." (Exodus 13:3a)*

> *[T]hen watch yourself, that you do not forget the Lord who brought you from the land of Egypt, out of the house of slavery. (Deuteronomy 6:12)*

> *It shall be a tassel for you to look at and remember all the commandments of the Lord, so as to do them and not follow after your own heart and your own eyes, after which you played the harlot. (Numbers 15:39)*

> *You shall remember all the way which the Lord your God has led you in the wilderness these forty years, that He might humble you, testing you, to know*

what was in your heart, whether you would keep His commandments or not. (Deuteronomy 8:2)

To remember Scripture in this context is to contemplate it in such a way that it makes a lasting impression on both the mind and the heart.

1:25 But one who looks intently at the perfect law, the law of liberty, and abides by it, not having become a forgetful hearer but an effectual doer, this man will be blessed in what he does.

"looks intently"—(GK) *parakypto*: consider carefully, inspect curiously out of interest, bend down to look closer

James was well-schooled in the Law of Moses. He now views it through the risen Christ and calls it "the perfect law, the law of liberty." This "perfect law" of verse 25 is the same as the "word" in verses 22 and 23 and the "word of truth" in verse 18. The doer, the Christian who has been supernaturally regenerated, is the "one who looks intently at the perfect law, the law of liberty, and abides by it." To believe in Christ is to abide in Christ. You can only abide in Christ if you have saving faith in Christ. Abiding faith and saving faith are inseparable. It is more than just hearing the biblical word; you have to be supernaturally transformed by God. That is what it is to be saved, to be justified by God, to be regenerated by the Holy Spirit.

Taking the ideas from verses 21 and 25 five together, "²¹ by the word implanted, which is able to save your souls . . . ²⁵ this [saved] man [who abides] will be blessed [because he is a doer] . . . ²¹ by the word implanted." Note that in the cases of verses 23 and 24, the lost person doing the listening has a choice to remember or forget what they have heard.

1:26-27 If anyone thinks himself to be religious, and yet does not bridle his tongue but deceives his own heart, this man's religion is worthless. Pure and undefiled religion in the sight of our God and Father is this: to visit orphans and widows in their distress, and to keep oneself unstained by the world.

The words translated here as "religious" and "religion" refer to the outward practice of ceremonies to honor a god. Jewish writers used them to refer to temple worship. Anyone can claim to be religious based on a wide range of interpretations and practices, but James insists that the words only apply to authentic Christianity when governed by strictly defined limitations. In these verses he presents examples of true Christian religious expression.

These verses are not meant to be exhaustive. James is presenting three examples to support his teaching.

1. Controlling the tongue—A Christian must learn to "bridle his tongue," to "rein in his tongue." The bridle and bit allow the rider to exert some degree of control over the horse. This does not demand complete control—sin is sin. But a high degree of spiritually mature, controlled speech is demanded by the Scriptures.

> "worthless"—(GK) *mateios*: vain, meaningless, nothing worth, used in the Bible to describe idolatry

> **Amplification:** *If anyone thinks himself to be religious [by way of ritual behavior], and yet does not bridle his tongue but deceives his own heart [with soul-less, heartless, intellectual head-faith], this man's religion is [vain], worthless, [and meaningless].*

His head-faith "deceives his own heart." He claims to be a Christian by his own standard, but God has judged his heart and does not agree. This is the time-bound religious expression of lost people hanging around in Christian churches while wagging their tongues in meaningless ways. This is the faith of the unconverted church dweller who is no better than a pagan idolater.

2. Concern for the helpless—There were no social welfare programs in those times. Widows and orphans left to themselves were helpless. We are not being told to go and specifically search out orphans and widows to the exclusion of everyone else. The phrase "orphans and widows" encompasses all of the downtrodden and disadvantaged in a society.

The Levite, because he has no portion or inheritance among you, and the alien, the orphan and the widow who are in your town, shall come and eat and be satisfied, in order that the Lord your God may bless you in all the work of your hand which you do. (Deuteronomy 14:29)

Wash yourselves, make yourselves clean; remove the evil of your deeds from My sight. Cease to do evil, learn to do good; seek justice, reprove the ruthless, defend the orphan, plead for the widow. (Isaiah 1:16-17)

TIME-BOUND: One test of the Christian religious experience is how and why we extend aid to the helpless in the world.

3. Avoiding worldliness—James's usage of "the world" in verse 27 represents the sinful lifestyle and worldview of the lost. The third point drives the first two. Outward actions such as controlling the tongue and being concerned for the helpless must be matched by the inner desire to be separated from sinful influences and actions.

...keep oneself unstained by the world.

> **Paraphrase:** *Keep yourself unstained, spotless, uncontaminated by the sinful lifestyle and worldview of the lost.*

Anyone can claim to be religious based on a wide range of interpretations and practices. But the Bible is a book of spiritual wisdom, not a book about being religious. Think how many times you hear the word *religion* in discussions about God. Then think about this: The word *religion* only appears two other times in the New Testament (Acts 26:5; Colossians 2:18).

TIME-BOUND: Religion is downstream from Christian conversion.

TIME-BOUND / TIMELESS: Religious behavior is only of eternal note when it is governed by strictly defined biblical limitations.

We have created a cultural Christian religion that says, *If you are a Christian, then Jesus loves you no matter what you do*—full stop. And while there truth in statements like that, it misrepresents the gospel of Jesus Christ by omission and is a woefully incomplete expression of the holiness of God. Scriptures about obedience and how and when to judge sinful actions are then twisted to teach that following Jesus means no one and nothing can tell us what to do or even what we should do. If you are not convicted to be obedient to the Bible, if you do not come under intense Holy Spirit conviction when you are disobedient, you may be in trouble.

If you are a hearer of the word only, and the Spirit of God is not in you motivating you to biblical action in your life, you are in trouble. The Bible insists that there are many, many nominal Christians sitting in churches hearing the biblical word every week who have not been justified by God. God judges the heart. Look into your own heart and see if this is you.

Everything in the Bible hangs on the issue of supernatural justification and conversion—what it means to be saved by grace through faith. James is writing about what your life should be like *if* you have been saved. He is not teaching salvation by works; he is not teaching the maintaining of salvation by works. James is teaching the synchronicity of salvation and sanctification. Jesus Himself defines this interdependence in John 14:23: "If anyone loves Me, he will keep My word; and My Father will love him, and We will come to him and make Our abode with him."

In John 15:14, Jesus is more terse: "You are My friends if you do what I command you." Said another way, "[If] you are My friends [by way of salvation] you [will] do what I command you." Justification, regeneration, and sanctification are separate topics that need to be understood separately, and they are inseparable. All or nothing.

The overall theme is this: True faith in Jesus Christ manifests in a lifestyle of obedience to God as defined by the Scriptures.

> **TIME-BOUND / TIMELESS:** Abiding faith and saving faith are inseparable.

2:1-13 Discrimination and Kingdom Law

2:1 My brethren, do not hold your faith in our glorious Lord Jesus Christ with an attitude of personal favoritism.

The expression "my brethren" marks a topic shift. Key ideas from verses 19-27 are now applied to the specific situation of discrimination against poor people within the Christian community.

> "glory"—(GK) *doxa:* the divine power and majesty of God that accompanies God's presence

To be "glorious" is the state of being like God. *Christ* means "Messiah." Jesus is the Messiah, the anointed One, the King of kings. So the title "glorious Lord Jesus Christ" means "Jesus the Messiah who is Lord of all and God." He is the deliverer who makes salvation possible for humanity. Jesus is Lord of our lives if we have saving faith.

> "personal favoritism"—(lit.) "receiving the face"—making judgments about people based on external appearances

Humans have a nasty tendency to rank and elevate people based on things like money, material possessions, or power. Honor and respect are given to those who have something we think we need, or we just worship the idols we have built around the wealthy or powerful person in our imaginations. But when a poor person or a homeless person shows up, the tendency is to avoid them, separate them away from the "regular" folks, or just drive them away. The details of any given culture change across time, but this phenomena remains and repeats all across human history. We discriminate, and we tend to do it based on superficial worldly standards.

> *For the Lord your God is the God of gods and the Lord of lords, the great, the mighty, and the awesome God who does not show partiality nor take a bribe. He executes justice for the orphan and the widow, and shows His love for the alien by giving him food and clothing. (Deuteronomy 10:17-18)*

> *You shall do no injustice in judgment; you shall not be partial to the poor nor defer to the great, but you are to judge your neighbor fairly. (Leviticus 19:15)*

A person who has faith that recognizes the glory of Jesus Christ should not make decisions about the spiritual condition of people based on any external factors. If you have faith in Jesus the Messiah who is Lord of all and God, do not demean it by only "receiving the face" of the people you deal with.

2:2-4 For if a man comes into your assembly with a gold ring and dressed in fine clothes, and there also comes in a poor man in dirty clothes and you pay special attention to the one who is wearing the fine clothes, and say, "You sit here in a good place," and you say to the poor man, "You stand over there, or sit down by my footstool," have you not made distinctions among yourselves, and become judges with evil motives?

"[A]ssembly" translates the Greek word *synagogue*—the Jewish meeting place for worship and instruction. So then, "your assembly" means "your Christian meeting place for worship and instruction."

"pay special attention"—look at with favor

Amplification: *You [rich man] sit here [beside me] in a good place.*

Amplification: *You [poor man] stand over there [away from me].*

"sit down by my footstool"—(lit.) "under my footstool"—an expression of disdain or contempt: *you are lower than my footstool.*

If an obviously wealthy or well-dressed person shows up at your Christian place of assembly, and an obviously poor or poorly dressed person shows up at the same service, and you find yourself favoring one over the other in your mind based on appearances, then James asks you two rhetorical questions in verse 4 that demand a "yes" answer: Have you not made distinctions among yourselves? Have you not become judges with evil motives?

> *[We] have . . . made [the above] distinctions among [ourselves] [and we have] become judges with evil motives.*

No one is closer to God because of the way they dress. No one is closer to God because of how they look. No one is closer to God because of their position in a church assembly.

> "make distinctions"—(GK) *diakrino*: separate and/or doubt, waver
>
> "make distinctions among yourselves"—external expressions of discrimination
>
> "doubt and waver in yourselves"—the internal cause of the external expressions

Here again is the divided heart of the double-minded from chapter 1, verse 6. When you hold people that way in your mind, you become "judges with evil motives." The sinful internal condition yields sinful outward expressions. Double-minded Christians exist full of spiritual doubt and uncertainty. This inner condition can then manifest into the evil of controlling and improperly judgmental behaviors in the Christian assembly.

TIME-BOUND / TIMELESS: Authentic expressions of Christian conduct can only come from an authentically Christian mind—a mind that has been regenerated by the Holy Spirit.

2:5 Listen, my beloved brethren: did not God choose the poor of this world to be rich in faith and heirs of the kingdom which He promised to those who love Him?

> "Listen, my beloved brethren"—Listen carefully, fellow Christians; I am shifting my focus again, so pay attention to my words.
>
> "did not God choose . . . ?"—Remember who ultimately makes a Christian a Christian.
>
> "poor"—(GK) *ptochos*: materially poor; used to translate the Hebrew word *'anaw*, which refers to the spiritually humble who rely on God

In this usage, "poor" points to both *ptochos* and *'anaw* as James adds another dimension to his lesson by way of the usage of "poor" in the Sermon on the Mount: "Blessed are the [spiritually humble], for theirs is the kingdom of heaven" (Matthew 5:3). "The [spiritually humble] of this world" have a deep and overwhelming sense of helplessness without God. The spiritually humble are blessed because they depend completely on God.

James challenges the sinfully biased outer expression of the double-minded discriminators:

> **TIME-BOUND:** "did not God choose the [materially poor] [in the eyes] of this world to be rich in faith...?"

James challenges the sinfully biased inner condition of the double-minded discriminators:

> **TIMELESS:** "did not God choose the [spiritually humble] of this world to be rich in faith...?"

James is writing to a Christian community made up of large amounts of materially poor people. Lots of poor people were getting saved. It should have been clear to them that material wealth and the social status it brings are not important to God.

> *For consider your calling, brethren, that there were not many wise according to the flesh, not many mighty, not many noble; but God has chosen the foolish things of the world to shame the wise, and God has chosen the weak things of the world to shame the things which are strong, and the base things of the world and the despised God has chosen, the things that are not, so that He may nullify the things that are, so that no man may boast before God. (1 Corinthians 1:26-29)*

There is a completely unbiblical works-based system spreading all over the world called liberation theology. It is a secular humanistic, works-based religious system that puts humanity in the spiritual driver's seat. This is one of the verses they use to support the claim that God only saves materially poor people and that people who meet some imagined level of material holdings cannot be saved. But there is no limiter in the original language of this verse to support that errant notion. In all instances, God judges the heart.

> *"Again I say to you, it is easier for a camel to go through the eye of a needle, than for a rich man to enter the kingdom of God." When the disciples heard*

this, they were very astonished and said, "Then who can be saved?" And looking at them Jesus said to them, "With people this is impossible, but with God all things are possible." (Matthew 19:24-26)

TIME-BOUND: None of us know which individuals God will or will not save.

2:6-7 But you have dishonored the poor man. Is it not the rich who oppress you and personally drag you into court? Do they not blaspheme the fair name by which you have been called?

"blaspheme"—(1) a violation, usually in speech, of God's person; (2) any slander that involves God whether direct or indirect

In the first century Middle East, a small number of landowners and merchants controlled the majority of the wealth and had considerable power. The rich were exploiting both the existing social structures as well as the legal system to get richer at the expense of the less powerful. In the case of James's dispersed flock, they did this while also mocking God.

In verses 6 and 7, James asks three rhetorical questions to point out the double-mindedness and hypocrisy of his spiritually immature Christian audience:

1. Is it not the rich who oppress you?
2. [Is it not the rich who...] personally drag you into court?
3. [Is it not the rich who...] blaspheme the fair name by which you have been called?

The Christians James writes to were discriminating against the same poor people whom God had honored while attempting to curry favor with the wealthy people who were discriminating against them. And to make matters worse, these rich or powerful people would turn around and slander the name of Jesus Christ.

TIME-BOUND: Showing favoritism toward the wealthy and powerful makes no sense in light of how they usually attain their status and what kind of people they more often than not tend to be.

TIMELESS: Showing favoritism based on any worldly standard violates God's standard. What would Jesus see?

2:8 If, however, you are fulfilling the royal law according to the Scripture, "You shall love your neighbor as yourself," you are doing well.

James was well-schooled in the Law of Moses. Here he attaches the word "royal" to the Law. He is filtering the Torah through his Jesus glasses. The "royal law" is the sum of all the biblical demands that God places on believers through Jesus, and the basis of this royal law is the law of love:

> And [Jesus] said to him, "'You shall love the Lord your God with all your heart, and with all your soul, and with all your mind.' This is the great and foremost commandment. The second is like it, 'You shall love your neighbor as yourself.' On these two commandments depend the whole Law and the Prophets." (Matthew 22:37-40)

TIME-BOUND: Love your neighbor as yourself.

TIMELESS: Love the Lord your God with all your heart, with all your soul, and with all your mind.

2:9 But if you show partiality, you are committing sin and are convicted by the law as transgressors.

The Law states,

> You shall do no injustice in judgment; you shall not be partial to the poor nor defer to the great, but you are to judge your neighbor fairly. You shall not go about as a slanderer among your people, and you are not to act against the life of your neighbor; I am the Lord. You shall not hate your fellow countryman in your heart; you may surely reprove your neighbor, but shall not incur sin because of him. You shall not take vengeance, nor bear any grudge against the sons of your people, but you shall love your neighbor as yourself; I am the Lord. (Leviticus 19:15-18)

The ancient Jews believed that these verses only applied to their fellow Israelites and tended to discriminate heavily against any and all Gentiles. Jesus corrected their errant theology in chapter 5 of Matthew:

> "You have heard that it was said, 'You shall love your neighbor and hate your enemy.' But I say to you, love your enemies and pray for those who persecute you." (Matthew 5:43-44)

Any elitism or favoritism in the body of Christ violates the demand of love for neighbor. The church is forbidden by Scripture to discriminate against anyone based on worldly standards of wealth, power, or appearance. The foundations of Christian culture should be built on the values of God's kingdom and not at all on the things that the lost world values.

2:10 For whoever keeps the whole law and yet stumbles in one point, he has become guilty of all.

No one can keep the whole Law of Moses. James is making a hypothetical point:

> **Amplification:** *[Suppose it were so that someone] keeps the whole law and yet stumbles in one point, he has become guilty of all.*

2:11 For He who said, "Do not commit adultery," also said, "Do not commit murder." Now if you do not commit adultery, but do commit murder, you have become a transgressor of the law.

The written Law is God speaking personally. Individual commandments are part and parcel of the whole of God's word. Each commandment is reflective of the will of God. So then, the violation of any single commandment is disobedience to God Himself.

> *"For truly I say to you, until heaven and earth pass away, not the smallest letter or stroke shall pass from the Law until all is accomplished. Whoever then annuls one of the least of these commandments, and teaches others to do the same, shall be called least in the kingdom of heaven; but whoever keeps and teaches them, he shall be called great in the kingdom of heaven." (Matthew 5:18-19)*

2:12 So speak and so act as those who are to be judged by the law of liberty.

> **Amplification:** *[Be constantly speaking and always acting in such a manner] as those who are [about] to be judged by [the Law of Moses as revealed through Christ].*

Abiding faith and saving faith are inseparable. Validate the reality of your faith by doing the biblical word. The final judgment beyond time will have its reflection in the life lived in time.

TIME-BOUND: If you are saved, act like it.

TIMELESS: If you are saved, one way or another you will act like it.

2:13 For judgment will be merciless to one who has shown no mercy; mercy triumphs over judgment.

"Blessed are the merciful, for they shall receive mercy." (Matthew 5:7)

Therefore, cursed are the merciless, they shall not receive mercy.

> **Amplification:** *[God's] judgment will be merciless to one who has shown no mercy [by God's standard].*

God, in His grace, provides a means of escaping judgment to condemnation—"mercy triumphs over judgment." The mercy He extends at salvation will reflect out from the life of a Christian.

TIME-BOUND: A merciful heart made right by God triumphs over a judgmental, sinful heart.

TIMELESS: God's mercy toward those who are saved triumphs over His judgment.

The royal law of holy love is central to understanding the Bible. God set forth His Law as the basis of judgment to condemnation. And then, in triumph of mercy over judgment, He allows His grace to be a means of escaping that judgment. We will always deserve judgment to condemnation, and none of us can perfectly conform to the law of love, but since God has saved us, our Christian hearts and minds will manifest actions that give evidence of the presence of Christ within us. By the power of the Holy Spirit in us, and with Jesus as our model, we are to be doers of the word—our faith will then radiate the holy love of God out into the world.

TIMELESS: Since we are the recipients of God's mercy . . .

> **TIME-BOUND:** . . . part of sanctification is to mirror that quality of mercy into the world.

2:14-26 The Relationship of Works to Faith

This passage has caused a lot of fuss over the centuries. It is the primary passage cited by people who believe that a person gets saved by doing works. And it is one of the passages cited by people who believe that if you do not do enough works, you can lose your salvation.

In verse 24 of chapter 2 we will encounter this statement:

You see then that a man is justified *by works and not by faith alone.*

Several theological traditions use this verse, and the rest of this part of chapter 2, to insist that Christians have to do good works to earn salvation, which is to say, to earn justification. They then reason that since salvation has to be earned by works on the front end, it must be maintained by works on the back end or it will be lost. But in chapter 3, verse 28 of the letter to the Romans, Paul writes,

[W]e maintain that a man is justified *by faith apart from works of the Law.*

And in the letter to the Ephesians, chapter 2, verses 8-9, we are told:

[B]y grace you have been saved through faith; and that not of yourselves, it is the gift of God; not as a result of works, so that no one may boast. (Ephesians 2:8-9)

So which is it? Are we justified by faith, or are we justified by works *plus* faith? And then, once we are justified, is God in control of our salvation, or are we?

The main problem with the works-based doctrines and doctrines that claim you can lose your salvation is that they put humans in control of grace and subordinate the will of God to the human will. Any works-based tradition, by its definitions, must then make some arbitrary degree of human works the standard for God's righteousness. This is core salvation doctrine we are talking about. This is not something that can be placed under the *unity in non-essentials—agree to disagree* banner.

If works-based theology is correct, then we also have a bigger problem. Both Paul and James were instructed by the risen Christ, and both were inspired by the Holy Spirit, to write documents that became part of the Bible. Paul's letters clearly state that we are saved by the grace of God and that our works contribute nothing to God's gracious and merciful decision to justify us. If James is teaching that Paul's salvation theology is wrong, then we have one book of the Bible in direct disagreement with other books of the Bible. If this condition exists anywhere in the Bible, then the doctrine of biblical inerrancy is wrong, and we can all toss our Bibles out and go find something else to do with our limited time on earth.

2:14 What use is it, my brethren, if someone says he has faith but he has no works? Can that faith save him?

The phrase "if someone says" establishes that James is questioning the supernatural reality of this type of faith. James begins his presentation with two rhetorical questions:

1. "What use is it . . . if someone says he has faith but he has no works?"

> "Use" can also be rendered as "good" or "profit" or "gain."

Two amplifications:

> *What [good] is it . . . if someone says he has faith but he has no works?*
>
> *What [profit] is it . . . if someone says he has faith but he has no works?*
>
> "works"—(GK) *ergon:* actions, deeds, accomplishments; behaviors with ethical and spiritual consequences; actions done in obedience to God

Three amplifications:

> *What use is it . . . if someone says he has faith but he has no [Christian works]?*
>
> *What use is it . . . if someone says he has faith but he [accomplishes nothing Christian]?*
>
> *What use is it . . . if someone says he has faith but he [accomplishes no actions done in obedience to God]?*

2. "Can that faith save him?"

   The English language Geneva Bible (GNV), and later the King James Version (KJV), rendered the second question as, "Can faith save him?" When you read it that way in English, look what can happen: "What use is it if someone says he has faith but he has no works? Can faith save him?"

   The Greek article used with "faith" looks back to previous uses of the word *faith*. According to the original Greek Scriptures, the question James is asking is, "Can that faith save him?"

   Amplification: *Can [that type of] faith save him?*

   The question is rhetorical. The Greek grammar used here expects a "no" answer: No, that kind of faith cannot save anyone. So what is that type of faith?

   James is building off of verses 2:12 and 1:21. The unregenerate head-faith of those not justified by God cannot save anyone, and that kind of faith proves itself false by its time-bound expression.

TIME-BOUND / TIMELESS: A non-Christian cannot produce Spirit-filled Christian works.

For by grace you have been saved through faith; and that not of yourselves, it is the gift of God; not as a result of works, so that no one may boast. (Ephesians 2:8-9)

Paul makes it clear, we do not do works to earn salvation. James is not writing about doing works to get or to keep salvation. James is writing about evidence of saving faith versus evidence of false faith. The "works" James is referring to is the natural outgrowth of salvation that will be present in a regenerated believer.

The first question could be asked this way: What good is it if someone says he has faith, but there is no evidence of the indwelling of the Holy Spirit playing out in their life?

In verse 12 of chapter 2, James tells us that we "are to be judged by the law of liberty" as final recognition that we did indeed get saved by God. Or, as James puts it in chapter 1, verse 21, our final judgment will prove that we did "in humility receive the word implanted" during this lifetime. And now James is clarifying the kind of faith that will provide security in that judgment and the kind of faith that will not.

The question is addressing the condition called head-faith—faith based on intellectual assent only. It is about a person who claims to know Jesus with their mouth but does not believe in their heart. A head-faith Christian is running on the mechanics of religion and never received the gift of the Holy Spirit.

Conversion to Christianity is not controllable by humans. Getting saved is not about mechanically reciting the sinner's prayer or engaging some kind of ritual activity presided over by a priest or a preacher. No one can declare themselves to be in right standing with God under their own power. No religious tradition has the authority to declare a person to be in right standing with God. Coming to saving faith is not just about intellectually believing the gospel or engaging in Christian ritual. That kind of faith cannot save anyone.

Justification is inseparable from conversion. At conversion, there is a mystical reconnection between God and the believer that takes place wherein the new believer is supernaturally transformed by the work of God. At conversion, a relationship has been engaged on God's terms by way of the power and presence of the Holy Spirit. There is a real, supernatural change of heart that takes place at conversion, and James is asserting that this supernatural intervention will be evidenced in time by ongoing obedience to Christ if a person is truly saved.

2:15-16 If a brother or sister is without clothing and in need of daily food, and one of you says to them, "Go in peace, be warmed and be filled," and yet you do not give them what is necessary for their body, what use is that?

This hypothetical situation applies to the first question from verse 14. The expression "brother or sister" makes it personal; this is a member of the immediate community. The phrase "without clothing and in need of daily food" points to a person in any kind of desperate condition.

"Go in peace" was a common biblical blessing; it was a Jewish benediction. It means, "Go in the blessings and well-being that God gives to those who walk with Him." It is personally passive; it is a prayer for God to supply their need. The second part, when coupled with the first part, takes on the passive meaning: "May God warm and fill you."

In context of verses 15 and 16, a person claiming to be Christian encounters a person in their community with obvious and immediate need. The Christian speaks a blessing over the person: "Go in the blessings and well-being that God gives to those who walk with Him. May God warm and fill you." Confronted with a situation that demands immediate action, the Christian responds with a lofty sounding biblical blessing but then does nothing practical to help. The implication here is that the person claiming saving faith is content to do this and nothing more.

The verbal blessing is painted here as elaborate religious cover for doing nothing. And James again asks a rhetorical question that demands a negative response: "[W]hat use is that?" This sits just after the command in verse 12 and the warning in verse 13. It is likely that James is pointing us directly at the teaching of Jesus as recorded in Matthew 25:

> *"But when the Son of Man comes in His glory, and all the angels with Him, then He will sit on His glorious throne. All the nations will be gathered before Him; and He will separate them from one another, as the shepherd separates the sheep from the goats; and He will put the sheep on His right, and the goats on the left. Then the King will say to those on His right, 'Come, you who are blessed of My Father, inherit the kingdom prepared for you from the foundation of the world. For I was hungry, and you gave Me something to eat; I was thirsty, and you gave Me something to drink; I was a stranger, and you invited Me in; naked, and you clothed Me; I was sick, and you visited Me; I was in prison, and you came to Me.' Then the righteous will answer Him, 'Lord, when did we see You hungry, and feed You, or thirsty, and give You something to drink? And when did we see You a stranger, and invite You in, or naked, and clothe You? When did we see You sick, or in prison, and come to You?' The King will answer and say to them, 'Truly I say to you, to the extent that you did it to one of these brothers of Mine, even the least of them, you did it to Me.' Then He will also say to those on His left, 'Depart from Me, accursed ones, into the eternal fire which has been prepared for the devil and his angels; for I was hungry, and you gave Me nothing to eat; I was thirsty, and you gave Me nothing to drink; I was a stranger, and you did not invite Me in; naked, and you did not clothe Me; sick, and in prison, and you did not visit Me.'" (Matthew 25:31-43)*

The inner motivation to action is not, *Someone is in need; I must do what is right under the Law so I can stay saved.* The inner motivation to action should be, *Someone is in need; I am doing what is right as a natural, Spirit-led outgrowth of the salvation I have experienced.*

2:17 Even so faith, if it has no works, is dead, being by itself.

"Even so"—in the same way

The actions of a Christian who consistently fails to live out the faith are as spiritually useless as an intellectual profession of faith that does not result in salvation. Faith that does not yield any spiritual action in time is "by itself" inwardly dead; it has some inherent defect that is making it inactive and useless. This defect can be caused by a genuinely saved person who is not being properly discipled and is not growing in grace and understanding. They are coasting through their days in spiritual neutral, and their sanctification process is undetectable to anyone around them and sometimes even to themselves. Or worse, this defect can reflect a person who confesses Jesus with their mouth but does not believe in their heart. They claim to know Jesus, and Jesus says, *Nope, I still don't know you.*

TIME-BOUND: You can memorize lots of theology. You can memorize the right answers to lots of Christian questions. And you can then be a biblically knowledgeable, doctrinally orthodox lost person.

TIME-BOUND: You can engage church as religious ritual and/or engage in sacramental practices and still be lost—still be spiritually empty. You can be a mechanically obedient, sacramental pagan.

TIME-BOUND / TIMELESS: James is not contrasting works-based salvation against salvation by grace through faith. He is contrasting a defective, false head-faith that yields no authentically Christian works against a saving faith that is Spirit filled and Spirit directed by its nature.

2:18a But someone may well say, "You have faith and I have works."

James uses a device called *diatribe*—a back and forth argument with an imaginary opponent. "But someone may well say," initiates the diatribe. In response to verse 17, his opponent claims that "you have faith and I have works." The opponent claims that one Christian can have just faith and another Christian have just works, as if they can exist separately. The opponent is claiming that a person can have genuine saving faith without yielding any spiritual fruit.

A note about verse 18: It is important to understand that almost all ancient Greek manuscripts contain no punctuation marks. There are no commas, no periods, no exclamation points, no quotation marks . . . nothing. There are also no paragraph or even sentence breaks. Bible translators must have a deep understanding of the source language's grammatical rules and must honor both the overall letter content as well as the immediate context to be able to determine where to put English language style punctuation marks.

In the verse 18 diatribe, it is clear where the quotation marks should begin, but for a variety of grammatical reasons it is difficult to decide where the quotation marks should end. In the case of this verse, translators are left to choose the placement that yields the fewest interpretive difficulties. Many older translations just leave the quotation marks out.

I am using the NASB1995 translation in this book. In this particular verse, however, I follow the approach taken by the overwhelming majority of modern Bible translations, which isolate the words of the imaginary objector at the phrase "You have faith and I have works." The commentators I trust also support this choice. Accordingly, I have placed the end quotation mark just after the word "works" in verse 18.

2:18b . . . show me your faith without the works, and I will show you my faith by my works.

"[S]how me" can also be rendered as "make visible to me." James challenges his opponent: "Make your faith visible to me without the works." The implication based on the next phrase—"and I will make my faith visible to you by my works"—is that his opponent cannot because one does not exist without the other.

James is saying, *Can you really show me that you are a Christian by your words alone? Is the ability to speak about Christian things evidence of salvation? I will show you my faith by the movement of the Spirit in my life, by the visible evidence of my transformed life.* James insists that genuine faith and Spirit-led works as an outgrowth of that faith always go together.

TIME-BOUND / TIMELESS: Saving faith and abiding faith are inseparable.

2:19 You believe that God is one. You do well; the demons also believe, and shudder.

"You believe that God is one" points to the *Shema*: "Hear, O Israel. The lord is our God, the Lord is one" (Deuteronomy 6:4). Every Jewish man, woman, and child knew this prayer. It was a fundamental statement of Jewish faith.

James continues his reply to his opponent from verse 18a by comparing head-faith to the faith of demons. He tells his opponent, "You do well" to believe the word of God; it is true. But just believing it in your mind does not grant salvation. Even demons believe in the one true God "and shudder."

"shudder"—(1) the reaction of fear provoked by contact with God; (2) the dread experienced by sinful people who know deep inside that they deserve the coming judgment

In Luke 4:34 a demon says to Jesus, "Let us alone! What business do we have with each other, Jesus of Nazareth? Have You come to destroy us? I know who You are—the Holy One of God!" This verse shows that the demon understood the nature of sin: "Let us alone!" The demon knew what is going to happen in the end times: "Have You come to destroy us?" The demon recognized the deity of Jesus Christ: "I know who You are—the Holy One of God!"

Demons are orthodox theologians. They know that God is real, and they know that the Bible is true. Demons know theology better than we do; they even shudder in fear of the coming judgment. Yet they do not have a faith that saves just because they have Bible knowledge and an intellectual acceptance of its truth.

The word "shudder" is also a picture of the dread experienced by sinful people who know deep inside that they deserve the coming judgment. With a hint of sarcasm, James is saying to liberal theologians from every age, "You believe that God [exists]. You do well [because it's true]; [but] the demons also believe, and [at least they] shudder."

To the biblically conservative theologian, James says, "You do well" to intellectually believe the Bible. But if it does not go any deeper than that, you are in trouble. Knowing the gospel without responding to it at the heart level does not save.

If you are doing Christian religion without saving faith, if you have some type or degree of intellectual faith without the indwelling presence of the Holy Spirit, you are at the moment no better off in the big picture than a demon.

2:20 But are you willing to recognize, you foolish fellow, that faith without works is useless?

"Fool" here refers to a spiritually ignorant person.

> **Paraphrase:** *Now that I have shown you by your own argument that you are spiritually ignorant, are you willing to recognize that head-faith without Spirit-driven works is spiritually useless?*

Good deeds that are not fueled by the presence of the Holy Spirit are useless spiritually. Faith that is not fueled by the conviction of the Holy Spirit is useless for salvation.

2:21 Was not Abraham our father justified by works when he offered up Isaac his son on the altar?

James uses Abraham as a test case to anchor his argument. The grammar dictates that the rhetorical question here demands a "yes" answer. Yes, Abraham was "justified by works when he offered up Isaac his son on the altar." But in Romans 4:3 and Galatians 3:6, Paul uses Genesis 15:7 as proof that Abraham was saved by faith and not works:

> *For what does the Scripture say? "Abraham believed God and it was credited to him as righteousness." (Romans 4:3)*

> *Even so Abraham believed God, and it was reckoned to him as righteousness. (Galatians 3:6)*

In Romans 3:28 and Ephesians 2:8-9, Paul insists that this principle applies to everyone:

> *For we maintain that a man is justified by faith apart from works of the Law. (Romans 3:28)*

> *For by grace you have been saved [justified] through faith; and that not of yourselves, it is the gift of God; not as a result of works, so that no one may boast. (Ephesians 2:8-9)*

Paul's teachings about justification, as recorded in English, seem at first glance to be in conflict with this section of the letter of James. Paul clearly uses "justify" to represent God declaring a sinner "not guilty" at the moment they place saving faith in Jesus Christ.

James wrote his letter before the letters of Paul were written. He did not have access to Paul's writings, so it is not possible that he is writing a rebuttal to Paul's letters. However, when James wrote this letter, Paul's teaching on justification was circulating by word of mouth. If James was aware of Paul's teaching, he may be writing here to address a misunderstanding people were having about what it means to be justified.

Whether or not James has Paul's teachings in mind, there is no conflict between the theology of Paul and James when the context of both writers is understood. An errant understanding of the usage of "justified" in James gave rise to the idea that James is contradicting the teaching of Paul and that one of them must be wrong about justification.

The Greek word that translates as "justified" has one of two possible meanings when used in the Bible for spiritual matters:

1. "declared innocent by God at the moment of salvation"
2. "demonstrated to be right; vindicated"

To understand which usage fits which letters, the meaning must be established by the surrounding context. In the cases of the letter to the Romans and the letter of James, each writer is using the term "justification" in a different context. Paul's writings clarify the distinction between faith and works in relation to conversion by God at the moment of salvation. So Paul uses the term "justified" to represent a sinner being declared "not guilty" by God at the moment of salvation. Therefore, in terms of salvation, Abraham was justified by God on the basis of his faith.

Now, look at the immediate context in James:

> *Show me your faith without the works, and I will show you my faith by my works.*

> *Show me your faith . . . and I will show you my faith.*

James is writing about the process of sanctification. He is demonstrating what salvation looks like playing out in time as we mature spiritually, yielding what we call our Christian witness. This, then, is the other biblical meaning of the word *justification*. In this usage, it means "demonstrating something to be right." So verse 21 has the meaning,

Was not Abraham our father [demonstrated to be right spiritually] when he offered up Isaac his son on the altar?

Was not Abraham our father [shown to be in right relationship with God by his actions] when he offered up Isaac his son on the altar?

With attention to the context, and some understanding of the original language, both James and Paul are shown to be in agreement with regard to how salvation happens and the sanctifying role that human works play in time *after* salvation has occurred. James is not arguing that works must be added to faith or that works generate faith. His point is that genuine saving faith will always yield some form of authentic Christian action. This is the work that James writes about here.

Obedience to biblical truth is an authenticating mark of a converted person. Obedience through works does not establish conversion—that would be a person saving themselves by their own power or by their own will. Works done by humans in time do not produce saving faith, but James insists that saving faith will always yield authentic Christian works. James offers us a test, or a measure, that we can use to diagnose the condition of our faith. It is not faith combined with works that saves. It is not either faith or works that saves. Saving faith is faithful according to the biblical standard. Saving faith is a faith that works.

Below is a paraphrase of verses 14 through 21:

14 What good is it, my brothers and sisters in Christ, if someone says he has saving faith but he has no Christian works? What use is it if someone says he has saving faith but he accomplishes no actions done in obedience to God? Can that type of faith save him? No, that kind of faith cannot save anyone.

15-16 If a person claiming to be Christian directly engages someone in their immediate community who has real and serious need, and all they do is offer a pious-sounding prayer and nothing else, what use is that?

17 In the same way, a proclamation of faith that does not yield authentic expressions of obedience to God, proves itself to be inwardly dead, a kind of faith that exists by itself apart from God.

18 But someone may disagree with me and declare, "You have faith and I have works." To which I reply, I challenge your assertion that you can make your faith visible to me without any works. On the contrary, I will make my faith visible to you by my works because saving faith always yields observable obedience.

¹⁹ Consider this: You believe in the God of the Bible. You are doing well to be at that point of understanding. But the demons also believe in God. They even react to God with fear.

²⁰ Now that I have shown you by your own argument that you are spiritually ignorant, are you willing to recognize that head-faith alone does not deliver salvation?

²¹ Consider the case of Abraham. Was not Abraham, our father in the faith, shown to be in right relationship with God by his actions when he offered up Isaac his son on the altar?

Long before circumcision, "Abraham believed God and it was credited to him as righteousness" (Romans 4:3). Abraham had faith in the promises of God, and by the grace of God, Abraham's faith was credited to him as righteousness. Abraham was saved by grace through faith.

In verse 18, James has just told his opponent, *You cannot make your faith visible to me without the obedient works, but I can make my faith visible to you by my obedient works.* And now he is saying the same thing about Abraham.

Justification: *Abraham believed God and it was credited to him as righteousness. (Romans 4:3)*

[And then later on in his life . . .]

Sanctification: *Was not Abraham our father [shown to be in right relationship with God by his actions] when he offered up Isaac his son on the altar?*

TIME-BOUND: Justification in James—"demonstrated to be right; vindicated"

TIMELESS: Justification in Romans—"declared innocent by God at the moment of salvation"

2:22 You see that faith was working with his works, and as a result of the works, faith was perfected; . . .

"You see"—The diatribe continues.

"faith was working"—Abraham already had faith (Genesis 15:6). James is showing Abraham's saving faith at work in the world.

"faith was working with his works"—Because the faith is authentic, the works will also be authentic. Saving faith is an active, ongoing force driving the life of a believer.

"perfect"—(GK) *teleios:* mature, complete (see 1:4)

"perfected," "completed"—evidence of a fully developed and matured Christian

Amplification: *. . . and as a result of the works, [Abraham's] faith was [shown to be complete and matured].*

Paraphrase: *You see that his faith and his actions were working together, and his faith was shown to be complete and mature by his actions.*

2:23 . . . and the Scripture was fulfilled which says, "And Abraham believed God, and it was reckoned to him as righteousness," and he was called the friend of God.

"[F]ulfilled" here means that something has been filled up—something has been brought to an ultimate significance.

Paraphrase: *And the Scripture that says, "Abraham believed God, and it was reckoned to him as righteousness" found an ultimate time-bound significance in Abraham's life of obedience when he offered up Isaac his son on the altar and in light of his obedience Abraham was called friend of God.*

"[Abraham] was called the friend of God"—See Isaiah 41:8; 2 Chronicles 20:7; James 4:4.

Abraham did not just intellectually believe God in Genesis 15:6. His heart was changed. God gave to Abraham a righteousness that did not inherently belong to him. Abraham's works in time then fulfilled God's reckoning of righteousness to him.

In Ephesians 2:8-9, Paul tells us, "For by grace you have been saved through faith; and that not of yourselves, it is the gift of God; not as a result of works, so that no one may boast." The next verse further clarifies the message of James:

For we are His workmanship, created in Christ Jesus for good works. (Ephesians 2:10a)

TIMELESS: salvation—For we are [God's] workmanship, created in Christ Jesus.... (Ephesians 2:10a)

TIME-BOUND: sanctification—For we are [God's] workmanship ... for good works.... (Ephesians 2:10a)

TIMELESS: We are not saved by good works.

TIME-BOUND: We are saved for good works.

God had already promised Abraham that Isaac would have a future beyond that moment. Abraham so completely trusted that God would do what God said, he was willing to sacrifice Isaac and trust that God would keep His word by bringing Isaac back from the dead. Abraham's works are intertwined with, and indistinguishable from, his faith. James uses the example of Abraham to show that when God justifies a person by faith, that faith will ultimately be justified before the world by the evidence of a transformed life.

2:24 You see that a man is justified by works and not by faith alone.

"faith alone"—the non-salvific head-faith that James has been attacking

Paul:

For we [insist] that a man is justified [only] by faith apart from works of the Law. (Romans 3:28)

TIMELESS: Justification in Romans is about God's once and future "not guilty" verdict pronounced over a sinner at the moment of salvation.

James:

You see that a man is [demonstrated to be in right relationship with God] by [his actions] and not by [head-faith] [that exists alone].

299

> **TIME-BOUND:** Justification in James is evidence of sanctification taking place. God's timeless "not guilty" verdict will always be demonstrated to be right in time by the Christian works that salvific justification by God will inevitably produce.

Real faith is a faith that works—a faith where obedience to God is central and on display for anyone to see. You do not need to say "show me" to Abraham; you can see his faith playing out in time.

> **TIMELESS:** God judges the heart; God sees faith.

> **TIME-BOUND:** You and I see a changed life and a biblically authentic Christian lifestyle.

2:25 In the same way, was not Rahab the harlot also justified by works when she received the messengers and sent them out by another way?

Rahab is used as another biblical test case. The test is, God's program works for a Jew. How about for a Gentile? How about for a Gentile prostitute?

Joshua records that the Gentile prostitute Rahab lived in the city of Jericho. She encountered two messengers from Israel who told her that they were men of God, that Jericho has been judged, and that it's going to fall to God's servant Joshua. Rahab said to the men, "I know that the Lord has given you the land . . . for the Lord your God, He is God in heaven above and on earth beneath" (Joshua 2:9a, 11b). She was then justified before humanity by protecting the messengers. The letter to the Hebrews says that because of her faith, Rahab did not perish when the city fell.

To use our terminology, at some point Rahab had come under conviction about who she was, what kind of world she was living in, and who the God of Israel is—and she was saved. She believed, and God justified her. Rahab had a faith that saves before the messengers arrived. Her works showed herself to be a friend of God and not a friend of Jericho. Her works did not get her saved; her works did not keep her saved. Her works simply evidenced her faith.

Amplification: *In the same way [as Abraham], was not Rahab the harlot also [demonstrated to be in right relationship with God] by [her actions] when she received the messengers and sent them out by another way?*

TIME-BOUND: Saving faith justifies itself before humanity by its actions in time.

2:26 For just as the body without the spirit is dead, so also faith without works is dead.

"body without the spirit," "body without [its small *s*] spirit"—the physical human body without the animating life principle

"faith without works"—intellectually professed faith that is not the product of justification and regeneration and therefore yields no sanctification

Just as a human body without a human spirit in it is dead even though it still appears to have human form, so also head faith that does not yield Spirit-filled works is dead even though it appears to have a religious form.

O it is a living, busy active mighty thing, this faith. It is impossible for it not to be doing good things incessantly. It does not ask whether good works are to be done, but before the question is asked, it has already done this, and is constantly doing them. Whoever does not do such works, however, is an unbeliever. He gropes and looks around for faith and good works, but knows neither what faith is nor what good works are. Yet he talks and talks, with many words, about faith and good works.[4]

Head-faith is dead faith. You know you are saved and walking with the Lord when you find yourself doing what God tells you to do. It is not "faith plus works" but "faith that works." This harmony of timeless justification by God at salvation and time-bound justification before the world is the condition of faith that all of the New Testament writers insist on in perfect harmony.

The doctrine of "once saved, always saved" is often misunderstood on all sides of the theological divide. There is no loophole in the gospel that allows a person to make a verbal or mental profession of faith in isolation from the

4. Martin Luther, *Preface to the Epistle of St. Paul to the Romans*, trans. by Theodore G. Tappert, in *Luther: Selections from His Writings*, ed. John Dillenberger (New York: Anchor Books, 1961), 24.

Holy Spirit, experience no change, and then maintain a life of disobedience to God. Even demons believe that way. A more semantically precise way to sum up the doctrine of assurance is, "if saved, always saved." If you are saved, you are always saved . . . and only you and God can know for certain.

> **TIME-BOUND / TIMELESS:** At salvation the Spirit changes the new believer—transforms the believer into a new spiritual creation. The (small *s*) spirit and the (big *S*) Spirit must meet, or nothing happens.

James is not arguing that works must then be added to faith. His point is that genuine saving faith will always yield some form of biblical outward expression. These verses also clarify James's presentation on true religion that started in verse 21 of chapter 1. He told us that we must "accept the implanted word." Only this Spirit-driven experience of inner transformation can bring a person into alignment with God and then produce works that are pleasing to God.

This "faith that works" passage is a further development of the theme James put forward earlier in the letter: "[P]rove yourselves doers of the word, and not merely hearers who delude themselves" (James 1:22). It is not faith and works that saves. If God changed your heart, you have faith, and your works will ultimately prove out your faith in time.

3:1-12 Sanctifying Speech

The words we choose to think, the words we use to order our conscious thoughts, are important. They shape and define who we are. The words we then choose to speak out into the world are no less important. Jesus put it this way: "I tell you that every careless word that people speak, they shall give an accounting for it in the day of judgment. For by your words you will be justified, and by your words you will be condemned" (Matthew 12:36-37). James would have been aware of this teaching and its centrality to any discussion of sanctification. So now, he moves from the general principle of Christian works to the specific issue of words as works.

3:1 Let not many of you become teachers, my brethren, knowing that as such we will incur a stricter judgment.

The office of teacher in the early church was roughly equivalent to the office of rabbi in Jewish communities. The teacher was tasked with explaining the truths of Christianity based on the growing oral and written tradition. James begins his admonition about the destructive potential of human speech by warning about the seriousness of the teaching role in the Christian community.

Let not many of you become teachers.

It is reasonable to infer from this beginning that too many people without the necessary moral and/or intellectual qualifications were setting themselves up as teachers.

. . . knowing that as such we will incur a stricter judgment.

James doesn't include here whatever specifics he had heard about that prompted him to write this part. We can use the teachings of Jesus to point in at least two directions.

In His teaching [Jesus] was saying: "Beware of the scribes who like to walk around in long robes, and like respectful greetings in the market places, and chief seats in the synagogues and places of honor at banquets, who devour widows' houses, and for appearance's sake offer long prayers; these will receive greater condemnation." (Mark 12:38-40)

Here we have Jesus criticizing people who set themselves up as teachers and then use the position to feed their ego or fill their pockets. Even their prayers are just for show.

It is reasonable to believe, from both the conditions in the Jewish Christian communities as James addresses them and from this teaching of Jesus, that too many people with sinful motivations were setting themselves up as teachers.

And that slave who knew his master's will and did not get ready or act in accord with his will, will receive many lashes, but the one who did not know it, and committed deeds worthy of a flogging, will receive but few. From everyone who has been given much, much will be required; and to whom they entrusted much, of him they will ask all the more. (Luke 12:47-48)

Jesus talks about willful, mindful disobedience done by people who know better. In light of this teaching of Jesus, it is reasonable to believe that too many people knew what and why they should be teaching and yet were not teaching the way they should.

Paul:

Therefore, I testify to you this day that I am innocent of the blood of all men. For I did not shrink from declaring to you the whole purpose of God. (Acts 20:26-27)

Paul:

Retain the standard of sound words which you have heard from me, in the faith and love which are in Christ Jesus. Guard, through the Holy Spirit who dwells in us, the treasure which has been entrusted to you. (2 Timothy 1:13-14)

If any of us accepts the office of elder, we are expected to fulfill the teaching role to the best of our abilities, all of the time "knowing that as [teachers] we will incur a stricter judgment." Elder leadership in the Christian community is a serious business with eternal consequences.

Paul was well aware of this line of thought:

Therefore, I testify to you this day that I am innocent of the blood of all men. For I did not shrink from declaring to you the whole purpose of God. (Acts 20:26-27)

And he gives this counsel to Christian teachers in 2 Timothy:

Retain the standard of sound words which you have heard from me, in the faith and love which are in Christ Jesus. Guard, through the Holy Spirit who dwells in us, the treasure which has been entrusted to you. (2 Timothy 1:13-14)

Paraphrase: *Not many of you should become teachers, my brothers, because you know that we who teach will be held to a higher standard.*

3:2 For we all stumble in many ways. If anyone does not stumble in what he says, he is a perfect man, able to bridle the whole body as well.

A general principle of sin is this: ". . . we all stumble in many ways." Everyone sins in a wide variety of ways, both great and small. If anyone's speech had absolutely no sin driving it, that would amount to a perfectly sinless person able to keep the entirety of his being from sinning as well. Only Jesus, the God-Man, could do that. It is not a possibility for the rest of us. Given this premise, Bible teachers are more likely to incur judgment due to improper speech because they are called on to regularly exercise the activity that is most prone to sinful expression—speaking.

In verses 3 and 4, James delivers two illustrations to support his assertion about the power of words.

3:3 Now if we put the bits into the horses' mouths so that they will obey us, we direct their entire body as well.

Even though the tongue is small, when it is unrestrained, the rest of the human creature is likely to be uncontrolled and undisciplined as well.

3:4 Look at the ships also, though they are so great and are driven by strong winds, are still directed by a very small rudder wherever the inclination of the pilot desires.

"the pilot"—the conscious, willful component; the conscious human spirit

"a very small rudder"—the means of control; the tongue

"the ships"—that which is controlled; the body

"strong winds"—violent, rough forces external to the ship and its pilot, capable of destroying the ship and its pilot, and beyond the pilot's control; manifestations of sin in the world

The conscious human spirit, inhabiting and piloting a human body that is subject to the violent and rough forces of sin in the world, is given a tongue—words—as a means of balancing this dynamic.

3:5a So also the tongue is a small part of the body, and yet it boasts of great things.

All of the wisdom literature in the Bible insists that the human tongue, as spoken word, has considerable power.

3:5b See how great a forest is set aflame by such a small fire!

Like a small spark that can become an out-of-control fire and destroy an entire forest, the human tongue has enormous destructive potential all out of proportion to its size.

A worthless man digs up evil, while his words are like scorching fire.
(Proverbs 16:27)

3:6 And the tongue is a fire, the very world of iniquity; the tongue is set among our members as that which defiles the entire body, and sets on fire the course of our life, and is set on fire by hell.

> "world"—(GK) *kosmos* the fallen, sinful world system ("iniquity" = evil)

Yes, the tongue really is that dangerous—a potential world of evil.

> *It is not what enters into the mouth that defiles the man, but what proceeds out of the mouth, this defiles the man. (Matthew 15:11)*

> *Peter said to [Jesus], "Explain the parable to us." Jesus said, "Are you still lacking in understanding also? Do you not understand that everything that goes into the mouth passes into the stomach, and is eliminated? But the things that proceed out of the mouth come from the heart, and those defile the man. For out of the heart come evil thoughts, murders, adulteries, fornications, thefts, false witness, slanders." (Matthew 15:15-19)*

Here we see two effects:

1. The tongue "defiles the [entirety of our being]."
2. The tongue "[wreaks havoc on] the [whole] course of our life."

. . . and one cause: the tongue "is set on fire by hell." Our English word *hell* is in this case a translation of the Greek word *Gehenna*. The word *Gehenna* originally referred to the Valley of Hinnom just outside of Jerusalem. The prophet Jeremiah tells us what happened in the Valley of Hinnom to cause it to be used as an illustration of the place of eternal separation from God:

> *They built the high places of Baal that are in the valley of Ben-hinnom to cause their sons and their daughters to pass through the fire to Molech, which I had not commanded them nor had it entered My mind that they should do this abomination, to cause Judah to sin. (Jeremiah 32:35)*

The god Molech was worshipped with child sacrifices. If you were feeling particularly religious, or if you were just sick of your infant child, you could earn Molech's favor by throwing him or her into the fire in front of the Molech idol. Jeremiah records a time when that was taking place just outside of Jerusalem at Gehenna. Because of that dark past, Gehenna was considered to be evil and was only used as a place to burn trash. It was a stinking, putrid dump where all of Jerusalem's garbage was burned every day. Jesus used the term *Gehenna* eleven times in the New Testament to illustrate the place of ultimate condemnation and punishment that we call hell. The power of hell—the power of Satan—gives the tongue its great potential for destruction.

> *The wise of heart will receive commands, but a babbling fool will be ruined. (Proverbs 10:8)*

> *He who conceals hatred has lying lips, and he who spreads slander is a fool. (Proverbs 10:18)*

> *Truthful lips will be established forever, but a lying tongue is only for a moment. (Proverbs 12:19)*

> *Do you see a man who is hasty in his words? There is more hope for [an ignorant dullard] than for him. (Proverbs 29:20)*

3:7 For every species of beasts and birds, of reptiles and creatures of the sea, is tamed and has been tamed by the human race.

The expression "is tamed and has been tamed" represents the divinely mandated state and ongoing process of human stewardship over creation.

TIME-BOUND: Genesis amplification: "every species" of the animal world is grouped together as separate from the "human race." Humans are not animals.

TIMELESS: Animals are not created as imagers of God.

3:8 But no one can tame the tongue; it is a restless evil and full of deadly poison.

"Restless" here is the same word translated in chapter 1, verse 8, as "unstable." The "restless evil" tongue is spiritually unstable and full of the poison of sin.

> *Their throat is an open grave, with their tongues they keep deceiving, the poison of asps is under their lips. (Romans 3:13)*

The expression "no one" literally translates as "no one among people." Human beings can tame all of the animals in creation, but "no one among people" can tame the "restless evil" of the tongue. The "deadly poison" of sin runs too deep in humanity.

> **Amplification:** *But Jesus looked at them and said, "With people [as far as it depends on them,] [salvation] is impossible, but with God all things are possible." (Matthew 19:26)*

TIME-BOUND: The tongue cannot be perfected by human effort.

TIME-BOUND / TIMELESS: But with God's help in the process of sanctification, it can be reined in.

TIME-BOUND: It is our responsibility as Christians to make this a part of our Christian work.

3:9 With it we bless our Lord and Father, and with it we curse men, who have been made in the likeness of God; . . .

This is the duality inherent in the "restless evil" of the tongue. The double-minded person claiming faith tries to please God and the lost world at the same time. At the extreme, this type of person claims to have faith in God while showing no signs of a saving faith yielding sanctifying works. The opposing nature of blessing and cursing is rooted in God's polarizing proclamations:

> *"I call heaven and earth to witness against you today, that I have set before you life and death, the blessing and the curse. So choose life in order that you may live, you and your descendants." (Deuteronomy 30:19)*

In ancient times, cursing was held as far more than just abusive or mean-spirited, time-bound language. Cursing someone was the act of calling on God to cut a person off from all blessings and to consign that person to hell. So then, praising God is the highest form of human speech; cursing one another is one of the lowest forms of human speech.

> *But I say to you who hear, love your enemies, do good to those who hate you, bless those who curse you, pray for those who mistreat you. (Luke 6:27-28)*

> *Bless those who persecute you; bless and do not curse. (Romans 12:14)*

3:10a ... from the same mouth come both blessing and cursing.

They have counseled only to thrust him down from his high position; they delight in falsehood; they bless with their mouth, but inwardly they curse. (Psalm 62:4)

3:10b My brethren, these things ought not to be this way.

TIME-BOUND: For the glory of God, things ought not to be this way.

TIMELESS: For your own ultimate good, things ought not to be this way.

"But I tell you that every careless word that people speak, they shall give an accounting for it in the day of judgment. For by your words you will be justified, and by your words you will be condemned." (Matthew 12:36-37)

3:11 Does a fountain send out from the same opening both fresh and bitter water?

James offers his first illustration here. Fresh water springs were essential to survival. Some springs produced a mixture of fresh and bitter water and were as unusable as the ones that only produced bitter. No spring produced fresh water one day and bitter water the next.

3:12a Can a fig tree, my brethren, produce olives, or a vine produce figs?

James's second illustration.

"You will know them by their fruits. Grapes are not gathered from thorn bushes nor figs from thistles, are they?" (Matthew 7:16)

3:12b Nor can salt water produce fresh.

A third illustration.

"So every good tree bears good fruit, but the bad tree bears bad fruit. A good tree cannot produce bad fruit, nor can a bad tree produce good fruit. Every tree that does not bear good fruit is cut down and thrown into the fire. So then, you will know them by their fruits." (Matthew 7:17-20)

A regenerated mouth should not pour out blessings to God one moment and curses on humanity the next.

"My brethren, these things ought not to be this way."

The simple, terse, and direct style of these verses demands meditation on this simple, terse, and direct command: "[P]rove yourselves doers of the word, and not merely hearers who delude themselves." Christians who have been supernaturally transformed by the power of the Holy Spirit ought to be on the path of authentically acting like it.

3:13-18 True Wisdom

The first part of chapter 3 dealt with the dangers and evils inherent in our sin-poisoned tongues and the care we should all take when we speak, especially those of us who teach the Bible. Now, the focus shifts from the problem of human speech to the solution: wisdom. And not just any wisdom—God's wisdom.

3:13 Who among you is wise and understanding? Let him show by his good behavior his deeds in the gentleness of wisdom.

"gentleness"—(GK) *prautes*: meekness; humility

Amplification: *"Blessed are the [meek/gentle/humble]." (Matthew 5:5a)*

Meekness of spirit does not mean weakness of spirit; it means we are to exercise self-control over our behaviors. The spiritually humble are broken before God and moving away from self-absorbed, self-centered, self-willed living.

TIME-BOUND / TIMELESS: True wisdom originates in the recognition of where we stand as sinful creatures in relation to the glory of God.

The fear of the Lord is the beginning of knowledge. (Proverbs 1:7a)

James teaches that only two kinds of wisdom exist: wisdom that comes from God and everything else. Acquiring true wisdom is not dependent on how much mental horsepower you have in your brain. True wisdom is not related to how clever your speech is or how much you know about this or that topic. The pursuit of true wisdom is more than mere intellection. True wisdom deals with the totality of who and what you are as an imager of God. For James, this means that behavior is as much a part of spiritual wisdom as thought.

> **Paraphrase:** *Who among you claims spiritual wisdom and special understanding? By the God-honoring obedience of his good behavior, let him make visible his works done in the spirit of humility that is true wisdom.*

3:14 But if you have bitter jealousy and selfish ambition in your heart, do not be arrogant and so lie against the truth.

"[B]itter jealousy and selfish ambition" are contrasted against the spirit of humility from verse 13.

> "jealousy"—(GK) *zelos*: positive sense, zeal; negative sense, envy
>
> > **Positive sense:** *His disciples remembered that it was written, "Zeal for Your house will consume me." (John 2:17)*
> >
> > **Negative sense:** *But the high priest rose up, along with all his associates . . . and they were filled with envy. (Acts 5:17)*
>
> "bitter jealousy"—the envy some people display when their ideas are effectively challenged
>
> "selfish ambition"—a sinful willingness to achieve personal power and prestige no matter what the cost to others
>
> "arrogant"—boastful

> *Thus says the Lord, "Let not a wise man boast of his wisdom, and let not the mighty man boast of his might, let not a rich man boast of his riches; but let him who boasts boast of this, that he understands and knows Me, that I am the Lord." (Jeremiah 9:23-24a)*

> **Amplification:** *But if you have bitter [envy] and selfish ambition in your heart, [you do not have wisdom and understanding, so] do not arrogantly boast [about your wisdom] and [in so doing] [sin] against the truth.*

3:15 This wisdom is not that which comes down from above, but is earthly, natural, demonic.

"from above"—from heaven; from God

"earthly"—human reasoning and human feeling with no allowance for God's will

"natural"—(GK) *psychikos*: unspiritual; natural in the negative sense that it is disconnected from God's will

"demonic"—(GK) *daimoniodes*: pertaining to demons; demonic in origin

Amplification: *[This kind of] [arrogant, bitter, selfish] wisdom is not [from God], but [having no allowance for God's will], it is unspiritual, and is demonic in origin.*

3:16 For where jealousy and selfish ambition exist, there is disorder and every evil thing.

"disorder"—(GK) *akatastasia*: confusion; another form of the word translated as "restless" from 3:8 and "unstable" from 1:8

. . . for God is not a God of akatastasia *but of peace. (1 Corinthians 14:33a)*

"When you hear of wars and akatastasia, *do not be terrified; for these things must take place first, but the end does not follow immediately." (Luke 21:9)*

The akatastasia caused by "envy and selfish ambition" yields "every evil thing."

Amplification: *"every [kind of] evil thing," "every kind of evil [practice]"*

Specific: A worldly church, pursuing things of the world, is always a place of spiritual disorder and spiritual confusion, and the result will always be spiritual chaos. Churches that teach people to draw close to the world instead of turning away from the world and drawing close to God, give birth to "every evil thing"—every kind of spiritually worthless practice.

General: Moving away from the true wisdom of God can and does bring about every kind of evil practice.

3:17 But the wisdom from above is first pure, then peaceable, gentle, reasonable, full of mercy and good fruits, unwavering, without hypocrisy.

This wisdom comes "from above," which means it comes to humanity by the Holy Spirit. James does not use the term "Holy Spirit" in his letter, but the Spirit was commonly associated with wisdom in Jewish writings. The Old Testament writings develop a profile of the character of a godly person with true wisdom as a God-given orientation that will always have profound practical effects playing out in time. James attributes these characteristics to the power and presence of true wisdom. If he is not using the word "wisdom" as an equivalent to "Spirit," he is at least using "wisdom" as an effect of the Spirit.

True wisdom, the wisdom of the Spirit, is "first pure." True wisdom is innocent, morally blameless. Everything that follows is conditioned by the words "first pure."

God's wisdom is "peaceable" in the heart of a believer. It compels a Christian to be peace loving—to be "gentle" and "reasonable." True wisdom compels us to engage people with consideration and to be open to reason when working through the Bible with each other. Those moving in this wisdom will be "full of mercy and good fruit."

"mercy and good fruits"—"Blessed are the merciful" (Matthew 5:7a).

No particular object of this mercy is specified; this mercy is a general function of being Jesus's disciple and applies to all situations. We have received God's mercy and demonstrate it by extending mercy to others. We are blessed when we love others as Christ loves us.

TIME-BOUND: True wisdom will produce the good fruit of genuine mercy.

"unwavering"—(GK) *adiakritos*: impartial; straightforward

TIMELESS: The true wisdom of God is ultimate truth. As such, it is impartial and straightforward. It does not vary from one person to another or from one situation to the next.

"without hypocrisy"—(GK) *anypokritos*: sincere; not playing a part

313

True wisdom is sincere. It does not play at the superficialities of religion. True wisdom is not capable of thinking one thing and saying another. A Christian hypocrite is working against the Spirit.

> **TIMELESS:** True wisdom is by its nature heavenly, is spiritual in essence, and originates with God.

The Bible is unwavering, straightforward, and stands as an impartial judge of all humanity on its own terms. I am doing my best to get out of my own way and be as clear about those terms as I can. With careful study over a long period of time, you will find that the Scriptures are not near as open to interpretation as some people like to tell you, especially when it comes to the basics of our faith. There are just a whole lot of people out there looking for loopholes to fit their earthly opinions into, instead of surrendering their earthly opinions to God's "unwavering" truth.

As a Christian teacher, I do my best to not care about my own earthly opinions. And while I care deeply about all of my students, I genuinely do not care about their earthly opinions either. I want us all to be about the business of mining the Scriptures so as to get away from our own earthly opinions and get to the heart of the matter: true wisdom—the heart of Christ as revealed in the Bible by the Spirit.

3:18 And the seed whose fruit is righteousness is sown in peace by those who make peace.

> "the seed whose fruit is righteousness"—conduct that is pleasing to God; the opposite of "every kind of evil"
>
> "the seed . . . is sown in peace"—"Blessed are the peacemakers" (Matthew 5:9a).

We must live the Good News of Jesus Christ out in the world. It is an active state of being and doing. While this blessing includes the idea of cultivating friendship and harmony with those around us, the primary expression of Christian peacemaking is living faithfully in alignment with the Bible's precepts so that we can authentically share biblical truth with others.

TIME-BOUND / TIMELESS: The seed is sown in the peace of God by those who are at peace with God and who then help others make peace with God.

TIME-BOUND: Helping others come to peace with God is the primary expression of Christian peacemaking.

TIME-BOUND / TIMELESS: The peace God speaks of can never exist outside of God's truth.

TIME-BOUND: We are never to avoid God's truth in an effort to "go along to get along."

TIME-BOUND / TIMELESS: God's truth is "first pure" and it must be first in our lives.

TIME-BOUND: The "seed . . . is sown in peace" when we give witness to the possibility for peace between God and humanity.

TIMELESS: Our reward—"[We] shall be called the children of God" (Matthew 5:9b).

4:1-10 Sanctifying Obedience

What is sin? At its essence, sin is separation from God. To move in sin is to move away from God. When lost people embrace and engage in thoughts and actions that the Bible calls out as sinful, their separation from

God is amplified as "the wrath of God is revealed from heaven against all ungodliness and unrighteousness of men who suppress the truth in unrighteousness" (Romans 1:18).

A large chunk of the church in this day and age is separating itself from God by separating itself from the biblical definitions of sin and by embracing the resultant sinful activities that grow out of sin. Too many assemblies are filled with people who cannot or will not see sin for what it is, or who refuse to identify as sin those things that the Bible calls out as sinful.

> **TIME-BOUND:** When people play at Christianity, the result is always the same: secular humanism in the form of liberal theology. The definition of sin, or even the acceptance that there is sin, is then left up to each individual.

Without the biblical doctrine of sin, humans become their own standard for what is right and wrong, and there is no spiritual dynamic for conviction and repentance. That is the path of secular humanism and the end game of liberal theologies. The end result is that no ultimate truth exists and standards of right and wrong are left up to the tyranny of the earthly humanists.

James is writing to Christian converts from Judaism in this letter. James's initial target audience, and his extended target audience for the last two thousand years, consists of people claiming faith in Christ who know and accept that God will not save them from sin if they are denying the reality and presence of sin. These are people—including us—who are exhibiting sinful actions both gross and subtle and should know better. These are people who do know better, and they are missing the mark in their Christian walks.

In these next verses, James is going to remind us about what is really going on when quarrels and conflicts rear their heads in a Christian community. He is going to remind us about what happens when there is too much world in our walks and in our assemblies.

4:1a What is the source of quarrels and conflicts among you?

> "quarrels"—(GK) *machai:* battles or controversy of any kind (physical violence or as a metaphor for bitter arguing or inward anxiety)
>
> "conflicts"—(GK) *polemoi:* war; battle; strife (actual or metaphorical)

James does not mention the details that were being fought over; he just calls out the bitterness of the fighting itself. He doesn't get lost in the superficial details; instead he asks, "What is the source. . . ?" He is more concerned with the underlying frequencies of earthbound and unspiritual thinking that have allowed demonic forces to drive the church.

4:1b Is not the source your pleasures that wage war in your members?

"pleasures"—(GK) *hedone*: desires; sinful, self-indulgent desires; this is where the English word *hedonist* comes from—a hedonist is given over to the self-absorbed pursuit of personal pleasure.

"members"—(GK) *mele*: parts of the human body; parts of the Christian community (in the case of this verse, I think James is pointing in both directions)

Beloved, I urge you as aliens and strangers to abstain from fleshly lusts [desires] which wage war against the soul. (1 Peter 2:11)

Amplification 1: *Is not the source your [sinful self-indulgent desires] that wage war in your [bodies]?*

For the body is not one member, but many. . . . so that there may be no division in the body, but that the members may have the same care for one another. (1 Corinthians 12:14, 25)

Amplification 2: *Is not the source your [sinful self-indulgent desires] that wage war in your [communities]?*

These are the desires that are at war in each of us and that get between each of us. Left to ourselves, we all default to wanting what we think is best for ourselves.

TIME-BOUND: No one this side of glorification is immune to self-indulgent desires and controlling covetousness.

4:2a You lust and do not have; so you commit murder.

"You have heard that the ancients were told, 'You shall not commit murder' and 'Whoever commits murder shall be liable to the court.' But I say to you that everyone who is angry with his brother shall be guilty before the court; and whoever says to his brother, 'You good-for-nothing,' shall be guilty before the supreme court; and whoever says, 'You fool,' shall be guilty enough to go into the fiery hell." (Matthew 5:21-22)

People always covet; people always want to get something they do not have. Frustrated desire to obtain possession of things, or control over people or situations, always escalates in the intensity of its expression if left unchecked.

TIMELESS: The murderous damage done is real and has real eternal consequences whether or not physical murder takes place in time.

4:2b You are envious and cannot obtain; so you fight and quarrel.

Amplification: *You [lust for] and cannot obtain [things in the world]; so you fight and quarrel [like the love of the Father is not in you].*

TIME-BOUND: Do not love the world nor the things in the world. (1 John 2:15a)

TIMELESS: If anyone loves the world, the love of the Father is not in him. (1 John 2:15b)

4:2c You do not have because you do not ask.

Amplification 1: *You do not have [what you really need] because you do not ask [God].*

Amplification 2: *You do not have [true wisdom] because you do not ask [God].*

In 4:1a James asks us, *"What [causes the] quarrels and conflicts among you?"*

Paraphrase: *They happen because you want your own way and fight for it deep inside yourselves. You want control over people and things, you lust for what you do not have, and you are willing to sin against God and humanity to get your way. You do not get these things from God because they are not yours to have; God does not respond to that kind of asking. And you do not have true wisdom because you do not ask God for it.*

4:3 You ask and do not receive, because you ask with wrong motives, so that you may spend it on your pleasures.

Jesus said, "Ask and it will be given to you" (Matthew 7:7a). But He said that right after saying, "Pray, then, in this way: 'Our Father who is in heaven, let Holy be Your name. Let Your kingdom come. Let Your will be done, on earth as it is in heaven'" (Matthew 6:9-10). We are not supposed to pray selfishly or self-indulgently. Our prayers should not be reflective of the "[sinful self-indulgent desires] that wage war in our [bodies]" (James 4:1b).

> **Paraphrase:** *You ask God for things and you don't receive because you ask with sinful, self-indulgent motives that are out of alignment with the will and way of God. You ask God for things and you don't receive because you're really just trying to indulge your own sinful desires and have things your own way.*

4:4 You adulteresses, do you not know that friendship with the world is hostility toward God? Therefore whoever wishes to be a friend of the world makes himself an enemy of God.

The Old Testament prophetic books often portray the relationship between God and His people as a marriage relationship with the Lord as the husband and Israel as the wife. When Israel turns to idolatry, she is accused of committing spiritual adultery against God: "But like a woman unfaithful to her husband, so you, Israel, have been unfaithful to me, declares the Lord" (Jeremiah 3:20). Jesus carried this theme forward when He called those who rejected Him "a wicked and adulterous generation" (Matthew 12:39a).

If you are doing things in the world that create "hostility toward God," then you make yourself "an enemy of God." When you behave in a worldly way, you are demonstrating that your allegiance is to the world and not to God.

TIME-BOUND / TIMELESS: The word "enemy" cuts both ways. If you are an enemy of God, God is your enemy.

4:5 Or do you think that the Scripture speaks to no purpose: "He jealously desires the Spirit which He has made to dwell in us"?

> *"You shall not bow down to them or worship them; for I, the Lord your God, am a jealous God, punishing the children for the sin of the parents to the third and fourth generation of those who hate me." (Exodus 20:5)*

"Do not worship any other god, for the Lord, whose name is Jealous, is a jealous God." (Exodus 34:14)

"This is what the Lord Almighty says: 'I am very jealous for Zion; I am burning with jealousy for her.'" (Zechariah 8:2)

TIME-BOUND / TIMELESS: God is jealous for His people; He will not share us with the world. He claims total ownership over our lives and demands faithful obedience.

4:6a But He gives a greater grace.

God's grace is sufficient for us to meet the requirement of verse 5. The wrath and anger of God are terrifying things, but His grace, mercy, and holy love give us everything we need to meet His requirements for salvation.

4:6b Therefore it says, "God is opposed to the proud, but gives grace to the humble."

God's gift of grace is only available to those who humble themselves before the person and work of Jesus Christ and surrender their lives to Him by way of faith.

4:7a Submit therefore to God.

For the mind set on the flesh is death, but the mind set on the Spirit is life and peace, because the mind set on the flesh is hostile toward God; for it does not subject itself to the law of God, for it is not even able to do so. (Romans 8:6-7)

For not knowing about God's righteousness and seeking to establish their own, they did not subject themselves to the righteousness of God. (Romans 10:3)

Therefore humble yourselves under the mighty hand of God, that He may exalt you at the proper time. (1 Peter 5:6)

TIME-BOUND / TIMELESS: Surrender your life to God and live surrendered to God.

COMMENTARY: THE LETTER OF JAMES

4:7b Resist the devil and he will flee from you.

Stand against the devil's authority. Whatever power Satan has, the Holy Spirit gives us the ability to overcome that power. At the heart of sin is trusting in the devil while distrusting God.

> **TIME-BOUND:** Anything Satan offers is nothing but a cheap, time-bound counterfeit of what God offers.

4:8a Draw near to God and He will draw near to you.

> *Therefore, return to your God, observe loyalty and justice, and wait for your God continually. (Hosea 12:6)*

When we have failed a test God puts before us, when we stop resisting the devil as we go into temptation and willfully embrace sinful actions, here is a promise to the faithful of ongoing forgiveness and time-bound spiritual restoration.

4:8b Cleanse your hands, you sinners; and purify your hearts, you double-minded.

Remember that the letter of James is written to converted Jews who are now Christians. James is writing to Christians who have fallen into sinful lifestyles. He is accusing this type of Christian of attempting to be friends with both God and the world at the same time.

If you are not living right, "cleanse your hands"—repent of the external behavior. If you are not thinking right, "purify your hearts"—repent of your internal attitude that is causing the sinful external behavior. You cannot do either of these without the other.

4:9a Be miserable and mourn and weep; . . .

This is the repentance language of the Old Testament prophets.

> **TIME-BOUND / TIMELESS:** A saved person should experience and manifest heartfelt repentance for sinful actions.

4:9b . . . let your laughter be turned into mourning and your joy to gloom.

> "laughter"—the metaphorical mark of the biblical fool; laughing in response to God's word
>
> "joy"—worldly joy, finding joy in sin; the opposite of rejoicing in the Lord

For as the crackling of thorn bushes under a pot, so is the laughter of the fool. And this too is futility. (Ecclesiastes 7:6)

"Woe to you who laugh now, for you shall mourn and weep." (Luke 6:25b)

"Blessed are those who mourn." (Matthew 5:4)

Christians are supposed to mourn, to grieve over sin. The more you grow spiritually, the more both your sinful actions and the condition of sin itself should bother you—if you are saved. Do not have a casual attitude toward sin and sinfulness.

TIME-BOUND / TIMELESS: Sins should deeply bother and trouble anyone experiencing the process of sanctification.

4:10 Humble yourselves in the presence of the Lord, and He will exalt you.

"The Pharisee stood and was praying this to himself: 'God, I thank You that I am not like other people: swindlers, unjust, adulterers, or even like this tax collector. I fast twice a week; I pay tithes of all that I get.' But the tax collector, standing some distance away, was even unwilling to lift up his eyes to heaven, but was beating his breast, saying, 'God, be merciful to me, the sinner!' I tell you, this man went to his house justified rather than the other; for everyone who exalts himself will be humbled, but he who humbles himself will be exalted." (Luke 18:11-14)

Here is a test of whether or not true wisdom is working in you. When was the last time you were deeply grieved over your sinfulness? When was the last time you broke down inside like the tax collector in Jesus's story and cried out something like, "God, I am sinner! Be merciful to me!"? You cannot humble yourself in the presence of the Lord if sin, especially your own, does not grieve you. The presence of sin breaks you down deep inside.

This passage from Luke is an antidote for works-based thinking. There is no blessing in attempting to lift yourself up by your own power in the presence of the Lord, "for everyone who exalts himself will be humbled." Sanctification is about learning to trust and rely on God more and more in everything we do—in every thought, in every action.

> **TIME-BOUND / TIMELESS:** The sanctifying walk is not an easy path, but God would not ask us to walk it if it cannot be done. He gave us His word.

4:11-12 Do Not Speak Against One Another

4:11a Do not speak against one another, brethren.

James brings us from "brethren" through "adulterous . . . double-minded . . . sinner" and back to "brethren" again. He moves from exhortation to repentance and now back to exhortation again.

> "speak against"—(GK) *katalaleo*: slander, defame, or denigrate—the absence of the person spoken against is implied, evil is implied; backbite—the person cannot see the attack, and they are unable to defend themselves

Katalaleo has at its root the word *laleo,* which means "mindless sound" or "sound without thought." *Laleo* means "sound made carelessly" or "careless noise." *Laleo* is attached to the preposition *kata,* which means "down." When you put them together as *katalaleo,* it means speaking down against a person and speaking evil against a person in a careless, thoughtless way—what we call slandering a person.

Slandering God:

> *The people spoke against God and Moses, "Why have you brought us up out of Egypt to die in the wilderness? For there is no bread and no water, and we loathe this miserable food." (Numbers 21:5)*

Slandering others internally:

> *Whoever secretly slanders his neighbor, him I will destroy; no one who has a haughty look and an arrogant heart will I endure. (Psalm 101:5)*

Slandering others externally:

> *You shall not bear false witness against your neighbor. (Exodus 20:16)*

> **Amplification:** *Do not [slander] one another, brethren.*

Slandering is a sinful activity you can do anytime, anyplace, regardless of circumstances, and you can do it with equal intensity with either your heart or your mouth.

4:11b He who speaks against a brother or judges his brother, speaks against the law and judges the law; . . .

> *"You shall not go about as a slanderer among your people, and you are not to act against the life of your neighbor; I am the Lord. You shall not hate your fellow countryman in your heart; you may surely reprove your neighbor, but shall not incur sin because of him. You shall not take vengeance, nor bear any grudge against the sons of your people, but you shall love your neighbor as yourself; I am the Lord." (Leviticus 19:16-18)*

> **Amplification:** *He who [slanders] a brother or judges his brother [to condemnation], speaks against the law and judges the law.*

> **TIME-BOUND / TIMELESS:** Slandering a fellow believer contradicts the "royal law" (from James 2:8).

4:11c . . . but if you judge the law, you are not a doer of the law but a judge of it.

You cannot claim to be under the authority of God's law if you deny its authority. You cannot claim to be a doer of God's law if you will not submit to biblical precepts and live them out on God's biblical terms. When you slander a brother or sister, you are elevating yourself to a place above the law of God. You are acting as if you are no longer subject to God's law; you are making God's law subject to you. And because the second command is like the first, to participate in gossip or slander is also to dishonor God. To willfully, mindfully engage in gossip or slander is to place yourself above the law of God. If you go all the way and are claiming the authority to judge the heart of another human to condemnation, then you are slandering both the law of God and God personally by claiming God-level authority. 4:12a There is only one Lawgiver and Judge, the One who is able to save and to destroy; . . .

> (capital *L*) "Lawgiver"—God is the One who put the law in place.

> (capital *J*) "Judge"—God is the One who ultimately applies the law.

> **TIMELESS:** "to save and to destroy"—Only God can rescue a person from

spiritual destruction. Only God can spiritually destroy a person through eternal separation.

"See now that I, I am He, and there is no god besides Me; it is I who put to death and give life. I have wounded and it is I who heal, and there is no one who can deliver from My hand." (Deuteronomy 32:39)

Therefore you have no excuse, everyone of you who passes judgment, for in that which you judge another, you condemn yourself; for you who judge practice the same things. (Romans 2:1)

"Do not fear those who kill the body but are unable to kill the soul; but rather fear Him who is able to destroy both soul and body in hell." (Matthew 10:28)

TIMELESS: The law comes from God. Only God has the authority to judge to salvation or judge to condemnation.

TIME-BOUND: None of us have the right to slander a neighbor or judge him to condemnation.

There are six things which the Lord hates, yes, seven which are an abomination to Him: haughty eyes, a lying tongue, and hands that shed innocent blood, a heart that devises wicked plans, feet that run rapidly to evil, a false witness who utters lies, and one who spreads strife among brothers. (Proverbs 6:16-19)

4:12b ... but who are you who judge your neighbor?

James does not ask, "Who are you to judge your neighbor's sins?" He asks, "[W]ho are you to judge your neighbor?"

Amplification: *"Do not judge [to condemnation] so that you will not be judged [to condemnation]. For in the way you judge, you will be judged; and by your standard of measure, it will be measured to you." (Matthew 7:1-2)*

Amplification: *But you, why do you judge your brother [to condemnation]? Or you again, why do you regard your brother with contempt? For we will all stand before the judgment seat of God. For it is written, "As I live, says the Lord, every knee shall bow to Me, and*

> every tongue shall give praise to God." So then each one of us will give an account of himself to God. Therefore let us not judge one another [to condemnation] anymore, but rather determine this—not to put an obstacle or a stumbling block in a brother's way. (Romans 14:10-13)

Amplification: *But to me it is a very small thing that I may be examined by you, or by any human court; in fact, I do not even examine myself. For I am conscious of nothing against myself, yet I am not by this acquitted; but the one who examines me [to salvation or to condemnation] is the Lord. Therefore do not go on passing judgment before the time [of final judgment], but wait until the Lord comes who will both bring to light the things hidden in the darkness and disclose the motives of men's hearts; and then each man's praise will come to him from God. (1 Corinthians 4:3-5)*

TIME-BOUND: When we judge a person to condemnation, we are "judging the law"—exceeding our disciplining mandate; in effect taking the place of God.

> *"Why do you look at the speck that is in your brother's eye, but do not notice the log that is in your own eye? Or how can you say to your brother, 'Let me take the speck out of your eye,' and behold, the log is in your own eye? You hypocrite, first take the log out of your own eye, and then you will see clearly to take the speck out of your brother's eye." (Matthew 7:3-5)*

We are only to judge the manifestations of sin; only God can judge the heart of the sinner. We are to discern sinful actions by the biblical standard and then disciple each other by the biblical standard. We are commanded by Jesus to disciple each other. We are to confront each other's sinful thoughts and actions while maintaining an authentic Christian bond of self-sacrificial love for one another.

> *Therefore do not go on passing judgment [to condemnation] before the time [of final judgment], but wait until the Lord comes who will both bring to light the things hidden in the darkness and disclose the motives of men's hearts; and then each man's praise will come to him from God. (1 Corinthians 4:3-5)*

Acting as if we have the authority to judge an individual to condemnation, instead of compassionately judging just their (and our) sinful actions, is an act of spiritual violence against God's law and an affront to the holiness and sovereignty of God.

> **TIME-BOUND / TIMELESS:** Humble yourselves in the presence of the Lord. (James 4:10)

The mark of a true believer is humility before God. *Humility* in ancient Greek means "lowliness of mind." We lower our minds, and we elevate God. A Christian humbly submits to God by submitting to the precepts and commands of God as absolute truth because a true Christian recognizes sovereign God as the giver of that truth. A true Christian recognizes and submits to the absolute authority of the Bible because it is the specific revelation of God.

Since the second command is like the first, the measure of a true believer is humility before humanity. This is another test of saving faith. Are you given over to malicious gossip? Do you habitually tell stories and lies that paint false pictures of those around you? According to James, these behaviors expose an evil nature and an unregenerate heart—something far away from a new creation in Christ.

Here is how Jesus responded to those who slandered Him:

> *"You are of your father the devil, and you want to do the desires of your father. He was a murderer from the beginning, and does not stand in the truth because there is no truth in him. Whenever he speaks a lie, he speaks from his own nature, for he is a liar and the father of lies."* *(John 8:44)*

A warning from the apostle John:

> *If someone says, "I love God," and hates his brother, he is a liar; for the one who does not love his brother whom he has seen, cannot love God whom he has not seen. (1 John 4:20)*

The word *devil* translates "*diabolos*"—the slanderer.

4:13-17 You Are Just a Vapor

4:13 Come now, you who say, "Today or tomorrow we will go to such and such a city, and spend a year there and engage in business and make a profit."

"Come now, you who say" is a rebuke. Christians should not move through life this way. James is not stating that a business person should not make a profit; this is not a lesson in economics. The problem is focusing on business to the exclusion of God. He is also not telling Christians to exist only for the moment and not make any plans or put any attention toward possible futures.

> *"[W]e will go to such and such city, [we will] spend a year there and [we will] engage in business and [we will] make a profit."*

> *But you said in your heart, "I will ascend to heaven; I will raise my throne above the stars of God, and I will sit on the mount of assembly in the recesses of the north. I will ascend above the heights of the clouds; I will make myself like the Most High." (Isaiah 14:13-14)*

James is warning us against the sin of prideful arrogance and its companion, worldly self-absorption. We can become so consumed with our business in the world that we lose sight of the spiritual. And it is a habitual kind of thing. The more we indulge that kind of life frequency, the easier it becomes to stay lost in it.

We have to make plans, and we have to invest in them to varying degrees. The problem is making plans as if God is not involved. Christians are not supposed to act like we are in control of God's universe. That kind of thinking is sinful at its essence.

TIME-BOUND: Christians are not supposed to move around in time with no regard for the will of God.

4:14 Yet you do not know what your life will be like tomorrow. You are just a vapor that appears for a little while and then vanishes away.

"Yet you" can be literally translated "people such as you." There are some grammatical complexities in the Greek that make it equally possible to render the first part of this verse as a statement followed by a question:

> **Amplification:** *Yet [people such as you] do not know what will happen tomorrow. [What kind of life is yours?]*

TIME-BOUND: There is an inherent uncertainty in the time-bound human condition left to itself; human life is fragile.

TIME-BOUND / TIMELESS: Christians do not have a sovereign overview, just a view into sovereignty through the Bible and the indwelling of the Spirit.

Question: What kind of life is yours?

Answer: *You are just a vapor that appears for a little while and then vanishes away.*

"vapor"—(GK) *atmis*: mist; smoke

Behold, You have made my days as handbreadths, and my lifetime as nothing in Your sight; surely every man at his best is a mere breath. Surely every man walks about as a phantom; surely they make an uproar for nothing; he amasses riches and does not know who will gather them. (Psalm 39:5-6)

Individual humans appear for a few movements in time, and then time blows us away like vapor, mist, or smoke in a strong wind. Our time here is already short, and God promises tomorrow to no one. You are not even promised your next breath. If you inhale your next breath, it is because God continues to exhale life into you.

TIME-BOUND: Human life is transitory—here today, gone tomorrow.

4:15 Instead, you ought to say, "If the Lord wills, we will live and also do this or that."

It is not enough to recognize the truth of verse 14. A person can have an overwhelming sense of their smallness in time and still act like the universe is a closed system. It is not enough to be generally spiritual-minded. Lots of ancient religious traditions used the expression "if the gods will it." James marks his teaching as being expressly Christian by using the phrase "if the Lord wills."

"Lord"—(GK) *kyrios:* master, supreme, or one who has power and authority; *Kyrios* is used throughout the Bible to refer to Yahweh, God the Father; *Kyrios* is used in the New Testament to refer to Jesus Christ.

James is addressing Christians here. As Christians we must maintain focus on the spiritual realm. God is testing us, refining us, getting us to a place where we realize that everything we are and everything we have is unfolding under the sovereign will of God. We are to come to a place where we are consciously living right in the middle of the tension caused by the paradox of time playing out in context of God's absolute sovereignty. That is a place of deep and daily surrender to the mystery of life in Christ. James tells us plainly: throughout the course of your doings, be in submission to God.

¹⁴ You are just a vapor. . . . ¹⁵If the Lord wills, [you] will live.

We only remain alive in time for a little while because the Lord wills it. The expression "if the Lord wills" or "God willing" is not to be mindlessly recited as magical, ritual religious-speak; it should become a deep, inner way of thinking about anything and everything all of the time.

> **TIME-BOUND / TIMELESS:** Whatever we do, our baseline stance should be dependence on the Lord.

4:16 But as it is, you boast in your arrogance; all such boasting is evil.

Even though you know about God, "You [put confidence in and rejoice in] your arrogance." You take a certain pride in yourself in planning your future with such confidence. This is the attitude underlying any kind of solely time-bound human planning. Anything that elevates humanity over God is evil; anything that excludes God is evil; an arrogant sense of self-sufficiency is evil; "all such boasting is evil."

4:17 Therefore, to one who knows the right thing to do and does not do it, to him it is sin.

We have been told to seek the will of the Lord in everything that we do. We have been told to consider the will of the Lord in everything that we do. This is "the right thing to do" in any and all circumstances. We know what we are supposed to do; we know how God wants us to live our lives; we know how God wants us to organize our thoughts, and so we must sanctify.

> **TIME-BOUND:** Humble submission to God means humble obedience to God. You cannot have one without the other.

When we think of our sins, we have a tendency to think of some express sinful activity or thought that we have intentionally done. We do not tend to think in terms of all the things that the Lord tells us to do and that we do not do. But James is telling us that sins of omission are as real and serious as sins of commission. In other words, disregarding what we ought to do runs right alongside doing what God tells us not to do. This takes sinfulness beyond each letter of the law about any given express sinful activity. We are as accountable to God for internal states of sinful inaction as we are for externalized sinful actions.

> **TIME-BOUND:** To not live, think, and be the way God wants us to live, think, and be is sinful.

5:1-6 The Trap of Wealth and Power

Chapter 5 begins with, "Come now, you rich. . . ." The first part of this chapter is about the test of riches—the deadly trap of wealth and power. James will now drive home the spiritual danger inherent in the sinful misuse of wealth.

James is writing a letter to be read in Christian churches. He is going to use the specific behaviors of certain non-Christian rich landowners as part of his example, but his message is to the church. This is a warning to all of us. For those claiming to follow Christ, this test of wealth is also a warning against trying to hold on to worldly wealth and power with one hand while reaching for God with the other.

> **5:1 Come now, you rich, weep and howl for your miseries which are coming upon you.**

A rich person, by the biblical standard, is a person who has much more than he needs to survive. The person who only has pretty much what they need to get by has little or no discretionary income to get lost in. But any person with more than a little discretionary income has been blessed with wealth and is rich according to the Bible. You can be a little bit wealthy, somewhat wealthy, pretty darn wealthy, or ridiculously wealthy, and in all cases, you have extra riches, and according to the James, you are rich.

> **TIMELESS:** "miseries which are coming"—eternal condemnation

Weeping and howling are used throughout the prophetic writings to depict the reaction of the lost to the "miseries which are coming upon [them]" at the final judgment. People with varying degrees of riches are not condemned just for being rich. The Bible does not condemn degrees of wealth, but it uniformly condemns misuse of wealth. "Come now, you [unrighteous] rich" is the implication in this verse.

"But woe to you who are rich, for you are receiving your comfort in full. Woe to you who are well-fed now, for you shall be hungry. Woe to you who laugh now, for you shall mourn and weep." (Luke 6:24-25)

The characteristic of this type of rich person is that they lust after wealth. While wealth is not sinful in and of itself, Jesus warns about the ever-present potential for sin inherent in the pursuit and acquisition of wealth:

And Jesus said to His disciples, "Truly I say to you, it is hard for a rich man to enter the kingdom of heaven." (Matthew 19:23)

This is also a statement of damning judgment against lovers of money and hoarders of stuff, who accumulate massive amounts of wealth that they spend on themselves while claiming that they are living surrendered to Jesus Christ.

TIME-BOUND: If you are serving money, you are not serving God.

5:2 Your riches have rotted and your garments have become moth-eaten.

The Greek word for "riches" comes from the name of one of the ancient Greek gods. His name meant "the abundance of the earth," and he was the son of the goddess of the earth. Back then, people primarily held their riches to be stores of food and collections of fine clothing—earth stuff subject to decay. They tried to get security from perishable, earthly things. But at some point, those things come to nothing; they eventually rot away with time.

5:3a Your gold and your silver have rusted; . . .

"rusted"—(GK) *katioo*: corroded; (metaphorically) decayed

Next, James references something that people would have thought more durable: "Your gold and your silver have rusted." You stored up money thinking it would provide security, but time passes, you are headed toward death, and your gold and silver has metaphorically "decayed" in its usefulness to you.

5:3b . . . and their rust will be a witness against you and will consume your flesh like fire.

Every worldly thing that can be possessed exists in a state of decay. Even the things that seem to remain longer lose whatever utility you thought they had because even though they may remain in time in some form, you will not. Even though the unrighteous rich cannot or will not see it, their wealth is already in a state of spiritual decay. And the visible relationship of lost rich people to wealth and the world will ultimately stand as witness to the invisible state of spiritual decay in their souls.

> *"They will fling their silver into the streets and their gold will become an abhorrent thing; their silver and their gold will not be able to deliver them in the day of the wrath of the Lord. They cannot satisfy their appetite nor can they fill their stomachs, for their iniquity has become an occasion of stumbling." (Ezekiel 7:19)*

TIMELESS: If you have stored up more wealth than you need, it "will be a witness against you" when you are judged.

TIME-BOUND: If you are a Christian and God blesses you with any degree of wealth, He is testing you to see what you do with it.

TIMELESS: You are accountable to God for what you do with your wealth.

5:3c It is in the last days that you have stored up your treasure!

> **Paraphrase:** *We are in the last days. The Messiah has come, the turning point of history has been revealed, and yet you focus on worldly wealth and possessions. Your relationship to wealth is destroying you. You think you have stored up something powerful, something that will last. All you have really stored up is judgment.*

> *"Do not store up for yourselves treasures on earth, where moth and rust destroy, and where thieves break in and steal. But store up for yourselves treasures in heaven, where neither moth nor rust destroys, and where thieves do not break in or steal; for where your treasure is, there your heart will be also." (Matthew 6:19-21)*

> *"No servant can serve two masters; for either he will hate the one and love the other, or else he will be devoted to one and despise the other. You cannot serve God and wealth." (Luke 16:13)*

> **TIME-BOUND:** The first warning sign that points to "your miseries which are coming upon you" is habitual use of wealth for selfish purposes—"for where your treasure is, there your heart will be also" (Matthew 6:21).

5:4a Behold, the pay of the laborers who mowed your fields, and which has been withheld by you, cries out against you; . . .

When James wrote this letter, more and more land was being held by a small group of very wealthy landowners. Many farmers had to hire themselves out to these landowners in order to survive, and many of the landowners were not treating them fairly. By their mistreatment of the farmers, the wealthy landowners were violating God's Law whether they knew it or not.

> *"You shall not oppress your neighbor, nor rob him. The wages of a hired man are not to remain with you all night until morning." (Leviticus 19:13)*

> *"You shall not oppress a hired servant who is poor and needy, whether he is one of your countrymen or one of your aliens who is in your land in your towns. You shall give him his wages on his day before the sun sets, for he is poor and sets his heart on it; so that he will not cry against you to the Lord and it become sin in you." (Deuteronomy 24:14-15)*

These landowners were oppressing and robbing those who had less wealth and power. So James writes,

> *Behold, the pay of the laborers . . . cries out against you. (James 5:4a)*

This hearkens back to the Old Testament:

> *[God] said [to Cain], "What have you done? The voice of your brother's blood is crying to Me from the ground." (Genesis 4:10)*

> *And the sons of Israel sighed because of the bondage, and they cried out; and their cry for help because of their bondage rose up to God. (Exodus 2:23b)*

5:4b . . . and the outcry of those who did the harvesting has reached the ears of the Lord of Sabaoth.

> "the Lord of Sabaoth"—the Lord of Armies, the Lord of Hosts, the title for God as leader of the armies of heaven

Everything that happens everywhere in time "has reached the ears of the Lord of Hosts." God is holy, God is all-powerful, and we are living out some part of the biblical last days. No one can escape judgment.

Woe to those who add house to house and join field to field, until there is no more room, so that you have to live alone in the midst of the land! In my ears the Lord of hosts has sworn, "Surely, many houses shall become desolate, even great and fine ones, without occupants." (Isaiah 5:8-9)

TIME-BOUND: The second warning sign that points to "your miseries which are coming upon you" is the acquisition of wealth at the intentional expense of others.

5:5a You have lived luxuriously on the earth and led a life of wanton pleasure; . . .

The first accusation: "You have lived luxuriously on the earth." Is it wrong to live in luxury? Is it wrong to have degrees of soft living in this life? Nehemiah tells of a time of luxury provided by God in response to obedience:

"They captured fortified cities and a fertile land. They took possession of houses full of every good thing, hewn cisterns, vineyards, olive groves, fruit trees in abundance. So they ate, were filled and grew fat, and reveled in Your great goodness." (Nehemiah 9:25)

If you are living in obedience to God, and God provides you with some degree of comfort, that is OK; it can be a good thing. To have some degree of soft conditions in this life is not sinful. But a Christian must always be asking the following questions: *How much is enough? How much is too much?* And the answer to these questions must be discerned from careful examination of the Scriptures.

To indulge in extremes of luxury, to live out a sinful, self-indulgent lifestyle—which will always be at the expense of others in some way, shape, or form—is always wrong.

The second accusation: "You have . . . led a life of wanton pleasure." You gave yourself over to excess. You became consumed by your indulgence in pleasure. A life given over to wanton pleasure becomes a living spiritual death.

[S]he who gives herself to wanton pleasure is dead even while she lives. (1 Timothy 5:6)

It is always wrong to lead a life of wanton pleasure.

"Behold, this was the guilt of your sister Sodom: she and her daughters had arrogance, abundant food and careless ease, but she did not help the poor and needy." (Ezekiel 16:49)

335

TIME-BOUND: The third warning sign that points to "your miseries which are coming upon you" is this: "You have lived luxuriously [in sinful self-indulgence] on the earth and led a life of wanton [sinful] pleasure."

TIMELESS: Three warning signs, one result. . . .

5:5b . . . you have fattened your hearts in a day of slaughter.

If you are lost in money and power, your sinful desire for extreme pleasures became uncontrollable immersion in wanton pleasure. You are living just like cattle being fattened before being led off to the slaughterhouse. The difference is the animal's death has no eternal consequences; yours does.

The result of being the unrighteous rich is,

"a day of slaughter"—God's imminent judgment

Then I saw an angel standing in the sun, and he cried out with a loud voice, saying to all the birds which fly in midheaven, "Come, assemble for the great supper of God, so that you may eat the flesh of kings and the flesh of commanders and the flesh of mighty men and the flesh of horses and of those who sit on them and the flesh of all men, both free men and slaves, and small and great." (Revelation 19:17)

TIMELESS: The Messiah has come. We are in the last days. Eternal judgment is imminent on all of humanity . . .

TIME-BOUND: . . . and still, "you [unrighteous rich lost people] have fattened your hearts in a day of slaughter."

5:6a You have condemned and put to death the righteous man; . . .

"[T]he righteous man" here is the follower of God experiencing persecution by the wicked rich.

Thus says the Lord, "For three transgressions of Israel and for four I will not revoke its punishment, because they sell the righteous for money and the needy for a pair of sandals." (Amos 2:6)

For I know your transgressions are many and your sins are great, you who distress the righteous and accept bribes and turn aside the poor in the gate. (Amos 5:12)

They covet fields and then seize them, and houses, and take them away. They rob a man and his house, a man and his inheritance. (Micah 2:2)

"Recently My people have arisen as an enemy—you strip the robe off the garment from unsuspecting passers-by, from those returned from war. The women of My people you evict, each one from her pleasant house. From her children you take My splendor forever." (Micah 2:8-9)

"Hear now, heads of Jacob and rulers of the house of Israel. Is it not for you to know justice? You who hate good and love evil, who tear off their skin from them and their flesh from their bones, who eat the flesh of my people, strip off their skin from them, break their bones and chop them up as for the pot and as meat in a kettle." (Micah 3:1-3)

"Now hear this, heads of the house of Jacob and rulers of the house of Israel, who abhor justice and twist everything that is straight, who build Zion with bloodshed and Jerusalem with violent injustice. Her leaders pronounce judgment for a bribe, her priests instruct for a price and her prophets divine for money. Yet they lean on the Lord saying, 'Is not the Lord in our midst? Calamity will not come upon us.' Therefore, on account of you Zion will be plowed as a field, Jerusalem will become a heap of ruins, and the mountain of the temple will become high places of a forest." (Micah 3:9-12)

"Can I justify wicked scales and a bag of deceptive weights? For the rich men of the city are full of violence, her residents speak lies, and their tongue is deceitful in their mouth." (Micah 6:11-12)

If you are living the lifestyle of the unrighteous rich, "You have condemned [the industry of the righteous man] and put to death the [rights of the] righteous man [in this world]."

TIME-BOUND: If you are living in the lifestyle of the unrighteous rich as expressed in these verses, you have both knowingly and unknowingly destroyed people in the process of your lustful self-indulgence . . .

TIMELESS: . . . and you will be judged by God for it.

5:6b . . . he does not resist you.

Non-resistance can take this form:

> *"But I say to you, do not resist an evil person; but whoever slaps you on your right cheek, turn the other to him also." (Matthew 5:39)*

Or this:

> *Bless those who persecute you; bless and do not curse. (Romans 12:14)*

Or, non-resistance can be the inability to resist.

In all instances and situations, the rich are not condemned because they are wealthy or powerful; they are condemned because of what they do with their wealth and power, how they relate to it, and how they hurt others to get it or maintain it.

> *"Sell your possessions and give to charity; make yourselves money belts which do not wear out, an unfailing treasure in heaven, where no thief comes near nor moth destroys." (Luke 12:33)*

In the case of this test, if the accumulation of wealth and stuff rules your life, "their rust will be a witness against you and will consume your flesh like fire" (James 5:3b).

> *"[F]or where your treasure is, there your heart will be also." (Matthew 6:21)*

Whatever wealth you have has been given to you by God. Use it to care for the people God puts around you. Take care of your immediate family and then use the better part of your discretionary income as God directs you. If you think you are doing right by God because you regularly tithe ten percent, you need to learn the difference between Old Testament tithing (which was a mandatory group of taxes that amounted to about twenty-five to thirty percent) and Old Testament freewill giving (which was what the widow that Jesus noted was doing). There is no more theocratic Israel; the laws pertaining to the mandatory tax-tithe have been put away. Now there is only freewill giving like that which took place at the Temple offering box referenced in Mark 12:41-44 and Luke 21:1-4.

TIME-BOUND: As a Christian, what you give, when you give, and why you give is now to be worked out between you and God on an ongoing basis.

5:7-11 Sanctifying Endurance

5:7a Therefore be patient, brethren, until the coming of the Lord.

"coming"—(GK) *parousia*: presence; the coming of the Lord, the arrival of the Lord, or the coming presence of the Lord

Even though the lost unrighteous rich have wealth and power in this life and all of their crazy games are playing out all around us, they face certain condemnation on the day of judgment if they remain lost. Therefore, Christians should move through time in patient anticipation of the "coming of the Lord."

"patient"—(GK) *makrothumeo*: *makros* = long; *thumos* = anger; long-angered as opposed to short-angered; long-tempered as opposed to short-tempered

Amplification: *Therefore be [long-tempered, long-suffering. . . .]*

The command has no specific pointer or detail. We are to be generally patient with people as things play out. We are to live resigned to the condition we find ourselves in as we keep our spiritual attention forward focused on the promises of God. James is also implicitly forbidding Christians from taking vengeance on their oppressors: "be patient . . . until the coming of the Lord."

Never take your own revenge, beloved, but leave room for the wrath of God, for it is written, "Vengeance is Mine, I will repay," says the Lord. (Romans 12:19)

TIME-BOUND: To endure whatever the world throws at you . . .

TIMELESS: . . . remain focused on the hope of your faith.

5:7b The farmer waits for the precious produce of the soil, being patient about it, until it gets the early and late rains.

In Palestine, the rains that came briefly at the beginning and end of the growing season were critically important. If either the early or the late rains did not happen, there was going to be a food problem:

"[God] will give the rain for your land in its season, the early and late rain, that you may gather in your grain and your new wine and your oil." (Deuteronomy 11:14)

James drives home the point that, despite all of our efforts and inventions, we are never in control of things the way we like to think we are. There is only so much farmers can do by their actions.

TIME-BOUND: A lost farmer does what he can do and waits.

TIME-BOUND / TIMELESS: A Christian farmer prayerfully does what he can do and then prays as he waits.

5:8a You too be patient; strengthen your hearts; . . .

There is only so much Christians can do by their actions. A Christian prayerfully does what he can do and then waits and prays. We do what we can do, and then we are to be patient with the things that are beyond our abilities.

"strengthen"—(GK) *sterixate*: be resolute; set your heart; establish your heart

When the days were approaching for His ascension, [Jesus] was determined *to go to Jerusalem. (Luke 9:51)*

When the days were approaching for His ascension, [Jesus] set His heart *to go to Jerusalem. (Luke 9:51)*

When the days were approaching for His ascension, [Jesus] set His face *to go to Jerusalem. (Luke 9:51)*

Amplification: *You too be [long-tempered, long-suffering; be in the sanctifying process of standing yourself up by your heart].*

Remember: "[A] double-minded man, [is] unstable in all his ways" (James 1:8).

[A]nd may the Lord cause you to increase and abound in love for one another, and for all people, just as we also do for you, so that He may establish your hearts without blame in holiness before our God and Father at the coming of our Lord Jesus with all His saints. (1 Thessalonians 3:12-13)

5:8b . . . for the coming of the Lord is near.

"is near"—(GK) *engizo*: nearness in space or time

Many early Christians, when they heard things like this about the second coming, expected Christ to return in their lifetime. But the expression "is near" is relative to the context of its usage.

"But of that day or hour no one knows, not even the angels in heaven, nor the Son, but the Father alone." (Mark 13:32)

The context of that statement is that it was made by the incarnate Jesus before His resurrection. Jesus did not claim the prerogatives of deity in His incarnation. He displayed surrendered obedience and humble confidence in the will of the Father. His expression of divine Sonship binds Jesus to humanity as our example to follow.

TIME-BOUND: The mystical lesson for all of time is that if the incarnate Jesus did not know, no one else in time can make a claim to know.

The risen Christ then reinforced the truth He had previously taught:

So when they had come together, they were asking Him, saying, "Lord, is it at this time You are restoring the kingdom to Israel?" [Jesus] said to them, "It is not for you to know times or epochs which the Father has fixed by His own authority." (Acts 1:6-7)

The death and resurrection of Jesus, and the giving of the Holy Spirit do mark the beginning of the last days, but only God knows the duration. The meaning of "is near" must be viewed in context of the entirety of salvation history from the beginning.

TIMELESS: But do not let this one fact escape your notice, beloved, that with the Lord one day is like a thousand years, and a thousand years is like one day. (2 Peter 3:8)

TIME-BOUND: The end of all things is near; therefore, be of sound judgment and sober spirit for the purpose of prayer. (1 Peter 4:7)

> **TIMELESS:** By God's way of reckoning, "the coming of the Lord is near."

> **TIME-BOUND:** A Christian is supposed to live in a constant state of preparedness.

5:9a Do not complain, brethren, against one another.

> "complain"—(GK) *stenazo*: grumble or murmur; in the Bible, "groans" (as a result of oppression)

Trials and temptations are persistent. It is easy and common for us to do our best in the world and then turn our frustrations on each other. But if we are commanded to be patient with the lost world, then we should be even more so within our Christian family.

> *We urge you, brethren, admonish the unruly, encourage the fainthearted, help the weak, be patient with everyone. See that no one repays another with evil for evil, but always seek after that which is good for one another and for all people. (1 Thessalonians 5:14-15)*

> *Therefore I, the prisoner of the Lord, implore you to walk in a manner worthy of the calling with which you have been called, with all humility and gentleness, with patience, showing tolerance for one another in love. (Ephesians 4:1-2)*

5:9b . . . so that you yourselves may not be judged.

> "be judged"—(GK) *katakrino*: be condemned; be damned; be judged to condemnation

> **Amplification:** *"Do not judge [to condemnation] so that you will not be judged [to condemnation]." (Matthew 7:1)*

James began chapter 5 reminding us about the judgment coming upon the lost. Here, he reminds us that we, too, will be judged, and that we need to be certain that our judgment is not going to include condemnation. We should all remember where we came from so as to keep our lives firmly fixed on where we are going.

> *So then, my beloved, just as you have always obeyed, not as in my presence only, but now much more in my absence, work out your salvation with fear*

and trembling; for it is God who is at work in you, both to will and to work for His good pleasure. (Philippians 2:12-13)

TIME-BOUND / TIMELESS: We should all remember where we came from so as to keep our lives firmly fixed on where we are going.

5:9c . . . behold, the Judge is standing right at the door.

But you, why do you judge your brother? Or you again, why do you regard your brother with contempt? For we will all stand before the judgment seat of God. (Romans 14:10)

TIMELESS: Even believers will be judged.

TIME-BOUND / TIMELESS: And we are all one breath away from standing before Jesus Christ.

TIME-BOUND: Act like it. Live like it.

5:10 As an example, brethren, of suffering and patience, take the prophets who spoke in the name of the Lord.

[O]thers received the trial of mockings and scourgings, yes, also chains and imprisonment. They were stoned, they were sawn in two, they were tempted, they were put to death with the sword; they went about in sheepskins, in goatskins, being destitute, afflicted, ill-treated (men of whom the world was not worthy), wandering in deserts and mountains and caves and holes in the ground. (Hebrews 11:36-38).

The prophets not only suffered injustice but spoke out against it. This is the way of practical Christianity.

"These things I have spoken to you, so that in Me you may have peace. In the world you have tribulation, but take courage; I have overcome the world." (John 16:33)

After they had preached the gospel to that city and had made many disciples, they returned to Lystra and to Iconium and to Antioch, strengthening the souls of the disciples, encouraging them to continue in the faith, and saying, "Through many tribulations we must enter the kingdom of God." (Acts 14:21-22)

TIME-BOUND: Patient endurance, even in the face of suffering, is supposed to be our default stance before the world.

5:11a We count those blessed who endured.

In this verse, "blessed" is a verb representing the objective state of our relationship with God. James is about sanctification. Then there is "blessed" as an adjective representing the state of receiving divine approval from God:

"Blessed are you when people insult you and persecute you, and falsely say all kinds of evil against you because of Me. Rejoice and be glad, for your reward in heaven is great; for in the same way they persecuted the prophets who were before you." (Matthew 5:11-12)

Christian existence is frictional against evil. There is no way to escape this dynamic in time. We are blessed when we endure both the active persecution Christians experience for the sake of Christ and the passive persecution we live with as a result of existing in a fallen world with a heart changed by God.

5:11b You have heard of the endurance of Job and have seen the outcome of the Lord's dealings, that the Lord is full of compassion and is merciful.

God tested Job. Job struggled and questioned, but he never abandoned his faith. He finally came to a place where he considered it all joy.

TIMELESS: God has purpose in everything that takes place in His universe.

TIME-BOUND: God tests your faith to prove it is real—to you.

TIME-BOUND / TIMELESS: God tests your faith to refine it so that you can see God more clearly.

In the last six verses, James uses the word *patience* four times. And in verse 11, he uses *endurance* twice. We are learning about the spiritual discipline of patient endurance. Whatever suffering you experience in this life is to be patiently endured. Your situation will be completely transformed when Christ is revealed in glory because "the Lord is full of compassion and is merciful." Look for blessings, not stuff, in this life.

> *For I consider that the sufferings of this present time are not worthy to be compared with the glory that is to be revealed to us. (Romans 8:18)*

Trials, difficulties with the world, various degrees of suffering—they all go with the Christian territory. We deal with these things by keeping our focus on the promise of God—the person and work of Jesus Christ. God is testing you, shaping you, refining you. The more you align yourself with God's will in your life, the greater the blessings, and that has nothing to do with wealth or power in this world. Remember that patient endurance does not equal weakness or spinelessness before the world; meekness does not equal weakness, "for God has not given us a spirit of [cowardice], but of power and love and discipline" (2 Timothy 1:7-14).

> *Therefore do not be ashamed of the testimony of our Lord or of me His prisoner, but join with me in suffering for the gospel according to the power of God, who has saved us and called us with a holy calling, not according to our works, but according to His own purpose and grace which was granted us in Christ Jesus from all eternity, but now has been revealed by the appearing of our Savior Christ Jesus, who abolished death and brought life and immortality to light through the gospel, for which I was appointed a preacher and an apostle and a teacher.*
>
> *For this reason I also suffer these things, but I am not ashamed; for I know whom I have believed and I am convinced that He is able to guard what I have entrusted to Him until that day. Retain the standard of sound words which you have heard from me, in the faith and love which are in Christ Jesus. Guard, through the Holy Spirit who dwells in us, the treasure which has been entrusted to you. (2 Timothy 1:8-14)*

5:12 Sanctifying Personal Integrity

James writes in the style of Old Testament wisdom literature. He presents short, terse, command-style presentations, each of which has implications in all sorts of directions. All of the sections of the letter work together as essential instructions for growing in grace and holiness. Each small section also stands on its own to deliver its specific goods. Verse 12 stands alone as a lesson and at the same time ties together much of what comes before.

5:12 But above all, my brethren, do not swear, either by heaven or by earth or with any other oath; but your yes is to be yes, and your no, no, so that you may not fall under judgment.

James begins with the word "but." The original Greek word translated here as "but" indicates a transition and not a contrast. We would get a better sense of the original meaning by using the word "now" or "and"—or by just leaving that word untranslated in modern English.

> **Amplification:** *[A]bove all, my brethren, [stop swearing].*

Underpinning all other considerations, what we say out loud and to ourselves, how we hold and use words, is indicative of how we are living out our faith.

Throughout the letter, James has pressed the importance of speech in context of sanctification:

> *If anyone thinks himself to be religious, and yet does not bridle his tongue but deceives his own heart, this man's religion is worthless. (James 1:26)*

> *[S]peak and so act as those who are to be judged by the law of liberty. (James 2:12)*

> *So also the tongue is a small part of the body, and yet it boasts of great things. (James 3:5)*

> *But no one can tame the tongue; it is a restless evil and full of deadly poison. (James 3:8)*

> *Do not speak against one another, brethren. (James 4:11)*

How we speak and how we use and hold words reflects our internal spiritual condition: "For the mouth speaks out of that which fills the heart" (Matthew 12:34). Your heart is a spiritual storehouse, and your mouth reveals what you have stored there. James presents this idea with a singular focus on swearing.

> "swear," "swear [an oath]"—invoking God's name to guarantee what one says

James is not writing about swearing in the sense of coarse or vulgar language; his focus is on swearing in the sense of swearing an oath. The Old

Testament law does not prohibit this type of oath, but it does condition it. The person swearing the oath is charged by God to be true to his word: "You shall not swear falsely by My name, so as to profane the name of your God; I am the Lord" (Leviticus 19:12). When you swear an oath, only swear it in the name of God: "You shall fear only the Lord your God; and you shall worship Him and swear by His name" (Deuteronomy 6:13).

An Old Testament oath made in the name of God asserted three things to the hearer: (1) I am telling the truth; (2) I am calling God as witness to my truth; and (3) may God punish me if I am not telling the truth. The guarantee of your word was the quality of your faith. To violate an oath was to consciously, mindfully invoke a curse from God.

Oath swearing was common practice in Old Testament times:

> Abraham said to his servant, the oldest of his household, who had charge of all that he owned, "Please place your hand under my thigh, and I will make you swear by the Lord, the God of heaven and the God of earth." (Genesis 24:2-3a)

It was not against the Law to swear an oath; it was against the Law to abuse the process.

> If a man makes a vow to the Lord, or takes an oath to bind himself with a binding obligation, he shall not violate his word; he shall do according to all that proceeds out of his mouth. (Numbers 30:2)

Swearing an oath and then breaking it also violates the Law all the way back to its foundation. Since an oath is sworn in the name of God, violating an oath also violates the third commandment: "You shall not take the name of the Lord your God in vain" (Exodus 20:7). And, if you are willfully, mindfully taking the name of the Lord in vain, how can you claim to be loving the Lord as your God with all of your heart, mind, and soul? Since someone is being hurt on the other end of the oath, you are violating the command to love your neighbor as yourself. All of this is why James begins this section with, "Above all, my brethren, stop swearing."

Part of what is going on with the Old Testament oath system is God reminding us that, left to ourselves, without God we are all a bunch of liars and cheats to one degree or another. Lost humanity is of Adam and exists in alignment with Satan. Satan is the father of lies, and lost humans are children of Satan. The fall wreaked havoc on the human conscience. God instituted a system of swearing in His Law both to reign us in and to amplify and expose us for the liars and cheats that we all have the potential to be in any given instance or circumstance.

Left to ourselves, we cannot be trusted for the most part. That is why people get sworn in during a trial. "Do you swear to tell the truth, the whole truth, and nothing but the truth?" And it used to end with, "so help you God?" The courts have to have penalties for perjury because lots of people will swear to tell the truth in one breath, fully intending to lie and mislead with their next breath.

The words we use, the way we use them, and the intent behind them are all vital in the process of sanctification.

In the time before Christ, there was a growing tendency to create varying degrees of oaths by swearing to less sacred things. Whatever the degree of bad faith or intentional deception that was taking place, the person giving the lesser oath felt like they were exploiting a loophole in the Law. They believed that they could compel someone to a place of trust while getting off of the spiritual hook with God.

Here is how Jesus addressed this kind of thinking:

> *"Again, you have heard that the ancients were told, 'You shall not make false vows, but shall fulfill your vows to the Lord.' But I say to you, make no oath at all, either by heaven, for it is the throne of God, or by the earth, for it is the footstool of His feet, or by Jerusalem, for it is the city of the great King. Nor shall you make an oath by your head, for you cannot make one hair white or black. But let your statement be, 'Yes, yes' or 'No, no'; anything beyond these is of evil." (Matthew 5:33-37)*

James 5:12 is a restating of Matthew 5:34-37. But we have to look to the teaching of Jesus to fully develop the idea. When Jesus uses an expression like, "You have heard that the ancients were told," He is referring to the traditions and the interpretive teachings of the rabbis.

> **Amplification:** *"[Your traditional teaching says]: 'You shall not make false vows, but shall fulfill your vows to the Lord.'" (Matthew 5:33)*

Jesus is not directly quoting from Old Testament Scripture in Matthew 5:33; He quotes a rabbinic paraphrase.

Sinful humans have a tendency to look for loopholes in God's Law. Same then as now. And that is what they did with the wiggle room in this rabbinic teaching: "I want you to believe me, so I will find a convincing way to

COMMENTARY: THE LETTER OF JAMES

swear without directly invoking the name of God because if I make a vow to something other than the Lord, I will not be violating God's Law if I break it."

This is what Jesus was addressing in the Gospel of Matthew when He rebuked the Pharisees:

> *"Woe to you, blind guides, who say, 'Whoever swears by the temple, that is nothing; but whoever swears by the gold of the temple is obligated.' You fools and blind men! Which is more important, the gold or the temple that sanctified the gold? And, 'Whoever swears by the altar, that is nothing, but whoever swears by the offering on it, he is obligated.' You blind men, which is more important, the offering, or the altar that sanctifies the offering?*
>
> *"Therefore, whoever swears by the altar, swears both by the altar and by everything on it. And whoever swears by the temple, swears both by the temple and by Him who dwells within it. And whoever swears by heaven, swears both by the throne of God and by Him who sits upon it."* (Matthew 23:16-22)

Many Jews created a tradition of swearing a bunch of different kind of oaths based on a faulty understanding of a paraphrase. The Pharisees then came along and invented a bunch of rules to govern the faulty application of the faulty understanding of the faulty paraphrase.

The same kind of thing has been playing out since then: "I swear on my mother's grave"; "I swear by all that's holy"; "I swear on a stack of Bibles." I want you to believe me, so whether or not I am lying, I will find a convincing way to swear. In response to this sinful tradition, James puts forward the teaching of Jesus: "Do not swear, either by heaven or by earth or with any other oath."

James is busting up the mechanical notion of sin. You cannot get around your spiritual accountability with clever word games. Heaven belongs to God. The Earth belongs to God. Jerusalem belongs to God. The hairs on your head belong to God. No matter what you think you are swearing by, any time you give your word you are giving it in the presence of God. Jesus tells us, and then He tells us again through James, to stop playing these kind of sinful games with your life.

James is writing to Christians. You are in the family of God now. Do not say things like, "As God is my witness" because now you are God's witness. If you are saved, do not lie, do not cheat, do not make foolish or dishonest vows, "but your yes is to be yes, and your no, no." Jesus said, "anything beyond these is of evil."

Our word as Christians should be so truthful that we do not need an oath to support it. Our word as Christians should be more trustworthy and binding than a signature on a legal document. This has nothing to do with the "oath" implicit in the signing of a legal contract or the "swearing in" that takes place in a court of law. Ideally, in Christian community, these things should not be needed, but they are often the best the systems of the world can do when no kingdom ethics are in play.

> *Every person is to be in subjection to the governing authorities. For there is no authority except from God, and those which exist are established by God. Therefore whoever resists authority has opposed the ordinance of God; and they who have opposed will receive condemnation upon themselves. (Romans 13:1-2)*

You are in no way violating the command of Jesus regarding vows, which is restated here in James, if you take an oath in a court of law or if you give your word in the form of a written contract.

> *Render to all what is due them: tax to whom tax is due; custom to whom custom; fear to whom fear; honor to whom honor. (Romans 13:7)*

A Christian who refuses to swear an oath within the confines of a courtroom scenario, or who refuses to engage in any business dealing where a contract needs to be signed, can create the impression of deceptiveness and falsehood in the eyes of the lost.

> *"[B]ut your yes is to be yes, and your no, no."*

Many of the secular systems of the world are built on the premises and lies of the enemy. Christians are supposed to live set apart from all of that. Regardless of the world's details, in any and all situations, speak plainly and honestly.

There is a consequence at the end of verse 12: "[Y]our yes is to be yes, and your no, no, so that you may not fall under judgment." James gives us tests that are also meant to be diagnostics as to whether or not we are saved. The Greek word translated here as "judgment" refers to a judge passing sentence in all other New Testament uses. It is never used to represent God chastening someone for a behavior. It is the same word James used in chapter 2, verse 13: "For judgment will be merciless to one who has shown no mercy." This is the judgment to condemnation. This teaching tracks back to the third commandment: "You shall not take the name of the Lord your God in vain, for the Lord will not leave him unpunished who takes His name in vain" (Exodus 20:7).

In chapter 23 of Matthew, after Jesus finishes taking down the Pharisees for their lying, cheating ways, He finishes with this: "You serpents, you brood of vipers, how will you escape the judgment of hell?" (Matthew 23:33).

As a baseline, James is telling you all of this "so that you may not fall under [judgment to condemnation]." While the letter of James helps you to sanctify, it also helps you to diagnose whether or not you are saved. He gives you all of these tests so you can look at the condition of your mind as it tries to function in a fallen world, and diagnose your spiritual condition.

If your yes *is not* yes, and your no *is not* no, and that is your constant default condition in the world, you are probably fooling yourself with regard to justification if you call yourself a Christian.

> *"He who overcomes will inherit these things, and I will be his God and he will be My son. But for the cowardly and unbelieving and abominable and murderers and immoral persons and sorcerers and idolaters and all liars, their part will be in the lake that burns with fire and brimstone, which is the second death." (Revelation 21:7-8)*

God judges the heart, and what comes out of our mouths is reflective of what is in our hearts. Serious stuff. The words you choose to live by, and then, the words you choose to live out, are vitally important. And so, by God's standard, "[Y]our yes is to be yes, and your no, no."

Your words as a Christian should be authentic, clear, solid, and true. As soon as you say, "I swear," as soon as you feel the need to make an oath-style statement, your words no longer stand as authentic. As soon as an oath is invoked, the ideal of spiritual truthfulness of heart has been compromised.

Jesus does not abrogate the Deuteronomy command; He shows that in a sense it is now unnecessary. As Christians, our bodies are now the temples, and we speak with God as our direct witness every time we speak.

5:13-18 Prayer and Healing

As the letter draws to a close, James presents a few verses about prayer and prayerful living. These verses are going to deal specifically with prayer as a response to suffering and sickness. The key to understanding these verses lies in understanding what kind of suffering and what kind of sickness James is writing about here.

Like any Bible passage that presents some interpretive difficulties in English, we look to the overall context of the specific book, the original biblical language, and our overall biblical theology to keep our cultural and linguistic status as latecomers to the biblical text in check.

James wrote this letter to Jewish Christians who left Jerusalem because of persecution. They are living in Jewish communities in foreign countries where they are experiencing persecution from both the Gentile populations at large and from the non-converted Jews. They are dealing with the anti-Christian hostility coming at them from the lost world around them, the friction caused by fellow Christians who cannot or will not conform their lives to Christ, and the personal temptations to sin that plague all believers.

It is not easy to live an authentic Christian life. No matter how far down the sanctifying path we go, there are always going to be times when the enemy gets the better of us one way or another. And when that happens, it hurts. It tears at the soul of anyone who has experienced the peace of Christ and the presence of the Holy Spirit.

TIME-BOUND: When the trials and sufferings we encounter get the best of us, they can leave us weak, physically and spiritually exhausted, mentally and emotionally crushed. It can seem that God is distant, that we have failed Him, or at least that we have failed Him as Christians.

5:13 Is anyone among you suffering? Then he must pray. Is anyone cheerful? He is to sing praises.

"Suffering" here is affliction and/or hardship. "Is anyone among you [afflicted, undergoing hardship, experiencing evil]?" It is the same word that was used back in verse 10 to reference the same type of suffering. In this verse, it is contrasted against being "cheerful," "joyful," or "well in spirit." Two polarized conditions are presented to represent the entire range of spiritual experiences that can occur "when you encounter various trials" (James 1:2b).

> [W]hen you encounter various trials. . . . [c]onsider it all joy, my brethren. (James 1:2b, a).

> Is anyone among you suffering? . . . Is anyone cheerful? . . . Then he must pray. . . . He is to sing praises. (5:13a, c, b, d)

Rejoice always; pray without ceasing; in everything give thanks; for this is God's will for you in Christ Jesus. (1 Thessalonians 5:16-18)

With all prayer and petition pray at all times in the Spirit, and with this in view, be on the alert with all perseverance and petition for all the saints. (Ephesians 6:18)

The word *pray* is used in every verse of this section. This letter is about sanctification. This section is about the power of prayer in the process of sanctification.

TIME-BOUND: Prayer is the constant in day-to-day Christian life regardless of circumstances.

5:14 Is anyone among you sick? Then he must call for the elders of the church and they are to pray over him, anointing him with oil in the name of the Lord.

"sick"—(GK) *astheneo*: physically weak or impotent; mentally ill; spiritually ill; physically diseased

Without becoming weak [astheneo] in faith he contemplated his own body, now as good as dead since he was about a hundred years old, and the deadness of Sarah's womb. (Romans 4:19)

For while we were still helpless [asthenes], at the right time Christ died for the ungodly. (Romans 5:6)

Now accept the one who is weak [astheneo] in faith, but not for the purpose of passing judgment on his opinions. One person has faith that he may eat all things, but he who is weak [astheneo] eats vegetables only. (Romans 14:1-2)

It is good not to eat meat or to drink wine, or to do anything by which your brother stumbles [is made astheneo]. (Romans 14:21)

Concerning this I implored the Lord three times that it might leave me. And He has said to me, "My grace is sufficient for you, for power is perfected in weakness [astheneia]." Most gladly, therefore, I will rather boast about my weaknesses [astheneia], so that the power of Christ may dwell in me. Therefore I am well content with weaknesses [astheneo], with insults, with distresses, with persecutions, with difficulties, for Christ's sake; for when I am weak [astheneo], then I am strong. (2 Corinthians 12:8-10)

James 5:14 asks, *Is anyone among you falling apart? Are you mentally, emotionally, or physically weak? Has your personal life of prayer and worship fallen apart? Are you feeling spiritually defeated?*

Then he must call. . . .

TIME-BOUND: No one is supposed to go it alone. We are to exist as disciples in discipling relationships. Ask for help when you need it.

Then he must call for the elders of the church. . . .

If you are spiritually weak, call out for help to the spiritually strong. Elders are called based on their spiritual maturity. Go to them and let them help you; draw on their spiritual strength.

Then he must call for the elders of the church and they are to pray over him. . . .

Elders are supposed to be the most spiritually mature Christians in any given Christian community. They have two primary responsibilities: immersion in the Bible and prayer. That is their specific function in the body and should be the focus of most of their time.

So the twelve summoned the congregation of the disciples and said, "It is not desirable for us to neglect the word of God in order to serve tables. Therefore, brethren, select from among you seven men of good reputation, full of the Spirit and of wisdom, whom we may put in charge of this task. But we will devote ourselves to prayer and to the ministry of the word." (Acts 6:2-4)

When you need to learn the Bible, call the elders. When you need biblical counsel, call the elders. When you need the intercession of powerful prayer warriors, call the elders.

. . . and [the elders] are to pray over him, anointing him with oil in the name of the Lord.

There are two Greek words that translate as "anoint" in the Bible: *chrio* and *aleipho*. *Chrio* is used for ceremonial anointing, like consecration to an office. To *aleipho* someone with oil is to physically rub or pour the oil onto a person. James uses the word *aleipho* in this verse.

The physical anointing could be cosmetic or hygienic. People would be anointed with oil after a bath. Athletes would be rubbed down with oil to soothe and relax sore muscles. Wounds would be anointed with oil to soothe irritation and inflammation. A visitor to a household would be anointed with oil on the parts of their body that had been exposed to the harsh desert climate.

> *You prepare a table before me in the presence of my enemies; You anoint my head with oil. (Psalm 23:5a)*

In Psalm 23 the anointing is an image—a poetic figure of speech for a spiritual blessing.

> *From the sole of the foot even to the head there is nothing sound in it, only bruises, welts and raw wounds, not pressed out or bandaged, nor softened with oil. (Isaiah 1:6)*

In Isaiah 1:6 Israel is represented as *astheneo*, as they receive no metaphorical healing anointing.

> **Amplification:** *Is anyone among you suffering? . . . Is anyone among you astheneo [to the point that you are spiritually broken, weary, defeated—even your prayer life has dried up]? Then he must call for the elders of the church and they are to pray over him, anointing him with oil in the name of the Lord. (5:13a-14)*

Since the physical action is in the name of the Lord, the physical anointing with oil is meant to have symbolic significance that brings focus to the event as it rides alongside the prayers of the elders.

This is the only place in the New Testament that mentions anointing a person who is *astheneo*. In other books of the New Testament, the healing of physical diseases takes place without anointing. This practice of anointing with oil is nowhere called out as part of praying for medical healing. Here the oil is the image of covering the person in ministerial comfort, soothing their spirit.

> *. . . [the elders of the church] are to pray over him, anointing him with oil in the name of the Lord.*

5:15 . . . and the prayer offered in faith will restore the one who is sick, and the Lord will raise him up, and if he has committed sins, they will be forgiven him.

> "the prayer offered in faith"—the prayer offered in alignment with the will of God
>
> "sick"—(GK) *kamno*: to grow weary or to be weary; exhausted; sick from exhaustion

Kamno is the same word used in Hebrews 12:3: "For consider [Jesus] who has endured such hostility by sinners against Himself, so that you will not *grow weary* and lose heart."

It is "the prayer offered in faith" and not medicinal or magical oil that "will restore the one who is [spiritually weary and exhausted]." And because the vehicle is prayer, the restoration will be according to God's will and way and not necessarily according to our specific wants.

Faithful prayer of the elders, joined with the faith of the person being prayed over, will restore the believer from the condition of spiritual *astheneo* and *kamno* they are experiencing—"the Lord will raise him up." We lift our prayers for restoration, and God willing, "the Lord will raise [the spiritually weakened brother or sister] up." The Lord will awaken and excite the believer.

> **TIMELESS:** Whatever type and degree of restoration that takes place, it is the power of God that heals and not some perfected level of praying or the proper use of sacramental magic oil.

You find yourself spiritually worn down. You are weak and despairing. You start to think you are losing the battle against evil. You feel done in, helpless. But if you are in this condition and saved, and you realize that you cannot and are not supposed to be going it alone, God promises that if you call on faithful elders of the church to gather around you, and you join with them as they pray over you, the Lord will restore you and lift you up. The Lord Himself will raise you up, lift your spirit, and get you back in the spiritual mix.

> **TIME-BOUND / TIMELESS:** These verses are about spiritual warfare—faith in action. The letter of James is about sanctification—sanctified living. These verses have nothing to do with the various faith-healing traditions.

James paints the picture of a weary, weakened believer whose prayer life has dried up. His ministry is barren and wasted, and his spirit is exhausted. And all that God asks for to deliver restoration is faithful prayer. This is a much higher promise than the curing of some physical ailment. We are not to treat God like some distant supernatural vending machine who will only perform a medical miracle if some super spiritual leader of the church gets the prayer and the oil just right. That is works-based faith. That is attempting to bind God by human ritual.

Along with the promise of personal restoration, "if he has committed sins [that have caused what he is going through], they will be forgiven him." If you come to whoever has elder authority over you, and take advantage of their pastoral ministry, the dynamic will encourage prayers of confession leading to the forgiveness of sin.

TIMELESS: These verses are spiritual in nature. Only God can forgive sins.

TIME-BOUND: As you are going, make disciples. To do that, someone has to disciple you. It is relational. Discipling is God's plan "A" for His church. There is no plan "B."

5:16a Therefore, confess your sins to one another, and pray for one another so that you may be healed.

Therefore, exist as Christians in discipling relationships. Learn the power of the discipling relationship, and invest in it. Do not hide your sinful actions—give a voice to them with a trusted mentor. Sin wants to have a Christian alone. Sin isolates. Sin wants you to live in the darkness, in the shadows of sinful separation.

God wants sin exposed in His light. He handles sin in the big picture. He asks us to handle manifestations of sin as one body here in time.

The word "healed" here has the same meaning as when Jesus uses it in Matthew 13:

> "For the heart of this people has become dull, with their ears they scarcely hear, and they have closed their eyes, otherwise they would see with their eyes, hear with their ears, and understand with their heart and return, and I would heal them." (Matthew 13:15)

Jesus speaks about the healing of spiritual restoration in terms of salvation. James writes about the healing of spiritual restoration in terms of sanctification.

5:16b The effective prayer of a righteous man can accomplish much.

Amplification 1: *The [powerful] prayer of a [justified] man can accomplish much.*

357

Closer to the Greek:

> **Amplification 2:** *The [powerful] prayer of a [justified] man [is very strong].*

Here is why James writes "call for the elders." Here is why every assembly needs spiritually competent elders. The real healing power of Christian fellowship derives from the faithful prayer of spiritually mature Christians. Faithful, earnest prayer provides nourishing comfort, spiritual restoration, and enhanced fellowship, and most importantly, it opens the floodgates of God's grace.

> **TIME-BOUND / TIMELESS:** "The effective prayer of a righteous man can accomplish much" because God says it can.

5:17-18 Elijah was a man with a nature like ours, and he prayed earnestly that it would not rain, and it did not rain on the earth for three years and six months. Then he prayed again, and the sky poured rain and the earth produced its fruit.

Elijah was a popular and celebrated figure in ancient Judaism. God did many miracles through him to authenticate his prophetic messages against sin. Elijah was also bodily taken up into God's realm. It was easy to elevate a man like Elijah. But James makes the point that "Elijah was a man with a nature like ours." What sets him apart as an example for us is the intensity of his personal faith evidenced here by the intensity of his prayer life.

The relevant Elijah story is in 1 Kings, but it does not mention this prayer. This detail is only mentioned here in James. There are also extra-biblical historical accounts of a three-and-a-half-year drought that occurred at that time. James tells us about a faithful man who prayed earnestly. He tells us, "The [powerful] prayer of a [justified] man [is very strong]."

> **TIME-BOUND / TIMELESS:** Every believer has the same access to God through prayer that Elijah had.

5:19-20 Disciple Each Other

Throughout the letter, James's style has been abrupt. He writes tersely to each point he wants to make and then moves directly to the next. He concludes the letter with one sentence about discipling, divided into two verses. Unlike most New Testament letters, there is no formal drawdown in these last two verses and no concluding greetings or prayers.

5:19 My brethren, if any among you strays from the truth and one turns him back. . . .

"strays"—(GK) *planao*: wanders; (metaphorically) falls away from the truth; is led away into error and sin; to cause to fall away; to lead away into error and sin

But Jesus answered and said to them, "You are mistaken, not understanding the Scriptures nor the power of God." (Matthew 22:29)

"For many will come in My name, saying, 'I am the Christ,' and will mislead many." (Matthew 24:5)

But evil men and impostors will proceed from bad to worse, deceiving *and* being deceived. *(2 Timothy 3:13)*

[F]orsaking the right way, they have gone astray. *(2 Peter 2:15)*

Amplification 1: *. . . if any among you [wanders away from God's biblical] truth*

"truth"—(GK) *aletheia*: certain truth; biblical truth; God's truth

. . . who hindered you from obeying the truth? (Galatians 5:7b)

If we say that we have fellowship with Him and yet walk in the darkness, we lie and do not practice the truth. (1 John 1:6)

Amplification 2: *. . . if any among you [is led away from God's] truth [into error and sin]*

"turns him back"—(GK) *epistrepho:* (transitive) to cause to return; bring back

"And he will turn *many of the sons of Israel back to the Lord their God." (Luke 1:16)*

"Simon, Simon, behold, Satan has demanded permission to sift you like wheat; but I have prayed for you, that your faith may not fail; and you, when once you have turned again, strengthen your brothers." (Luke 22:32)

We pray for each other. But what do we do when we are praying for a disciple of ours and there is no change? What do we do if a fellow Christian wanders away or is led away into error and sin? In both cases, we make effort to turn him back. We get personally involved, and we engage.

We are all supposed to have fellow Christians like this in our lives—someone who will cross the line and speak up when we slip sideways in our walks or wander away from some aspect of God's truth.

TIME-BOUND: Prayer does not exempt us from personal action.

5:20 . . . let him know that he who turns a sinner from the error of his way will save his soul from death and will cover a multitude of sins.

> "error of his way"—(GK) *planes autos hodou*: his wandering way; his erring way
>
> "death"—(GK) *thanatos:* spiritual death throughout the New Testament when sin is the issue

When a Christian wanders and stumbles in sin, they are living in the separation that is sin, and they begin to look and function like lost people. When you knock some spiritual sense back into that person, you help to create room for them to listen to the conviction of the Spirit. By the grace of God, they are then restored to Christian fellowship, and even a multitude of sins will then be covered.

God charges fellow Christians to look out for each other and to help each other if we stray from the Christian path. And James shows us one aspect of the discipling relationship as he encourages us to intervene in the lives of fellow Christians who are having spiritual difficulties in their walks.

Jesus clearly established the centrality of the discipling relationship at the end of the Gospel of Matthew:

> [T]he eleven disciples proceeded to Galilee, to the mountain which Jesus had designated. When they saw Him, they worshiped Him; but some were doubtful. And Jesus came up and spoke to them, saying, "All authority has been given to Me in heaven and on earth. Go therefore and make disciples of all the nations, baptizing them in the name of the Father and the Son and the Holy Spirit, teaching them to observe all that I commanded you; and lo, I am with you always, even to the end of the age." (Matthew 28:16-20)

Who is Jesus speaking to? His disciples. What does He do? He comes to them. He speaks to them to reassure them and restore them. The disciples do not speak here. Their role is to listen, to learn, to understand, and to obey.

The Great Commission is not explained in terms of the means—the proclaiming of the gospel. The Great Commission is explained in terms of the ongoing end: go . . . and make disciples. As you are going, make disciples—baptize them if they get saved, and continue to teach them. This is discipling that leads to conversion and then ongoing discipling for the rest of our lives.

The biblical model for Christian evangelism is the discipling relationship. The biblical model for sanctification is the ongoing discipling relationship. The letter of James is about practical Christianity; it is about what sanctification should look like playing out in time.

> **TIME-BOUND:** James is teaching us about who and how we are supposed to be in Christ in the here and now. He is also teaching us about who we are not supposed to be as well.

What can and does happen all too often is a person gets saved, receives the gift of the Holy Spirit, and then, for a variety of reasons, fails to be discipled. When that happens, all of the things James warns us about have the potential to manifest. A supernaturally converted Christian who is not walking rightly is not going to lose their salvation, but they can completely blow their witness and testimony before the church and the world and make a wide variety of huge spiritual messes.

All Christians are supposed to be in discipling relationships. All of us are supposed to have someone further down the path of Christian living than we are teaching us, looking over our shoulders, helping us. No one is supposed to be going it alone.

> **TIME-BOUND:** Plan "A" for the Christian life is discipling relationships. There is no plan "B."

CLOSING THOUGHTS

God sent His divine Son as a human man to die on the cross for the purpose of conquering the very real evil in the world. The result is that the penalty of sin was paid by Christ on the cross, and victory over the power of sin was proved out at the resurrection. Because of this shift in how God relates to sinful humanity, and because of how God will now let us relate to Him, saved people placed in Christ by God now share in divine life.

The only way God gets us into a position or state of being where we can sanctify is through the relational activity that happens at salvation, at conversion. That is when supernatural transformation takes place.

If you are lost, how do you experience the blessings of God—this power, this grace? All you have to do is accept Christ. But it has got to be real, and it has got to be on God's terms—total surrender. The question is not whether or not you have a master; the question is, *Which master are you serving?* Turn away from sin, and turn back to loving God with all of your heart, soul, mind, and strength. Let Christ's work, work for you. Romans 10:9 says, "[I]f you confess with your mouth Jesus as Lord, and believe in your heart that God raised Him from the dead, you will be saved," and your sinful actions—and God knows they are a multitude—are then covered forever. If you are lost, and you are wrestling with everything you have just read, find a faithful theologically conservative Christian assembly to help you sort yourself out.

TIMELESS: God does the saving.

TIME-BOUND: And He uses the community of believers in the process.

We are not perfected at salvation; that sort of thinking is an affront to Holy God. But our natural relationship to the power of sin is changed. God takes us where He finds us at justification, but He does not leave us there. Through regeneration we are supernaturally restored spiritually and made able to live in a way that pleases God.

When the Holy Spirit regenerates a person, there is going to be a huge difference in how that person thinks and acts. There will be a deepening of conscience and an ongoing sense of conviction when dealing with temptation and sin. There has to be. If a person has really been saved, a real supernatural transformation has taken place.

Spiritual life is now no longer a hypothetical something on the outside of us that the Law points to; it is an actual tangible reality inside of us. Christians who have been justified by God are children of God, born again of the Holy Spirit. This is the condition of sanctity—we are in Christ, and Christ is in us. Justification freed us from the penalty of sin. Regeneration loosed us from the power of sin. Someday down the road, we will be freed from the very presence of sin—but not yet. Sanctification, living a sanctified life in Christ, is the "not yet" period of existence between regeneration and glorification.

Will a supernaturally changed Christian still wrestle with the presence of sin? Yes. Will a supernaturally changed Christian constantly game the grace of God and willfully live like a lost person with no hint of Christian conscience or conviction? May it never be. It cannot be.

If you are saved and you have wandered away into the darkness of some sinful action or another, you turn back. Turn back to loving God with all of your heart, soul, mind, and strength. Christ's work has already paid for all of your sins past, present, and future. Let whoever is discipling you help you get back on your spiritual feet and back on the narrow path. This can only take place if you are living in the ongoing dynamic of a discipling relationship.

TIMELESS: God does the sanctifying.

TIME-BOUND: And He uses the community of believers in the process.

If you are saved, think about where you stand with Christ in contrast to where you used to stand with Adam. Realize the incredible, gracious gift you have been given. Surrender to the reality of your faith by being accountable to Jesus every day. Cultivate a life of private prayer and contemplation and extended periods of biblical immersion. Make private and corporate time for worship. When you are home alone, put on some God-honoring music, engage in some God-honoring silence, or immerse in a God-honoring devotional, and lift it up to God in private worship. If you do that regularly, it will dramatically increase your ability to immerse in public, corporate worship. The more you do it, the easier it gets.

To make room for these disciplines, let God take away the stuff that you do not need. Then, let God give you each day the only thing you have ever really needed—His presence.

> **TIME-BOUND / TIMELESS:** Trust in the Lord with all your heart and do not lean on your own understanding. In all your ways acknowledge Him, and He will make your paths straight. (Proverbs 3:5-6)

May grace be with you all.

Amen.

www.ingramcontent.com/pod-product-compliance
Lightning Source LLC
Chambersburg PA
CBHW021214090426
42740CB00006B/221